As near perfect a mallet bottle as one could wish for; this bottle exemplifies the typical shape and form of the period. The large seal is crisply and accurately delineated and, in addition to the date, 1734, carries the bottle's full provenance: 'The Rev^d/Doct Rumney/St. Albans/1734.'

Understanding
Antique Wine Bottles

Roger Dumbrell

Antique Collectors' Club
in association with
Christie's Wine Publications

© 1983 Antique Collectors' Club
World copyright reserved

ISBN 0 907462 14 6

Published for the Antique Collectors' Club by
the Antique Collectors' Club Ltd.

British Library CIP Data
Dumbrell, Roger
    Understanding antique wine bottles
    1. Bottles — Collectors and collecting
    I. Title
    748.8'62'075   NK5440.B6

Printed in England by Baron Publishing, Church Street, Woodbridge, Suffolk

Antique Collectors' Club

The Antique Collectors' Club was formed in 1966 and now has a five figure membership spread throughout the world. It publishes the only independently run monthly antiques magazine *Antique Collecting* which caters for those collectors who are interested in increasing their knowledge of antiques, both by greater awareness of quality and by discussion of the factors which influence the price that is likely to be asked. The Antique Collectors' Club pioneered the provision of information on prices for collectors and still leads in the provision of detailed articles on a variety of subjects.

It was in response to the enormous demand for information on "what to pay" that the price guide series was introduced in 1968 with the first edition of *The Price Guide to Antique Furniture* (completely revised 1978), a book which broke new ground by illustrating the more common types of antique furniture, the sort that collectors could buy in shops and at auctions, rather than the rare museum pieces which had previously been used (and still to a large extent are used) to make up the limited amount of illustrations in books published by commercial publishers. Many other price guides have followed, all copiously illustrated, and greatly appreciated by collectors for the valuable information they contain, quite apart from prices. The Antique Collectors' Club also publishes other books on antiques, including horology and art reference works, and a full book list is available.

Club membership, which is open to all collectors, costs £9.95 per annum. Members receive free of charge *Antique Collecting,* the Club's magazine (published every month except August), which contains well-illustrated articles dealing with the practical aspects of collecting not normally dealt with by magazines. Prices, features of value, investment potential, fakes and forgeries are all given prominence in the magazine.

Among other facilities available to members are private buying and selling facilities, the longest list of "For Sales" of any antiques magazine, an annual ceramics conference and the opportunity to meet other collectors at their local antique collectors' club. There are nearly eighty in Britain and so far a dozen overseas. Members may also buy the Club's publications at special pre-publication prices.

As its motto implies, the Club is an amateur organisation designed to help collectors to get the most out of their hobby: it is informal and friendly and gives enormous enjoyment to all concerned.

For Collectors — By Collectors — About Collecting

The Antique Collectors' Club, 5 Church Street, Woodbridge, Suffolk

Contents

Acknowledgements

Enthusiasm on the part of the author is only one of the requisites in a book of this nature. Undoubtedly more important is the assistance, encouragement and criticism I have received from friends, colleagues and numerous individuals. I should like to place on record my particular thanks to the following:

For initially fostering my interest in the subject, I owe much to both Robert Sadunajski and Derek Askey. In the same vein I have to thank Roger Lee and Jim Bull, whose enthusiasm on all aspects of the 'bottle scene' has proved a constant encouragement to me.

For information on wine bottles from the west country I am indebted to Alan Tomlin and Nick Halliday, both having supplied me with details of fresh seals when these have come to light. David Mackeen has also communicated details of important west country seals in the Plymouth Museum. For knowledge regarding bottle excavations in and around the Plymouth area I must thank Ray Rees; as a result of our discussions I have acquired much useful information.

In Dorset Michael Such has been of great assistance in keeping me up to date with bottle discoveries from that part of the country. For details of various bottles as well as detached seals I am grateful to Henry Chesterman and his son of Bristol, both noted collectors.

My warmest thanks are due to Michael Gibbs, of the Royal Institution of South Wales, not only for details concerning bottles in the Swansea Museum, but especially for his untiring research of my own '1674' bottle.

In London, both Steve Narraway and Neil Wilcox have most generously given me details of important bottle seals recovered from the Thames. Down river at Hampton Court, I have had the pleasure of meeting David and Beryl Harris and examining their bottle collection.

I am especially grateful to *Country Life* for allowing me permission to reproduce Chapters Seven and Eight of Sheelagh Ruggles-Brise's *Sealed Bottles*.

Thanks are also due to the following for permission to reproduce photographs in their possession or for allowing photographs to be taken of bottles in their collections:

Neil Wilcox, London; Derek Askey, Brighton; Robert Sadunajski, Eastbourne; David Harris, Hampton Court; Steve Narraway, London; Henry Chesterman, Bristol; Sotheby, King & Chasemore, West Sussex;

Sotheby's, London; Christie's, London; Lawrences, Crewkerne.

Finally I have to thank all those collectors and dealers who have allowed me to examine their bottles, generously given their advice and supported my project from its very beginning.

Roger Dumbrell
Sussex, 1982

1. Introduction

This book has been written first and foremost for the collector. It does not include an exhaustive account of the history of bottle making, and the accent is not on genealogy for this is a subject in itself. In this volume emphasis has been laid on the recognition of different forms, and the story of the evolution of the bottle itself.

The book begins with a detailed account of the evolutionary changes that occurred in glass wine bottles from the seventeenth century onwards, followed by a general guide to dating. Careful consideration is given throughout to details such as, size, structure, colour and weight, in addition to an individual section on each of the main wine bottle types. Extra information is provided by way of separate sections on European bottles, miscellaneous forms and individual seals.

Finally the book discusses bottles from the points of view of rarity, fakes, forgeries and restorations, as well as forming a collection and, for the sake of completeness, there is a price guide and selection of auction house records.

It was felt that the information mentioned above was either lacking or sadly deficient in more recent publications on the subject. Even today, certain writings on English glass give scant attention to bottles, and some even exclude them altogether. This is difficult to understand when one realises that bottles formed a very large proportion of all glass vessels actually made. That they were, and still are to some extent, taken for granted seems the only possible explanation.

Initially, quite the reverse was the case. In the early years of the seventeenth century wine bottles were still relatively scarce, expensive and difficult to acquire and, as such, were held in high esteem by their owners. The purely utilitarian image of bottles today was inconceivable at this early stage, when bottles were a luxury and the poorer classes still drank from vessels of leather, horn and earthenware.

Strange indeed, therefore, that items of such prestige and antiquity, should wait so long to receive the full recognition they now enjoy.

Museums took considerable interest in old bottles well before they received the attention of collectors, and many of the earliest and most desirable specimens were recovered when wine bottles were regarded with almost total indifference by the majority. As an aid in corroboration of site dating the glass wine bottle was to prove an invaluable asset to the archaeologist, as most post-medieval sites contain at least some glass bottle fragments. Both Rees-Price in 1908 and E.T. Leeds in 1914, and again in 1941, proved beyond doubt that the dating of the various forms even without the aid of seals was definitely possible.

Considerable impetus to the study and collection of bottles was given by Sheelagh Ruggles-Brise who published her now famous *Sealed Bottles* in 1949. Both prior to and after this date, much of the literature available to the student or collector is scattered throughout the pages of certain periodicals and learned journals, little, if anything, appearing in book form until comparatively recently.

The most recent factor to affect the status of the hobby was the dump-digging 'explosion' of about 1972. In many places throughout the country people became actively engaged in retrieving Victorian relics, particularly bottles, from long-forgotten dump sites. This fascinating hobby was soon pursued by thousands of people both at home and abroad, and a country-wide network of collectors and dealers soon sprang up to satisfy the growing demands of more discerning clients.

Few really early bottles were dug at first, but the activity did serve to re-awaken people to bottles in general and, at the same time, put the focus of attention on the real antiques of the bottle world, namely the wine bottles. Thus new adherents swelled the ranks of wine bottle collectors and early wines became no longer the sole province of the antique glass collector. Prices rose dramatically, especially with the early bottles, as the demand quite easily exceeded the supply.

The situation has changed very little today, and the hobby can now prove quite expensive if the collector wishes to acquire dated seals only. Having said this, the hobby has much to recommend it. The fascination of wine bottles will undoubtedly endure for, quite apart from age and rarity, their historical significance is often considerable. Few relics of the past centuries are as thought-provoking as these. It is difficult indeed to admire an early bottle without allowing the imagination to pose the following questions: how and why did this particular vessel survive? Who once owned and used it? Why was it eventually discarded? And by whom? Occasionally, by patient and untiring research, some of the mysteries can be unravelled, but by far the majority will remain forever unsolved. Such, however, are the pleasures of the hobby; there is room here for the romantic and the student, the collector and the investor. Collecting antique wine bottles, will provide a thoroughly satisfying and worthwhile interest, an opportunity to delve into the past, and reflect on the products of a bygone age.

2. History and Evolution of the Wine Bottle, c.1630-1900

Early developments

The early history of glass making in England is somewhat obscure; no doubt the Romans brought the craft to Britain, but no evidence of its adoption by the natives exists. Later Anglo-Saxon glass in the form of coloured beads and pendants has been unearthed, and some quite beautiful cups, beakers and vases of the later Saxon period exist. Many, however, are undoubtedly imports from the Low Countries, France, Belgium and the Netherlands, where the art of glass making was already well advanced.

It is interesting to note that in A.D. 675 Bede recorded the need for French workers to be employed in order to make window glass for the newly built monastery at Wearmouth. Almost a century later the position was no better, and foreign workmen had once again to be employed. Although evidence of one or two ninth and tenth century glass houses does exist, the state of affairs over the country as a whole was pitiful indeed.

The basic materials needed for the manufacture of glass are sand plus the addition of an alkali. In England such requirements led to the first of the glass workers establishing their furnaces at Chiddingfold on the Surrey-Sussex border in around 1226. Here both sand, wood and bracken were in plentiful supply. The small forest glass house was established with, again, the assistance of immigrant workmen. When the immediate supply of wood dwindled these itinerant glassmen simply moved on to a different spot.

Their furnaces were so constructed that the entire series of operations could be completed on one spot. The fire for melting the 'frit' (the term for the raw materials necessary to make glass) was at ground level, the work chamber above, and the annealing oven (for cooling) above this.

Translation of an ancient manuscript concerning the site shows that these small forest glass houses produced 'Brode glass and vessel', proving that in addition to window glass, certain other smaller articles were made such as phials, bowls, cups, urinals, and bottles, etc. Excavations at this and similar sites nearby have corroborated this information.

The Wealden 'industry' must have prospered, for glass furnaces in and around this area were still operating in 1556.

Glass was already in vogue in the homes of wealthy Tudors by the middle of the sixteenth century as an inventory of Henry VIII, dated 1542, amply illustrates. Bottles, bowls, ewers, flagons, basins, even candlesticks, are among the numerous vessels mentioned, some decorated, others of coloured glass, and all obviously of a high standard of craftsmanship. Even then there was a choice of glass to suit the pocket of the individual: the unpretentious greenish glass of the forest workmen, or the expensive and highly esteemed Venetian imports, to which no doubt the above inventory refers. In late Elizabethan times the English were still engaged in the manufacture of the pale and fragile soda glass, which proved wholly unsuitable for the vintner, who turned to the sturdy long necked shaft and globe bottles currently being imported by the French.

Production of 'green' or bottle glass

The establishment of glass houses specifically intended for the production of 'green' or bottle glass, did not occur until the closing years of the sixteenth century. During the early years of the next century even greater strides were made in this direction.

Up until now, fragile, pale green, often 'wanded', containers had been the order of the day, but the need for a stronger and darker coloured vessel had long been felt, and now at last, this demand was at least partially satisfied by home manufacture.

A man named Jean Carre, previously engaged in the production of window glass in the Weald, moved to London and, in 1567, applied for a licence to make 'Venice' glasses. The application was turned down, but undeterred Carre introduced Venetian workmen to assist in the running of the Crutched-friars glass house in 1570. Obviously very few of our countrymen, if any, were well versed in the art of glass making.

Upon Carre's death in 1572, Giacomo Verzelini took over the running of the Crutched-friars site, but when this accidently burnt down in 1575 he moved into new premises in nearby Broad Street. In the same year this able Italian obtained a monopoly to make Venice glasses for a period of twenty-one years.

Although the above sites and information relating to them are well documented, it is unfortunate but true that as yet we know very little about contemporary sites engaged in the manufacture of 'green' glass, which would include the so-called coarser products of the day, window glass, bottles, phials, etc. For evidence of these we have to rely more on the paintings of the period, old documents, inventories, and, of course, the result of modern day excavations.

Paintings prove quite conclusively that the use of bottles of one type or another was widespread in Elizabethan times. Documents, useful though they are, should be interpreted with caution, one of the main problems being their frequent failure to be specific. 'Bottles' could so easily be of ceramic composition, rather than glass. The results of archaeological digs one would assume to be of the utmost assistance, especially where these are accurately datable, but even here there are problems. Surprisingly little glass has survived from the sixteenth century; pottery being far more durable is the usual find on such sites, and glass even when present is often of a very fragmentary nature.

According to *The English Housewife,* London, 1615, bottles for ale were already in use in 1575, and the fact that their corks were 'tied down with stout string' infers that the string-rim was employed for this purpose. Various paintings show quite conclusively just such a bottle; of a pale greenish coloured metal, round in the body, with a moderately long neck and high pointed kick-up. Other bottles of the late Tudor period appear to have been more carafe- or flask-like in character, some approach the eighteenth century bladder onions in appearance, but lack the string-rim altogether. In many instances the bottles appear to have been protected by a coating of wicker or leather, and the actual mention of these 'wanded' bottles occurs as early as 1550. This once more points to the fact that most bottles of this period were totally unlike the later wine bottles, being of much thinner metal and hence less sturdy. Wicker covered bottles, or 'flasks' if you like, continued to be used in one form or another well into the eighteenth century, and those that could not be stood on their own, were almost certainly travellers' bottles, and may even have been carried on horseback. Indeed the flat oval shaped bottles with drawn necks and pincered string-rims so often referred to as spa water bottles were undoubtedly used for wine also.

But to return to the mainstream of our discussion. By 1577, glass vessels had become so popular and sought after by the nobility, that their possession was often ranked way above that of the precious metals like gold and silver. True, such remarks apply more especially to the Venetian glass, but the 1589 patent of Miller and Scott proves beyond doubt the growing importance of the bottle and vessel side of the industry. There were now fifteen glass houses operating in the metropolis, and by 1592 some already specialised in the production of bottles and like vessels, and this number takes no account of the innumerable smaller furnaces which must have existed in the provinces.

The art of making bottles

A recipe for bottle glass in the seventeenth century reads: 'any sort of ashes well powder'd and ordinary sea sand from Woolwich'. In more exact terms, most English wine bottles were made of glass containing sand, potash, lime, alumina and oxide of iron. The sand and lime being present in considerably larger proportions to the other three constituents. Lime in the mix helped to produce a harder and stronger glass, and the oxide of iron, a deep coloured, more opaque vessel.

Without doubt the exact materials employed at individual glass houses varied to a considerable extent. Evidence suggests that certain seaweeds were occasionally used for the potash constituent, and barilla imported from Spain. This latter material was a form of seaweed, similar to kelp. All these materials had the regular addition of cullet, which was quite simply broken, fragmentary, or otherwise discarded pieces of glass. Quite a trade in this commodity existed, and many poor folk became totally engaged in the collection and distribution of this valuable waste. (As far as bottle houses were concerned, the trading in 'flint' glass for cullet was strictly forbidden.) The inclusion of cullet in the glass mix permitted earlier fusion of the metal and much improved its quality.

The procedure for blowing a glass bottle can be summarised as follows: the frit was placed in a crucible (clay pot) above the fire, and upon fusion, the 'metal', as it is then called, was skimmed of a large percentage of its impurities. When once cooled to a semi-plastic state, the blower would gather a sufficient quantity on the blow pipe and, by twisting and turning it, work it into a manageable shape, the 'paraison' as it was then known. Using only lung power he would then proceed to inflate the glass, rolling it occasionally on a metal slab (the marver) to determine its shape, and constantly reheating it at the furnace mouth. The pontil rod was then dipped but lightly into the crucible, and attached to the extremity of the vessel. When secure, the blow pipe was removed from the opposite end by smartly tapping, and the neck and top finished by the aid of a pair of flat-bladed forceps. Then the pontil rod was detached, and the area of attachment pushed up into the base of the bottle to form the kick-up.

After this the bottle was taken to the cooling oven, or 'lehr', for the all important process of annealing to take place. Too sudden cooling would result in strains and stresses in the glass, which all too often led to the bottle shattering of its own accord. In the seventeenth century losses of this type were quite commonplace.

In the case of moulded bottles the gather of glass was blown into a pre-shaped wooden or metal mould, and in later varieties of hinged moulds only the neck top and string-rim remained to be finished by hand. Early moulds were tapered at one end in order to facilitate removal of the finished bottle. Moulded bottles of one type or another are as old as antiquity, but in the case of wine bottles moulding took place at a somewhat later stage in their development. However it is only fair to say that, with the advent of mechanical moulding for wine bottles, around 1811, the art of the glass blower in this field was drawing to a close.

Time was becoming a valuable commodity itself, and any means of

A glass house at Loughor, near Swansea, artist unknown, nineteenth century, oil on canvas. This glass house was known to be in operation by 1766; glass making appears to have been abandoned on this site by the late nineteenth century.

expediting production was carefully investigated. For the collector of today this state of affairs is much to be deplored, for it heralded the way to mass production and the characterless products we know today.

The seventeenth century

The 'invention' in 1610 of coal-fired glass houses shows that the continued devastation of the country's woodlands was fast becoming intolerable, even at this date, and shortly after this, in 1615 to be precise, James I totally prohibited the use of wood fuel in glass furnaces. This in no way appears to have slowed down the rise of glass as one of the country's foremost commodities, and many far-seeing people rightly saw a great future in it. After all England had a lot of catching up to do and, to further this end, another proclamation was made in the same year forbidding the importation of French bottles. In short, everything that could be done in order to foster and encourage the home manufacture of glass was quickly implemented.

The now famous Italian, Giacomo Verzelini, had retired from glass making in 1592, and in the same year bottle houses were established in London to specialise in the production of 'French quart wine bottles' as they were then known.

At the same time Sir Jerome Bowes took over the Broad Street glass house only to be ousted from this position by another glass entrepeneur, Sir Edward Zouche whose company acquired ownership in 1615. Sir Edward Zouche was obviously very much 'into' glass, so to speak, and must have been fully aware of its potential, for as early as 1611 we find him investing sums in the region of £5,000 towards the erection of other glass houses in London.

Yet another great name in English glass making appeared on the scene in 1623, when Sir Robert Mansell acquired his far reaching patent to cover virtually all kinds of glassware. It is interesting to note that the final wording of the grant reiterates the condition that all glass of whatever kind must be manufactured by the aid of coal-fired furnaces alone. Perhaps the 1615 edict of James I was not always adhered to.

As regards wine bottles, it is only fair to say that no indisputable evidence exists to prove their manufacture in this country prior to 1592 and, with one possible exception, no wine bottles appear to have survived from that era. The one tantalising exception was recorded in the pages of the *Journal of the Chester and North Wales Archaeological Society* for 1948, which described a bottle of pale green glass with the seal 'C.B.K.1562' unearthed at Chester in 1939. Only the bottom half of the bottle had survived and upon this base was the incredibly early seal. For some unaccountable reason this important find cannot now be located, and what would have been one of the most interesting finds for bottle collectors remains shrouded in mystery. One cannot help but wonder whether the date on the seal could actually have been 1662. The likelihood of a badly eroded seal bottle is very great, as witnessed by a large percentage of recoveries, and this could have lead to the date on the seal being misread.

The possibility of a dated bottle of the sixteenth century is not great, nor is it supported by the evidence we have been able to unearth to date.

It is generally agreed that the first wine bottles of the form now known as shaft and globe appeared during the opening years of the seventeenth century, the 'Mansell' period to be more exact. Unsealed bottles attributed to c.1630 do exist, and by 1633 glass bottles are specifically mentioned in household accounts and inventories. Furthermore, a patent of 1662, with its attendant wrangles, also points to their manufacture at about this date. Of wine bottles c.1592-1620 we can only conjecture, but what seems very likely is a switch from pale coloured thin walled vessels to those of darker, heavier metal, and sturdier form.

Production of English wine bottles was well under way by 1634, where they are already mentioned in customs records as export cargo, and in 1645 Oliver Cromwell found the taxation of glass, including bottles, a worthwhile venture.

The 1636 Act forbidding the sale of wine by the bottle was an attempt to regulate the measure of wine received by the customer. After all no two bottles could be blown exactly alike and considerable discrepancies occurred. The Act meant that the vintner could now keep his wine in the cask and private individuals could have their bottles filled with the contents of an entire butt. The Act had more profound effects, however; it led to an immediate increase in the private use of the wine bottle and, what is even more important, it was fundamental in introducing the practice of 'sealing' one's bottles for, with so many bottles arriving at the vintner's for filling it was an obvious precaution to have them marked.

Household account books from this period onwards make frequent reference to orders for glass wine bottles, and in rarer instances they are specified as being of the 'marked' variety, in short, sealed. It seems that certain individuals ordered literally hundreds of bottles annually using them, one assumes, at large social gatherings, feasts and banquets, where no doubt the revelry and drunkenness of the guests led to innumerable breakages. On such riotous occasions as these bottles were lost or left in the grounds, thrown into nearby lakes or ponds, even smashed by the more inebriated individuals purely to hear the sound of breaking glass, and yet others returned home with their users. How else can we account for the use by some large households of over five hundred bottles a year?

The withdrawal of the patent granted to Henry Holden and John Colenet in 1662 was of the greatest value in terms of establishing more exactly the date of the advent of the English shaft and globe bottle. The term 'invented' in the patent does suggest a new form of bottle or at least a new technique in manufacture, and possibly both. However the patent was withdrawn on the grounds that the bottle Holden and Colenet claimed to have made was already in circulation, and had been for some thirty years. In short, although wine bottles themselves were not 'new' in 1632, the shaft and globe form as we know it today undoubtedly was.

Samuel Pepys was among the ranks of those who aspired to having 'marked' bottles, and in 1663 there is a well-known reference concerning his visit to Mr. Rawlinson's at the Mitre Tavern, where he took obvious delight in watching his newly-made sealed bottles filled with wine, about five or six dozen. Three years later when the flames of the Fire of London swept swiftly and relentlessly through the timber-framed houses of the city, we find Pepys busily engaged in burying his wine and bottles in Seething Lane, from whence he was able to retrieve them, apparently undamaged, ten days later: 'Got my wine out of the ground again and set it in my cellar'.

By 1677 bottle making had become a separate part of the glass industry, and such was the demand and increasing popularity of these vessels that many establishments specialised purely in their manufacture. Bottles could then be purchased direct from the glass house, ordered from the local vintner, or even obtained from one of the glass carriers who peddled their wares in both town and country. Prices varied, but in 1671 the fifth Earl of Bedford is known to have paid 3s.6d a dozen for plain bottles, and 5s. a dozen for sealed ones. The extra 1½d. for the addition of a seal does not seem much when one considers that a brass die had to be made and cut by an engraver. Furthermore, for reasons not really apparent, with every repeat order for sealed bottles, a fresh die seems to have been cut. As yet no adequate argument has been put forward to explain this state of affairs. One would quite reasonably assume that any glass house manager, expecting the almost inevitable repeat orders, would have put the die to one side, rather than destroy it or re-cut it for use meanwhile. For the historian studying a series of bottles from a particular house or tavern, the resulting seal variations are most interesting; witness how E.T. Leeds covered the history of many of the Oxford tavern bottles in this manner, though such a search will be both laborious and time consuming.

The establishment of bottle houses continued unabated in England and, in 1695, just short of forty bottle houses were said to have a total annual output of over two million bottles. Whether this total takes into account the large percentage of breakages which took place during cooling is unknown, but such was the case, with far too little attention being given to the all important process of annealing. However, a ten per cent loss of bottles through shattering seemed to be acceptable in glass houses at the close of the seventeenth century — after all the resulting cullet was easily used in the next batch, and was even said materially to improve its quality.

The eighteenth century

A further duty levied on wine bottles appeared in 1695, and was to be just one in a whole series of such taxes that would burden the glass makers on and off over the next 150 years. However the bottle makers continued to prosper and, at the beginning of the eighteenth century, imports of bottles to this country had dwindled dramatically.

The Methuen Treaty, signed with Portugal in 1703, had far reaching effects on both the wine trade and the wine bottle. Port soon became a very popular drink and with it came the need for such wines to mature in the bottle. Totally free-blown, almost spherical bottles, like the onion, were far from suitable for the purpose, and so over the next forty or so years the straight-sided port bottle began to emerge. These bottles were easily binned horizontally and the liquid kept permanently in contact with the cork. This meant that the cork was unlikely to dry or shrivel, thus spoiling the contents — no mean consideration when wines were to mature in the bottle over reasonably long periods of time.

Bristol was second only to London as a major glass making area, and by 1725 it possessed no fewer than fifteen glass houses, which at that date supposedly exceeded those in operation in the metropolis. Daniel Defoe writing at the same time adds that Bristol's export trade was greater than London's: "They have indeed a very great expence of glass bottles by sending them fill'd with beer, cider and wine to the West Indies, much more than goes from London etc." The passage concludes with an interesting reference to the export of natural spring and mineral waters, without unfortunately specifying the exact type of bottle used. However, it is evident that glass bottles of one type or another were now regular cargo goods, and as such soon became widely dispersed throughout the trading countries of the world.

There followed in 1728 a Bill prohibiting the import of wine to this country in 'flasks, bottles and small casks', a measure which Parliament hoped might lessen the activites of smugglers and facilitate the detection of contraband goods. How effective the Bill was remains uncertain.

As early as 1661, Merret in his *Art of Glass* states that as regards the glass trade 'few foreigners of this profession are now left amongst us', pointing to the fact that English workmen were now quite proficient at their trade. None the less, as late as 1750 we find the large glass works at Alloa in Scotland introducing Bohemian workmen in order to assist them in the making of glass bottles. One can only infer from this that English workers in glass were still hard to find, or that their Continental counterparts were more able and willing to do the job. In much earlier times it had often been a proviso of the granting of licences to foreign workmen, that they should also instruct our own countrymen in the 'art and manner of making glass'; obviously this had not been as effective as was originally hoped.

In 1770, the continuing taxes on bottle glass were now levied according to weight — at this stage 2s. a cwt. However, bottle glass had always escaped the higher rates of duty payable on flint glass as it was made of simpler, less costly ingredients. Glass houses, and bottle makers in particular, were still able to make a good profit on their wares, and in addition to this much streamlining of the manufacturing process had taken place since the beginning of the eighteenth century.

The nineteenth century

Much of the accent on new bottle making techniques was directed towards moulding, although the search for methods of attaining an exact size of wine bottle had begun in the latter part of the seventeenth century. Initially the search for uniformity was in order to regulate capacity but, in the late eighteenth century, demand ensured that speed was of the essence. To this end, Charles Chubsee of Stourbridge, Gloucester, developed an iron bottle-making mould of three-piece design in 1802, which not only allowed the body of the bottle to be blown to a predetermined shape and size, but also the neck. Only the lip, and the seal should this be needed, remained to be finished by hand in the traditional fashion.

The firm of Henry Ricketts, Bristol, had been making similar experiments, and by 1811 some mould-formed bottles from this company were already on the market. By 1821, when Ricketts was granted a patent for his three-piece mould, bottles began to emerge from the glass house of a totally different character. The additional embossing of the company name to the base, and the Imperial measure and patent marks to the shoulder, were also entirely new concepts as far as wine bottles were concerned, but served somehow to alienate the new bottles from the previous tradition of truly free-blown and hand-made bottles. The present day appeal of moulded wine bottles, even when sealed, is not great, but at the time, moulding meant that the wine merchant and his customers were assured not only of equal measure, but also of consistent quality.

Even so, fewer and fewer people had their bottles sealed, it was becoming unnecessary and less prestigious to do so. The ownership of 'personalised' bottles had once held great distinction, but now that industry mass-produced the wine bottle the interest in sealing rapidly declined.

Almost fully automatic production was achieved just prior to 1890 by a Yorkshireman named Howard Ashley, but the first truly automatic machine was developed in the United States by Michael Owens in 1902. Such machines were soon installed in this country and, with further development, the Owen's machines were capable of manufacturing glass bottles at the alarming rate of over fifty thousand a day.

Just look at the hedgerows, ditches, rivers and streams of today; we are already building up a considerable legacy of glass containers for future generations to unearth. Is it at all possible that one day we shall look upon these as historic and curious artefacts of a bygone age?

Important facts and events

1542   Amongst an incredible array of glass vessels belonging to Henry VIII, were listed 'Twelve bottles of glasse with oone cover to them all, etc etc.'

1549   Eight Murano glass workers arrived in England and set up their furnace in the Crutched-friars Monastery in London.

1567   Jean Carre, who controlled the London glass house, petitioned for a licence to produce Venice glass, which failed.

1570   Undeterred, Carre introduced Venetian workmen in order to assist in the running of the Crutched-friars glass house.

1572   Carre died, and his foremost workman, Giacomo Verzelini became the glass house manager.

1575   The Crutched-friars site burned down, and Verzelini established a new glass house in Broad Street. In the same year he applied for a patent to make Venice glasses, and was granted this for a period of twenty-one years.
       The English-Housewife referred to 'round bottles with narrow necks for bottle ale, the corks being tied down with stout string.'

1578   Elizabeth I instituted the appointment of 'Yeoman of the Bottales', with an annual wage of £5. By 1690 the appointment included two horses in addition to the annual salary; from which we may infer that the position entailed more than mere 'head cellarman'. Indeed, it may well have extended to ensuring the actual purchase and safe transportation of the wine to and from its destination in the Royal Cellars.

1589   Hugh Miller and Acton Scott applied to the crown for a patent to make 'Urynalls, bottels, bowles, cuppis to drinck in and such lyke.' There were now fifteen glass houses operating in the metropolis.

1592	Verzelini retired, and Sir Jerome Bowes took over the Broad Street glass house. Two or three bottle houses established in London, purely to specialise in the production of 'French quart wine bottles' as they were then known.
1605	The Star Chamber accounts of James I for the year give another early reference to bottles and corks: 'item for bottles to bring the Lords wine in 13/4, item to him for corks to stop bottles, 2/6.' An early inventory of the same date refers to: '2 glasse bottles couerde wth leather'; 'One greate wanded bottle of glasse'.
1610	Licence granted for the invention of coal fired glass houses.
1611	Sir Edward Zouche spent sums in the region of £5,000 in the erection of glass houses at Lambeth.
1612	A glass house in existence at Southwark was engaged totally in the manufacture of 'green glass', this would almost certainly include bottles.
1615	James I prohibited the importation of French bottles and the use of wood fuel for glass furnaces. A company headed by Sir Edward Zouche took over the Broad Street glass house. Markham wrote: 'The corks of all bottles should be fast tied with pack thread.'
1621	The household account books of Lord William Howard of Naworth Castle recorded the following items over a short period of years: 1621 — two bottles to put wine in 8d. 1624 — XIX quarters of seck to fill the cellers of glasses. 1633 — glass bottells 3s.
1623	Sir Robert Mansell acquired the sole patent for the making of glasses. This included 'all manner of drinking glasses, broade glasses, windowe glasses, looking glasses, and all other kinde of glasses, glasses, bugles, bottles, violls or vessells whatsoever made of glass of any fashion, stuffe, matter or metall whatsoever...with seacoale, pittcoale, or any other fewell whatsoever, not being tymber or wood.'
1634	Customs' records of the period already show 'English bottles' as part of the merchandise exported from this country.
1636	Act prohibiting the sale of wine by the bottle.
1645	Oliver Cromwell taxed glass, including bottles.
1658	William Russell, fifth Earl of Bedford is known to have ordered twelve dozen glass bottles at this date, and a further twelve dozen, 'with my Lord's coat on yem' in 1671. These latter bottles cost 5s. a dozen.
1660	First mention in literature of bottled beer and wine as an export.

1662   Patent granted to Henry Holden and John Colenet to manufacture glass bottles, providing these were more standardised and of equal measure. As their claim of 'having invented and attained unto perfection the making of glass bottles' was later found to be false the patent was withdrawn. It was alleged that Colenet had assisted a certain Sir Kenelm Digby in making wine bottles at least thirty years previously.

1663   The well-known reference in Samuel Pepys' diary, when he went to Mr. Rawlinson's "and saw some of my new bottles made with my crest upon them, filled with wine, about five or six dozen."

1672   Between this date and 1676, Sir Robert Clayton ordered 181 dozen bottles from a Southwark glass house; of this amount, 107 dozen were 'marked' bottles, in short seals.

1677   Several glass houses in England now specialised purely in the production of bottles.

1689   Phillip Dallowes, a 'green-glass worker' claimed to have found a way of making bottles to an exact size, an interesting reference to an early form of cup mould.

1691   An inventory of this date gives the current price of plain bottles as 2s. per dozen.

1695   Thirty-eight bottle houses in operation in England, with a total annual output of over two million.

The Excise Act recorded that, "glass bottles fly and break to at least ten per cent loss whilst in the warehouse"; this all points to an inadequate annealing process.

William III put a duty on wine bottles of 1s. a dozen.

1696   The number of bottle houses increased to forty-two.

The writer John Houghton stated that home demand was now well catered for, and in 1694 he only knew of eight dozen bottles being imported.

1698   The duty payable on glass halved.

1699   The duty abolished altogether.

1703   The Methuen Treaty signed with Portugal; wines from that country now entered England at distinctly lower rates of duty, and in return we exported woollen goods on a like basis.

1725   Daniel Defoe mentioned the export of large quantities of glass bottles: 'fill'd with beer, cider and wine etc.'

Fifteen glass houses operating in Bristol alone.

1728   Parliament introduced Bill prohibiting the import of wine in flasks, bottles or small casks.

1735   Scenes from Hogarth's 'Rakes Progress' show the continued use of wanded bottles.

1736   Act settling the measure of wine sold in bottles.

1738	Bottle houses gave more detail to the all-important process of annealing.
1746	Excise duty again levied on all types of glass.
1750	The glass house at Alloa in Scotland is recorded as introducing Bohemian workers to assist in the making of glass bottles.
1770	The actual duty on glass bottles at this date is 2s. cwt.
1802	Charles Chubsee of Stourbrige made an iron bottle mould of three-piece design.
1811	Several moulded or semi-moulded wine bottles appeared on the market, none with the addition of embossing to the shoulder or base.
1813	The duty on glass bottles raised to 8s.2d. a cwt.
1821	Henry Ricketts of Bristol granted a patent for a fully standardised bottle-making mould.
1845	The duty payable on glass bottles finally dropped altogether.

Chronological calendar

Dates on bottles often mean very little unless one can immediately associate them with the period in which the bottles were made. It was therefore thought desirable to add a chronological calendar with some details of dated bottles relevant to particular monarchs' dates.

The bottles in this book were in the main part made during the Stuart and Hanoverian periods.

Stuart

CHARLES I, 1625-49. It is thought that at least two bottles dated in the 1630s are in private hands, albeit of a fragmentary nature, but apart from this no other dated seals for this very early period have yet come to light. As previously stated, the Holden-Colenet case, if taken at face value, makes the existence of bottles with seals dated after 1632 a definite reality. The shaft and globe with the Jermyn coat of arms is 1644-45 and a few other bottles are thought to be of this age.

COMMONWEALTH, 1649-60 (Oliver Cromwell, 1653-58, Richard Cromwell, 1658-59). In the period just prior to Cromwell's rise to power in 1653 we have the first dated seal, 'W.E.1650', followed by 'John Jefferson 1652'; the 'R.W.' bottles, although undated, are of a similar age.

First intact dated seal bottle, the celebrated shaft and globe 'R.P.M. 1657'. Almost certainly of the same period, although again undated, are Richard Billingsly' and a castle, 'R.M.R.' and a stag, and 'L.W.M.' and a Tudor rose. Being undated it is only fair to say that the latter bottles, and several others like them, could conceivably occur at the beginning of the following period. Precise dating to within a year or so is often very difficult.

CHARLES II, 1660-85. The two classic bottles at the outset of this period are 'C.R...R.A.B. 1661' and 'C.R. 1661'. Both examples carry the head and bust of the monarch and were undoubtedly made to celebrate the Restoration. As commemoratives these bottles were certainly issued some years after the event and a date nearer the 1670s would seem more appropriate. The form and construction of both examples would seem to bear this out.

Dated seals for the next ten years are very scarce; a mermaid and the date '16(6)7' is represented by a seal only; similarly, two (16)74 seals with the cipher of 'Anne Morrell' exist and a solitary (16)75 example without neck top. One of the best condition early bottles is provided by 'Bydder, THISTLE-BOON 1674'. Following this, 'Richard Church', a dolphin and 1676 is another good example. Post-1680 dated seals, although scarce, become a little more frequent. Some of the more important ones which take us through to the end of this monarch's reign are: 'M.W.' intertwined, plus the date, '8 & 1', for 1681; 'A.H.' and mermaid, '1682'; cipher of Anne Morrell, 1683; bottles with same seal, dated 1684 and 1685; R. How at Chedworth 1683; 'E.C. Cambridge', a dolphin, 1684; 'Anthony Hall' in Oxford, 1685.

JAMES II, 1685-88. The transition period, very few long-necked bottles were made; the squat onion-like form rapidly took their place.

Examples of this type of bottle are: 'C.P. 1686'; 'T.L. 1687'; cipher of Anne Morrell 1686, and a similar bottle dated 1688; 'R.H.' a (?) globe '1688'; 'T.T. 1688' and, lastly, 'E.S. 1688'.

WILLIAM III and MARY II, 1689-1702 (Mary II 1689-94). In the main, early onion forms exist, as exemplified by 'Cha. Turnor 1690'; 'R.W.' a King's head, '1690', (two variant types); 'W.T.C. 1690'; 'R.N. 1691'; 'I.I. 1693'; 'R.W.' flanking a King's bust, '1693'; 'H. Hooton, 1694'; 'R.W.' a King's head '1695'; 'R.W.' flanking a King's bust, '1696' and '1697'; 'D. Musgrave, (16)98'; 'R.E.W.' a King's head '1699'; 'R.E.W.' King's bust in armour, '1699'; 'G.S. 1699'; 'M.M. 1700'; 'Daniel Dowsing de Norwich, 1700'; 'I.C. 1700'; 'Edouard Gaston 1700'; 'Abraham Frost 1701'.

ANNE, 1702-14. The main onion period, dated seals became more frequent, but those with the magic '0' in the date remained few in number and much more difficult to find than post-1710 dated examples. The emergence of the bladder onion, or oval-bodied bottle, should also be noted. Early examples of this bottle are 'N.C. 1710' and 'Thos. Adams Senr. 1714'. Below are listed dated onion bottles, one for each year of Queen Anne's reign, the last of the Stuart monarchy:

'Coventry House, 1702'; 'Rice Wight 1703'; 'J. Collens 1704'; 'T. Browne Exon 1705'; 'F.G. 1706'; 'William Battishill 1707'; 'Anne Eilhering^{tn} 1708'; 'Tho. Edgar 1709'; 'Robt. Smith 1710'; 'M. Hinton 1711'; 'F.M. 1712'; 'I.H. 1713 PAX'; 'Mr Labbe de Lavillette 1714'.

With the exception of the penultimate bottle (an usually square shaped example) all those recorded above are of the typical rounded squat form. 'Rice Wight 1703' is one of the scarce decanter bottles.

Hanoverian

GEORGE I, 1714-27. Onion bottles remain the typical vessel in use until c.1720, by which time the introduction of straighter-sided bottles had already begun. By 1725 onions in their true form were uncommon and by 1728 they were scarce. The examples illustrative of this period include bottles of both types and these are marked accordingly. The majority will also be found in the plates.

'W. Pratt 1714'; 'W. Roe 1717'; 'R. Erisey 1718'; 'T. Ridge 1720' (true onions).

'J. Holme 1721'; 'D.V.O. 1724' (transitionals).

'E. Herbert 1721'; 'J. Fenn 1725'; 'Samuel Caston Wodbrig 1725'; 'Wm. Strode esq 1727' (straight sides).

GEORGE II, 1727-60. When the onion bottle faded from the scene, the mallet swiftly took its place. The octagonal made its debut c.1730, and the earliest of the cylindrical bottles were in evidence just a little later; examples of all three types are given below.

'O.G.M. 1732'; 'F. Fry, Dear Park 1736'; 'Evan Jones Llanellyd 1743' (mallets).

'M.C.R. Exon 1744'; 'W. Basterd 1753'; 'Wm. Daniel 1754'; 'G.D. 1758' (cylinders).

'C.E. 1734'; 'R.W. 1739'; 'Wm. Vallis 1741'; 'Jno. Jackson 1751' (octagonals).

GEORGE III, 1760-1820. The mallet bottle was superseded by the squat and true cylindrical forms, the latter far more suitable for binning. A further development was the appearance of the Nailsea bottles around 1800. Few of these bottles emanate from the eighteenth century, although the factory was known to be in existence by 1788. Most dated examples were made during the reign of George IV and William IV.

Examples of both squat and true cylinders may be found by reference to the plates; a few more, both typical of their respective types are given below.

'J.H. Haddon 1770'; 'I. Sharp 1781'; 'R.B. Bray Morrish 1786'; 'G. Olliver 1799'; 'Jno. Williams Ruan 1815' (squats).

'W. Pooly 1764'; 'T. Godden 1777'; 'James Oakes. Bury 1781'; 'T. Littlefair 1796'; 'Wm. Warren Taunton 1807' (cylinders).

GEORGE IV, 1820-30. The great majority of bottles are now three-piece moulds, the process becoming almost universal after 1822. First embossing is now seen on the shoulders and bases of wine bottles. Most bottles still carry the normal pontil scar but fewer of them have actual dated seals.

'John Dunning 1821'; 'Jos. H Arlett 1822'; 'Picton Castle 1827'; 'S.T. 1828' (three-piece moulds).

WILLIAM IV, 1830-37. Virtually all moulded bottles; in general fewer seals, examples here are:

'Jno George Pennant 1833'; 'T. Putt 1836'; 'Jas Gill 1836'; 'B 'a coronet' 1837' (three-piece moulds).

VICTORIA, 1837-1901. The continuation of moulded bottles, and the disappearance of the pontil scar around 1840. The practice of sealing bottles rapidly declined in Queen Victoria's reign never, it appears, fully to revive. Sealed examples are: 'N. Lawrance Launceston 1840'; 'Boynton 1848'; 'H.G. 1854'; 'Rousden Jubilee 1887'.

Development of design, 1630-1900

c.1630-60	Long parallel neck, bulbous body, string-rim applied well below lip, kick-up of small diameter and often shallow, bottle stands somewhat precariously on small base. Bottles invariably of green metal and often light in weight.
c.1660-70	Long neck tapering somewhat to shoulders, body more ample, egg-shaped or slightly angular shoulders, string-rim fractionally nearer lip.
c.1670-80	Neck distinctly shortened and becoming broader at shoulders, body often larger, shoulders of bottle more distinctly angular, string-rim becomes progressively nearer to lip, kick-up becomes both wider and deeper. Bottle sits on wider base and becomes more stable. Often of heavier green metal.

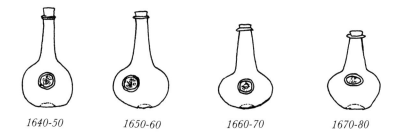

1640-50   *1650-60*   *1660-70*   *1670-80*

c.1680-90 Neck shorter still (in some cases becoming very abbreviated), body much larger, either bucket-shaped or considerably more bulbous, kick-up wider still and moderately deep, string-rim position to within 6mm of lip. Most bottles remain green in colour and heavy in weight.

c.1690-1700 Neck only moderate, body distinctly globular, angular shoulders virtually disappear, string-rim remains similarly positioned, base of bottle wider as is kick-up and pontil. Bottles mostly green but becoming darker, 'black' glass examples begin to emerge.

c.1700-10 Slender and more attenuated neck, body becoming wider and more squat, base wider than before and string-rim 3-4mm below lip, kick-up often quite shallow, 'black' glass bottles appear more frequently. Lighter in weight than in previous two decades.

c.1710-20 Form remains fairly constant, at end of period distinct signs of marvered sides to certain bottles. Mostly dark glass, but varying from green, through olive, to black.

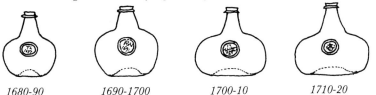

1680-90   *1690-1700*   *1700-10*   *1710-20*

c.1720-30 Neck gradually lengthens and marvered sides to majority of bottles results in squarer bodies, shoulders often narrower than bases, which are wide with kick-up deeper and more rounded.

c.1730-40 Neck longer still, slightly tapering to shoulder, body often

1720-30   *1730-40*   *1740-50*   *1750-60*

	almost square, sagged at base. Kick-up very deep occasionally reaching up into bottle to mid-body level, hummock shaped. String-rim in some examples is again fractionally lowered. Metal varies in colour.
c.1740-50	Neck increases in diameter but remains quite long, body either squarish or of more upright form. Other features similar.
c.1750-60	Neck remains moderately long, bottle becomes narrower and more upright, although somewhat short in the body. Kick-up rather more cone-shaped but still deep.
c.1760-70	Upright cylindrical bottles with sagged bases, kick-up deep and often acute. Neck moderately long, string-rim becomes 'double' in some cases, due to flattening over of rim. Bottles in various coloured metals but majority in dark glass.
c.1770-80	Necks vary in length during this period, bodies vary from cylindrical to squat cylindrical, double string-rim normal though fair amount of variation. Kick-up remains similar. Sagged base to bottles gives overall waisted appearance.
c.1780-90	True cylindricals are the order of the day, but the squat form of bottle still popular. Necks variable, but generally longer on the narrow bottles, and shorter on the squats. Kick-up deep, wider, and often shallower on squat forms. String-rim double but variable.
c.1790-1800	Continuation of cylindrical form but squats become fewer as not suitable for binning. String-rim becoming, if anything, more ample.

| 1760-70 | 1770-80 | 1780-90 | 1790-1800 |

c.1800-10	Fewer squats, mainly true cylindricals which sag very little at the base. Kick-up becoming once again shallower. Many now blown into 'chip mould', and wider at shoulder than base. String-rim ample, normally a double collar of glass. Mostly dark glass bottles.
c.1810-20	Emergence of three-piece mould bottles towards end of this period, with mould seams plainly traceable. Neck moderate and evenly tapering, string-rim becomes cone-shaped but remains double collar of glass. Disappearance of pontil scar to base of many bottles.
c.1820-90	Few free-blown bottles produced, mainly three-piece mould cylindricals; even these, however, produced in both cylindrical and squat forms. Lips and rims of bottles remain hand-finished, with cone-shaped top altering slightly in aspect on certain bottles c.1850. 'Blob tops', appear towards the end of this period. Base now concave and shallow with embossed lettering, rarely pontilled.
c.1890-1900	Moulded bottles of narrow cylindrical form. Mould seams eradicated on later examples, by 1900 many are machine-made.

1800-10 *1810-20* *1820-50* *1850-1900*

Two bottle forms which do not fit easily into the evolutionary process noted above are the bladder onion form and the moulded form.

c.1710-75   The bladder onion bottle appeared c.1710 with no apparent evolutionary form preceding it. Tenuous links *may* exist with figures j and k in section 17 but this is by no means certain.

1730-70   Moulded bottles were certainly not 'new' c.1730, but it was at this time that the octagonal form found favour as far as wine containers were concerned. Compared to other forms, its use was not widespread and true sealed wines in this form are hard to come by.

1710-75   *1730-70*

3. General Guide to Dating

Reference to the wine bottles illustrated at the end of the previous section will show the major changes that occurred in the construction of English wine bottles c.1630-1900. Following this, machine-made bottles became almost universal, and their charm and character rapidly declined.

The examples referred to provide broad guide lines only, as many differences in form occurred; it should always be borne in mind that we are dealing with vessels that were almost entirely free-blown and hand-finished, and certain anomalies and eccentricities are to be expected. Today, it is the very individual quality of these objects that renders them so particularly attractive to the collector. Nevertheless, with such an array of variant forms, the dating of unsealed bottles can at first prove a little confusing. Certain bottles can be placed quite easily within their respective age groups, others are more difficult. Where available, careful comparison with sealed and dated counterparts is essential. When this is not possible, the all important criteria of form, colour, weight, thickness of metal, kick-up, and pontil should be assessed collectively. By such means, the majority of bottles can be dated quite accurately, providing total reliance is not placed on any one factor.

A further pitfall worth mentioning is that certain dissimilar forms of bottle were often manufactured simultaneously; the onion and the bladder-onion are a case in point. In addition, some features are not always definitive of a precise age. The reasons for this are quite simple; no two glass houses operated identically, and the adoption of new techniques occurred at different stages in different glass houses. Having said this, reference to some actual examples can be made. Figures a and b show a pair of English wines which differ to a remarkable degree in form alone, yet they are both of a similar age. Figure a is a late onion bottle, c.1726. Figure b is a bottle of the same period crudely formed, but representing an early attempt at a more upright bottle. As one of the first efforts to regulate the shape and size of the vessel, it is an interesting and scarce

Figure a

Figure b

item, but one that upon first encounter fails to reveal its age.

As early as the seventeenth century, some onion bottles were blown into a cup-like mould in order to determine their actual body size; this however had little effect on their appearance, and was primarily designed to ensure equal measure. Other contemporary but dissimilar forms are illustrated in figures c-j. Figures c and d show an onion c.1720 and an early mallet of the same period. The mallet differs from the onion only in its 'marvered' sides, yet this small step has rendered the appearance of the two bottles totally different. Both forms were to exist side by side for a number of years. Indeed, some collectors refer to such transitional bottles as straight-sided onions, and not without some justification, as it is occasionally difficult to know just where the dividing line should be drawn.

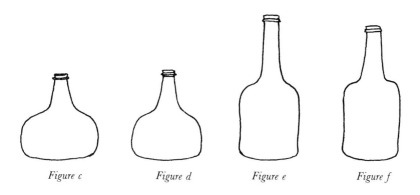

Figure c   *Figure d*   *Figure e*   *Figure f*

Even the cylindrical wines varied to a considerable degree. Both the squat and cylindrical forms were manufactured simultaneously as dated seals testify. The former more bulky form was not to fade from the scene until the early nineteenth century, which is all the more surprising when one considers how unsuitable the bottle must have been for binning purposes. Obviously not everyone's cellar arrangements were of the 'modern' kind, even at this late date.

Figures e and f represent two early cylindrical wines c.1750; figures g and h two bottles of the 1780 period, and figures i and j a pair of sealed bottles dated 1822 and 1824 respectively. Considering the small difference in age, the latter two bottles are remarkably dissimilar in form. In addition to this it is unusual to note that both are free-blown, and not of the moulded variety more frequent at this date.

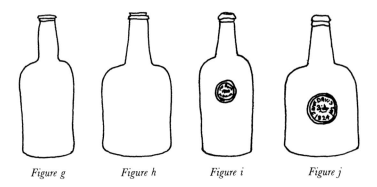

Figure g   Figure h   Figure i   Figure j

Bearing in mind all these facts, the collector, and especially the novice, may well doubt his chances of placing an unsealed bottle to within ten years of its manufacture. It does seem true, that the more bottles one examines, the more difficult it becomes to generalise at all; there are always enough exceptions to obscure the rule. The most sound advice one can offer the beginner is to examine as many wine bottles as possible, and so much the better if one can actually handle the pieces, and give them close scrutiny. Eventually, given experience, the dating of unsealed wines should not cause too much difficulty, although the necessary '*circa*' should always be added to new acquisitions of this nature.

Wine bottles in section, c.1650-1820

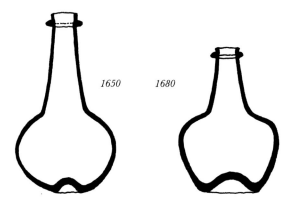

1650   1680

1710

1730

1770

1790

1820

Changes in the string-rim construction on English wines, 1640-1910 onwards

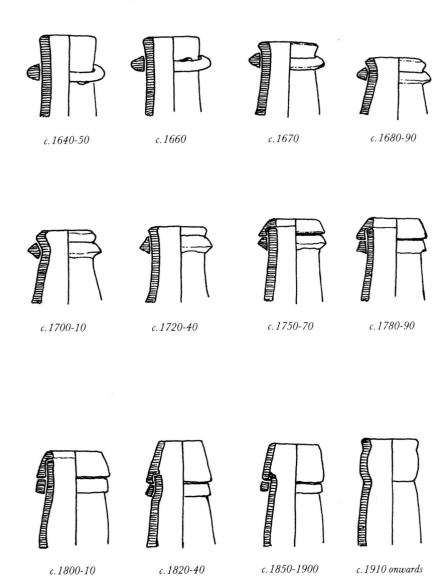

c.1640-50	*c.1660*	*c.1670*	*c.1680-90*
c.1700-10	*c.1720-40*	*c.1750-70*	*c.1780-90*
c.1800-10	*c.1820-40*	*c.1850-1900*	*c.1910 onwards*

String-rim variants on dated English wines, c.1770-1840

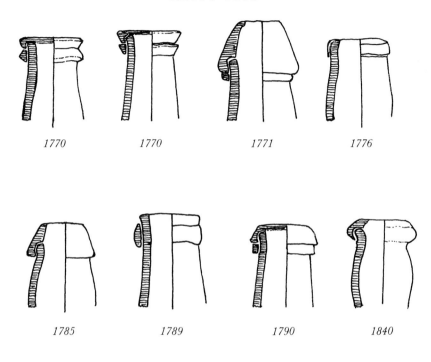

1770 *1770* *1771* *1776*

1785 *1789* *1790* *1840*

European string-rim types on unsealed wines

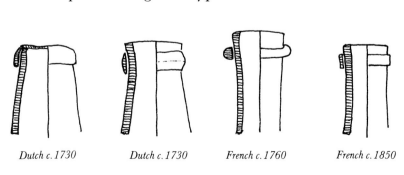

Dutch c.1730 *Dutch c.1730* *French c.1760* *French c.1850*

Plate 1. *English wine bottle kick-ups and pontil marks, c.1630-1820 (see also European Wine Bottles pp.130-133).*

c.1630-60

c.1660-80

c.1680-90

c.1690-1700

c.1725-30

c.1735-50

c.1770-1800

c.1770-1815

c.1822 onwards

c.1680

c.1685

c.1690

c.1700-10

Plate 2. *One hundred years in the development of the English wine bottle is shown by these 'typical' unsealed bottles of the period 1680-1780.*

c.1720-30

c.1730-40

c.1750-60

1770-80

43

4. Shaft and Globe Wine Bottles, c.1630-60

The very first wine bottles of the true shaft and globe form appeared during the reign of Charles I, probably shortly after 1630. A pair of bottles with seals dated c.1637 is thought to be in private hands. Its existence is certainly feasible if one examines the implications of the Holden-Colonet case of 1662 which is discussed on pp.19 and 20.

Several bottles thought to be pre-1650 are known, although the distinction of being the earliest intact dated seal bottle still rests with Northampton Museum's 'R M P 1657'. The recently discovered 'W E 1650' exists as a seal only, and is the earliest in that form. This important seal was recovered from the Thames at Queenhithe, and now rests in the Museum of London. Closely following this is another detached seal with a coat of arms and 'John Jefferson 1652'. However, even if undated, earlier intact bottles do exist, the shaft and globe bearing the arms of Henry Jermyn being a case in point. Sound documentary evidence exists (an article in *Country Life,* October 1952 by Ruggles-Brise) to prove the bottle dates c.1644-45. Among other examples which could be cited are the 'R W' sealed bottles discovered in both England and America. The history surrounding these bottles also suggests a date of manufacture prior to 1652. The half-bottle 'W H P' and the king's arms is another excellent example of a bottle almost certainly of this age, and there are several others.

These early bottles competed in their time with the 'black-jacks', bellarmines and Delftware wine pots of Lambeth but, by the end of the period under discussion, the future of the glass wine bottle was assured.

The first shaft and globe bottles were almost true to their name, having a long parallel neck and globular body with the kick-up often small in diameter, and only just sufficient to raise the jagged pontil scar clear of the table. The bottles rested somewhat precariously on a very small surface area.

In unsealed bottles attributed to 1630 the neck is long and narrow, the body globular with shoulders ill-defined, figure a. Circa 1640-50 the neck becomes wider but remains fairly parallel, the body size increases in diameter and, if anything, becomes more squat and egg-shaped; the shoulders however remain hardly, if at all, discernible, figure b. Circa 1655-60 the neck is very gently tapering and becomes moderately wide where it joins the body. The bowl of the bottle becomes truly egg-shaped with shoulders distinctly traceable, figure c.

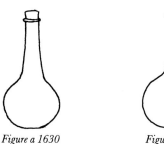

Figure a 1630 *Figure b 1645* *Figure c 1655*

Throughout this early period the string-rim remained well below the orifice of the bottle, at times by as much as 12-15mm. The string-rim itself deserves special mention, as on all shaft and globe bottles its position, construction and application are quite different from later bottles; only on the first onion bottles do we find lingering similarities. A wide strip of glass was quite loosely applied around the neck of the bottle and pinched on to the neck, or held there by the addition of small blobs of glass applied both from above and below. Thus, compared to later types of string-rim, it was more ample, but less an integral part of the bottle. This is borne out by several of these bottles which have come down to us with the string-rim completely missing but the actual neck undamaged.

Later string-rims were smaller, more closely fitting affairs, and when these suffered a blow it normally followed that the neck was damaged too. In shape the string-rim was disc-like, rounded at the edges and invariably wider than in later bottles.

The majority of these early bottles are of a fairly light apple green colour and many were surprisingly light in weight for their size, few if any of the really dark glass examples having yet been made.

Position and character of the string-rim on bottles c.1630-60

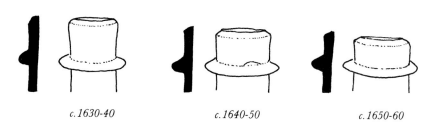

c.1630-40 *c.1640-50* *c.1650-60*

45

Plate 3. *Shaft and globe bottle, surface condition showing result of long burial in the ground; an early example c.1660.*

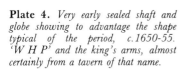

Plate 4. *Very early sealed shaft and globe showing to advantage the shape typical of the period, c.1650-55. 'W H P' and the king's arms, almost certainly from a tavern of that name.*

Unsealed shaft and globe wine bottles, c.1630-60

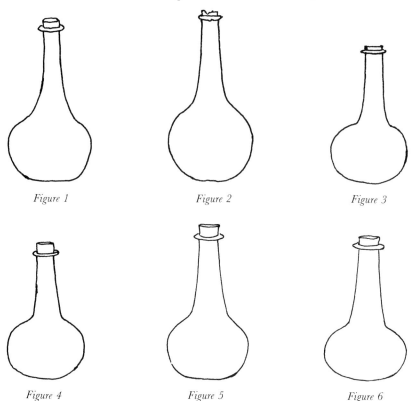

Figure 1   Figure 2   Figure 3

Figure 4   Figure 5   Figure 6

Figure 1. *Very early crudely-made bottle, ascribed by some students and collectors to the period of Charles I, c.1630-40. Note the spindly neck, poorly tooled string-rim and irregular shaped body. The kick-up is almost non-existent.*

Figure 2. *Bottle of the period 1640-50, of heavier metal. The ill-defined shoulders result in an almost bag-shaped body; the kick-up is once again minimal.*

Figure 3. *The body is now globular and more carefully formed, neck parallel, kick-up shallow but distinct. Most bottles now display some aptitude in their making; c.1650.*

Figure 4. *Body a little more oval, slight taper to neck, but otherwise similar to Figure 3; c.1655.*

Figure 5. *Neck now distinctly tapering and wider where it meets the body, kick-up moderately pronounced. Some bottles, such as this example, are now relatively broader in the base; c.1655-60.*

Figure 6. *The more normal form, c.1660; egg-shaped body with neck evenly but distinctly tapering.*

Sealed shaft and globe wine bottles, c.1650-60

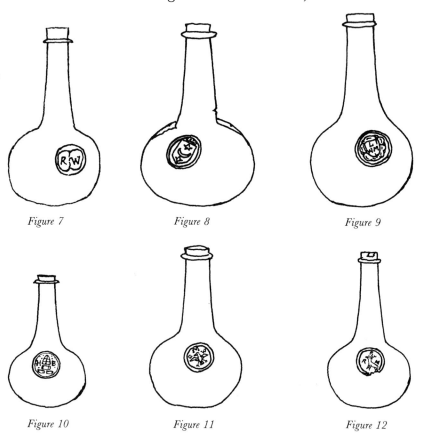

Figure 7

Figure 8

Figure 9

Figure 10

Figure 11

Figure 12

Figure 7. 'R W'. *Evidence suggests a pre-1652 date for this bottle and another like it, both found in London and traced to Ralph Wormeley a plantation owner of Jamestown, Virginia, where identical seals to those on the London bottles have been discovered. There is some dispute as to the exact date of his death but c.1650 would seem appropriate.*

Figure 8. *Coat-of-arms of Henry Jermyn, created a Baron in 1643 and Earl of St. Albans in 1660. Evidence surrounding the discovery of this bottle suggests that it could date prior to 1650.*

Figure 9. *'W M L' in a Tudor rose; William and Mary Long of the Rose Tavern, Covent Garden, London, c.1655.*

Figure 10. *'H B', a vintner's brush and three tuns, c.1655. Belonged to Humphrey Bodicott of the Three Tuns Tavern, Oxford, tenancy period 1639-60.*

Figure 11. *'G W M' and a bird with wings displayed, c.1655-60. A classical shape and typical of the period.*

Figure 12. *'R M R' and a stag; almost certainly a tavern bottle, c.1655-60.*

48

Sealed shaft and globe wine bottles, c.1657-60

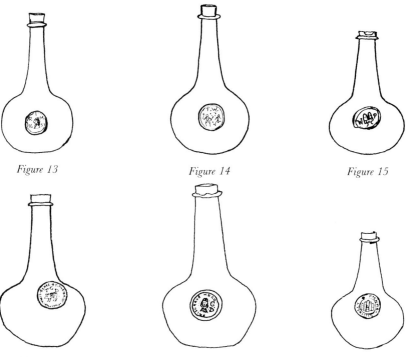

Figure 13   Figure 14   Figure 15

Figure 16   Figure 17   Figure 18

Figure 13. 'R M P 1657' and a king's or Turk's head. Although the earliest dated intact bottle, its ownership remains unsolved. Possibly from a King's or Turk's Head Tavern.

Figure 14. 'T. W.' and two tennis players; Thomas Wood of the Salutation Tavern, Oxford, 1651-63. The bottle is c.1660 and is unlikely to pre-date the 1657.

Figure 15. 'W P' and a mitre, c.1660. Traditionally associated with William Piers, one-time Bishop of Peterborough, Bath and Wells, but now thought to have belonged to William Proctor of the Mitre Tavern in Wood Street, London. A further candidate, is William Pagett of the Fleet Street Mitre. Other Mitre Taverns and seals are known from London in the seventeenth century.

Figure 16. 'T D C' and 'THE WHIT BEARE AT THE BRIDG FOOT'. A tavern bottle with the initials those of the licensees. A White Bear Tavern once stood near the Old London Bridge; c.1660.

Figure 17. 'C.D/PALSGRAVE HEAD' and a man's head; c.1660. The Palsgrave Head was a tavern in the vicinity of Temple Bar, London. A seal formerly in the Guildhall Museum, London, has the letters 'THE PAULSGRAVE HED TAVERN' and initials 'C D S' and may well have emanated from the same premises.

Figure 18. 'Richard Billingsly' and a five-turreted castle; a shorter necked bottle than is usual at this period but no later than 1660.

49

5. Shaft and Globe Wine Bottles, c.1660-80

Of the few shaft and globe wine bottles that have come to light most fall within this period, roughly the reign of Charles II. A few bottles actually exist which portray the bust of the monarch carefully delineated on the seal. These examples, 'King's bottles' as they are occasionally known, had their originals in the numerous King's Head Taverns, which existed in the seventeenth century. Bottles from these and the previous decades are often in very poor, even fragmentary, condition, and a small percentage only have survived the ravages of time in anything like their original condition.

By 1665 noticeable changes had already taken place in the construction of wine bottles. The neck in many instances had become somewhat shorter and the parallel neck was slowly disappearing. The string-rim had moved nearer the bottle top, the body had become less globular, and shoulders to the vessel were now discernible. By 1670 all these changes were more marked, furthermore the body had become cup-shaped with more angular shoulders. With further development along these lines, the wine bottle c.1680 had a much abbreviated neck and a distinct bucket-shaped body. Very few bottles of the true shaft and globe shape were still manufactured. In general bottles had become heavier, sturdier and stood firmly upon a broader base as the four illustrations, figures a-c, show. It should be added that the kick-up became deeper and wider, and that the string-rim moved yet again a little nearer the bottle top (see opposite). Its disc-like construction remained similar but, if anything, it was a little narrower and smaller in diameter towards the end of the period.

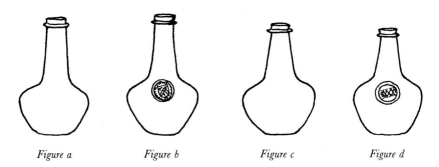

Figure a   *Figure b*   *Figure c*   *Figure d*

Although the long-necked globular-bodied bottle must have been a very natural form for the early glass blower to produce, it is evident that the fashion at this period for length and elegance also influenced the wine bottle's initial shape and form.

The change by 1680 to a heavier more squat bottle was probably one of necessity. It is suggested, quite feasibly, that in the crowded taverns of the period long-necked bottles were particularly vulnerable and prone to breakage, and replacement, even then, was quite costly. It was the tavern keepers who accounted for a large proportion of the bottles produced, for they, the noblemen, clergy and others of high rank were the only people able to afford them.

Neck top formation on bottles dated c.1665-80

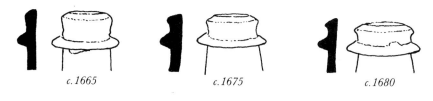

c.1665   c.1675   c.1680

Plate 5. *Half-size shaft and globe in almost mint condition and in much darker metal than is normal at this period; c.1665.*

Plate 6. *Early sealed (as yet unresearched) shaft and globe, c.1660-65. This is about the earliest date that a slight bucket shape to the body (the result of minimal marvering) is at all noticeable; the feature is more often noted on bottles c.1670 onwards. The bottle bears an original label showing it to have been dug up in London in 1884. Formerly in the Pitt Rivers Museum, Dorset.*

Plate 7. *A previously unrecorded shaft and globe sealed with a shield enclosing a chevron and three fleur-de-lis; in the apex of the chevron a hand appraised denoting a baronet. From Gloucester.*

Plate 8. *'W M' intertwined and the numerals 8 and 1 for (16)81; an early dated transitional form midway between shaft and globe and onion wines.*

Plate 9. *This immaculate shaft and globe half bottle c.1665 is rare on two counts. Firstly, it would be hard to find another bottle of this period in such fine condition; secondly, the bottle glass is exceedingly dark, virtually the true black glass so sought after by collectors.*

Sealed shaft and globe wine bottles, c.1660-75

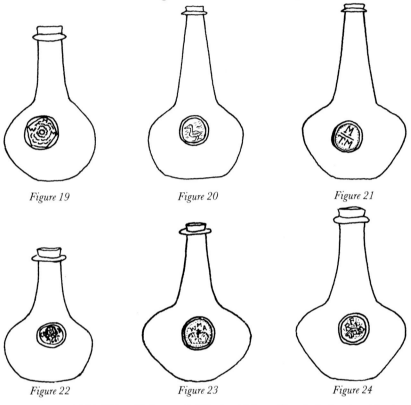

Figure 19

Figure 20

Figure 21

Figure 22

Figure 23

Figure 24

Figure 19. *'W M H' in a Tudor rose; half bottle with just a hint of a bucket-shaped bowl; c.1660-65.*

Figure 20. *Goose seal; in many respects a similar bottle to the following one. This example appears to have the inclusion of a gridiron beneath the bird motif, and therefore probably originated from a Goose and Gridiron Tavern in London; c.1665.*

Figure 21. *'T.M M' with a vintner's spray; belongs to a distinct group of bottles with somewhat contradictory dating features. The long neck has led most authors to assume a 1650-60 date for this form, but careful examination of all the criteria points to a somewhat later date, c.1665-70.*

Figure 22. *'C R B/1661' and a king's head. A Restoration commemorative and almost certainly manufactured some years after the actual event, c.1670.*

Figure 23. *'W A M' and a crown within a beaded border; William and Anne Morrell of the Crown Tavern, Oxford. Joint tenancy 1660-79, Anne Morrell as widow 1679-96. This example c.1670.*

Figure 24. *'R I F' and a bear; a good example of the typical form c.1675. Ralph and Joan Flexney of the Bear Inn, Oxford.*

Sealed shaft and globe wine bottles, c.1670-80

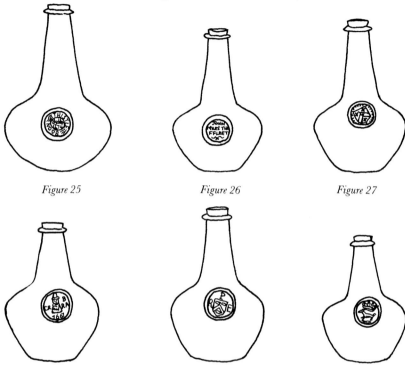

Figure 25   Figure 26   Figure 27

Figure 28   Figure 29   Figure 30

Figure 25. *'THISTLE BOON/Bydder/1674'. Few dated seals of the 1670s exist and this bottle provides a useful comparison for undated examples. The bottle belonged to Thomas Bydder of Thistle Boon, a small village in the parish of Oystermouth, south of Swansea.*
Figure 26. *'John/Miles The/Ffleet', c.1670-75. Possibly a tavern bottle but may have been connected with the Fleet Prison, London.*
Figure 27. *Shield enclosing a chevron, three fleur-de-lis and a hand appraised; the hand of Ulster denotes a baronet; original owner unknown; c.1670-75.*
Figure 28. *'C R/R A B/1661' and a king's head; very similar bottle to the bottle dated 1661 in Figure 22, and again unlikely to be as old as the date on the seal suggests; c.1675.*
Figure 29. *'R E P', a chevron and three tuns; Richard and Elizabeth Pont of the Three Tuns Tavern, Oxford, c.1678. Several detached seals are known, and a total of five or six complete bottles. The joint tenancy period extends from 1666 to 1687 and the bottles are datable according to their seals.*
Figure 30. *Stag with an earl's coronet above, c.1678-80. No provenance.*

6. Onion Wine Bottles, c.1680-1700

The gradual transition from a long-necked to a short-necked bottle had almost taken place by 1685. In many cases, however, bottles c.1680-90 certainly retained very strong resemblances to those of the previous decade, but even these soon faded with the further shortening of the neck and change in body size and shape around 1690.

In certain places up and down the country moderately long-necked bottles were still manufactured, but they had altered considerably since the long-necked, globular bodied bottles had first appeared on the scene. In general bottle necks were now much shorter and wider at the shoulder, while the body remained moderately high-shouldered and angular. These were truly transitional bottles, often spoken of by the collector as 'shaft and globe form onions', an apt enough term and one that levies a high value upon this type of bottle.

The string-rim remained ample and disc-like with evenly rounded edges and was applied in much the same way as before, it had, however, moved yet again fractionally nearer the orifice of the bottle, at a distance of approximately 6mm.

Three dated tavern bottles which show the progression in form, 1682-99

Figure a 1682 *Figure b 1690* *Figure c 1699*

Between 1690 and 1700 the necks of bottles shortened even further, as reference to figures a-c shows. Bodies became larger and more rotund and the characteristic bucket shape of the previous decades disappeared.

It is during this time, too, that subtle but important changes were made to the string-rim. These changes are most easily seen by reference to the drawings below, but in short the rim alters from a neat parallel coil of glass to one with a wider base and more bevelled edge set, yet again, a little nearer the bottle top. By 1700 it is positioned in most instances at a distance of some 4mm from the top of the bottle. One further characteristic which appears c.1685-1700 is the distinct flare given to the neck top above the string-rim. This resulted in a nipped or waisted appearance, and no doubt served to tighten the string-rim securely to the neck, and also to assist in pouring.

Neck top formation on bottles, c.1680-1700

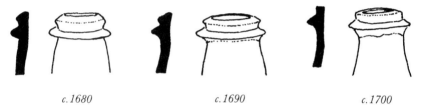

c.1680   c.1690   c.1700

Reference to the three onions on the previous page will show to advantage the precise changes which have been discussed. It is interesting to note the amount of change that has taken place in each bottle during what is a relatively short space of time. The shoulders of each bottle are gradually seen to slope away, the slight bucket-shape on the 'A H 1682' example (figure a) gives way to a distinctly more squat form in the 'R W 1690' (figure b) and eventually results in the even more squat and broad-based bottle 'R E W 1699' (figure c). These dated tavern bottles provide a very sound basis for the study of bottle evolution, the 'R E W 1699' bottle already reflecting the slightly more elegant neck form typical of bottles in the next decade.

Plate 10. *Two excellent tavern bottles; left: from the King's Head; right: from the Crown, both in Oxford; dated 1690 and 1684 respectively. The olive green king's head 1690 bottle bears a good likeness to King William on the seal with the letters 'R W' for Richard Walker, then tenant of that tavern. The long-necked 1684 bottle in green metal bears the cypher of William and Anne Morrell with a crown above and the letters 'OXON'. There are several variations according to date, etc.*

Plate 11. *Later King's Head Tavern bottle of Richard Walker dated 1699. In this example the seal has been completely redesigned and, in addition to a new effigy of the king, incorporates the extra letter 'E', for Walker's wife Elizabeth.*

Sealed onion wine bottles, c.1681-85

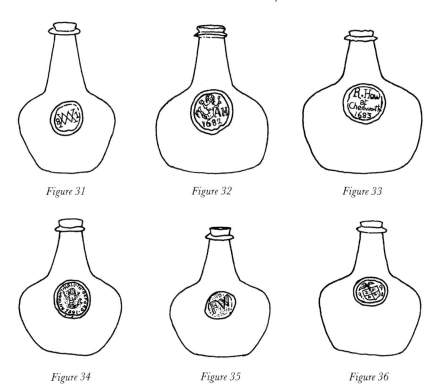

Figure 31   Figure 32   Figure 33

Figure 34   Figure 35   Figure 36

Figure 31. *'M W' intertwined, either side the digits '8 1', for (16)81; one of the earliest dated bottles extant. Probably the seal of Whicker-Moreton, who held the leases for the Mermaid Tavern in Oxford.*
Figure 32. *'A H/1682' and a mermaid; Anthony Hall, junior, 1675-91, of the Mermaid Tavern, Oxford. His father's seals incorporated a ship in addition to the mermaid device, and a single example appears to be dated 1667, although the third digit is somewhat poorly defined.*
Figure 33. *'R How/at/Chedworth/1683'. A large clearly sealed bottle, belonging to Richard How, Lord of the Manor at Chedworth, near Bristol, in the seventeenth century.*
Figure 34. *A mermaid, surrounded by the words 'ANTHONY HALL IN OXFORD 1685'; another Mermaid Tavern bottle of Anthony Hall, junior.*
Figure 35. *'F W', c.1685.*
Figure 36. *Possibly coat-of-arms and crest of the Lowther family, c.1685.*

Sealed onion wine bottles, c.1686-91

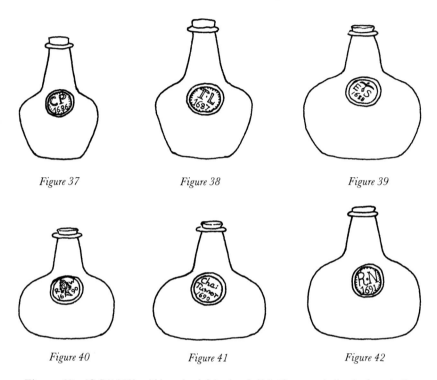

Figure 37   *Figure 38*   *Figure 39*

Figure 40   *Figure 41*   *Figure 42*

Figure 37. *'C P/1686' within a beaded border; half bottle, very similar in form to the following bottle. Excavated in London, owner unknown.*

Figure 38. *'T·L/1687' within a beaded border; as the figure shows some bottles were still made with a smaller body and contracted sides, thus retaining their 'earlier' characteristics at a time when other bottles of a more squat variety were already in production. See figures 32, 34, and 35.*

Figure 39. *'E S/1688'.*

Figure 40. *'R W/1690' and a king's head. Richard Walker of the King's Head Tavern, Oxford 1687-1704. There are several bottles and seals connected with this tavern, but only one is known dating from the first year of his tenancy.*

Figure 41. *'Cha:/Turnor/1690'. There are two of these bottles, one complete, the other broken, both found in Oxford where the name Turner was quite frequent at this date.*

Figure 42. *'R·N/1691', within a beaded border; Robert Newman, merchant-mariner of Dartmouth, 1676-1739.*

Sealed onion wine bottles, c.1693-99

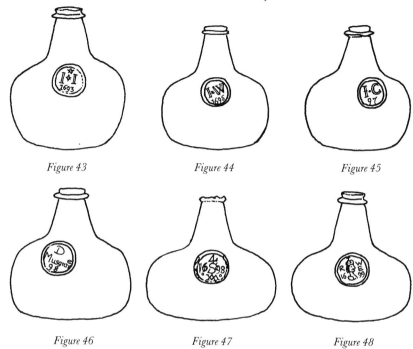

Figure 43

Figure 44

Figure 45

Figure 46

Figure 47

Figure 48

Figure 43. 'I I/1693' and two stars.

Figure 44. 'I W/1695'.

Figure 45. 'I·C/97'. Unfortunately it is always difficult to trace the owners of bottles with initials only, and the history surrounding the discovery of the bottle needs to be known if any success is to be achieved. The practice of using single digits to represent the date drew to a close with the passing of the seventeenth century.

Figure 46. 'D/Musgrave/98', for 1698. Musgrave or Musgrove, as it is occasionally spelt, crops up quite frequently in eighteenth century Oxford. A certain Musgrave was apparently a fellow of All Souls College in 1747, and it is quite possible that the family had been in Oxford during the seventeenth century.

Figure 47. A merchant's mark and date '1698'. Believed to be the only complete example of its type in England. As bottles are known to have travelled far and wide during their lives, it is not unreasonable to suppose that this example could have been brought to this country from the colonies. Several early settlers had their bottles marked in this fashion, but as most glass vessels were still ordered from England, it is equally possible that this example never actually reached its destination. Purchased at an auction in the West Country.

Figure 48. 'R E W/1699'. Another King's Head Tavern, Oxford, bottle, this time with the inclusion of Walker's wife's initial 'E' (for Elizabeth) incorporated in the seal. Many of the Oxford tavern bottles have been recovered from the sites of the original taverns, whilst others have been excavated from rubbish dumps on the town's outskirts.

7. Onion Wine Bottles, c.1700-30

By the year 1700 the onion bottle, as most people understand it, was well-established. The body of the bottle had now become very squat and wide, with the neck attenuated and often sunk well into the shoulders. Although short, the neck was often more tapering and elegant than in bottles of the previous decade and accounted for approximately half the total height of the vessel (figure a).

The kick-up was wide but varied a little in depth and was occasionally quite shallow. The scar left by the pontil rod was wide, ring-like in appearance and, depending on the amount of glass used when the rod was first applied, it varied from a faint trail-like circle, to a considerable mass of jagged glass.

The changes which had taken place to the string-rim were now quite apparent; gone were the ample disc-like rims of the previous decade which were replaced by a neatly bevelled form which was both smaller in diameter and more acute at its outer edges (figures b and c). Callipers were used in the operation needed to achieve this string-rim. While the bottle was slowly rotated on the pontil rod, the callipers were applied both above and below the rim levelling and shaping. The consequent mark left on the bottle's neck can often be traced as a shallow groove or very slight constriction. It seems unlikely that these finishing irons were in regular use prior to 1680 as very few bottles show any evidence of this.

As the period progressed more and more bottles were subject to the marvering process, by which the still warm bottle was rolled on a slab

Figure a 1704 *Figure b c.1715* *Figure c 1727*

(marver) in order to straighten its sides. This process was to result in the onion bottle gradually losing its true identity. Slight marvering resulted at first in the so called straight-sided onion bottle, typical of the period 1715-25 (see figures b and c and plate 15), at this stage a distinct enough form as it retained all the true onion characteristics. With more heavily marvered bottles the body size and form became much impaired, the bottle became more upright and similarity to the rounder-bodied onions rapidly faded (plate 16).

By 1722 some true mallet forms already existed and by 1730 this bottle became almost universal.

The onion neck, too, had undergone change; in many bottles it had lengthened considerably and become more parallel in form. It is true, however, that many exceptions occur; typical onions with dates as late as 1730 are recorded and, conversely, mallet bottles with dates as early as 1722. In matters of evolution it is obviously unrealistic to attempt to draw distinct dividing lines, but in this case change may have been dictated to some extent by a search for uniformity in bottle production and the need for even more suitable storage vessels.

However, that the onion proved a most successful bottle, stable and therefore well-suited to being passed back and forth across the oak tables of the period, is evinced by its lengthy popularity, the bewildering array of forms in which it was manufactured, and the not inconsiderable amount of such vessels which has survived to the present day.

Neck top formation on bottles, c.1700-25

c.1700-10

c.1710-20

c.1720-25

Plate 12. *'W. Skammell 1704'. The quite radical change in shape and design can be seen if this bottle is compared to the bottle in Plate 11. It should be emphasised, however, that considerable 'overlaps' occurred.*

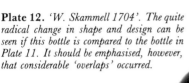

Plate 13 *(left). Partially iridescent onion bottle 'I L/1712' of exceptionally squat form. However, reference to figures 63, 68 and 74 in this section will serve to remind the reader that the straight-sided form of onion was also in existence at this date.*

Plate 14 *(right). Large onion wine bottle sealed 'John/Garneys/1724'. By this date there are probably as many straight-sided onion bottles as there are those of more rounded form, as reference to the figures for this period will show.*

Plate 15. *This straight-sided onion wine is considerably more difficult to date than the previous example but the few sealed and dated bottles the author has been able to examine of closely similar form bear dates between 1707 and 1725. See also figures 61 and 76 and, to a somewhat lesser extent, figure 89.*

Plate 16. *An early straight-sided onion bottle, c.1715, dredged from the Thames in London. Note the excellent proportions; pale metal and retention of a rather coil-like string-rim at a time when the later form of more bevelled construction was almost universal.*

Sealed onion wine bottles, 1700-10

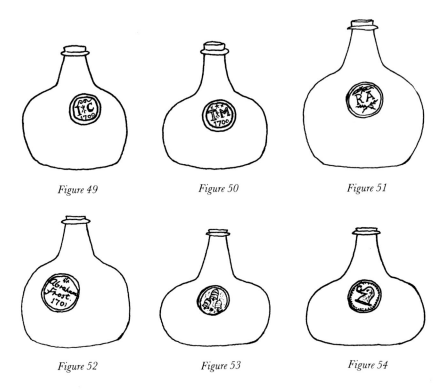

Figure 49　　　　　*Figure 50*　　　　　*Figure 51*

Figure 52　　　　　*Figure 53*　　　　　*Figure 54*

Figure 49. *'I C/1700'; decorative scrolls above and fleuret between the letters.*

Figure 50. *'T M/1700'; decorative fleurets above and between the letters. Bottle found in Sussex in 1898.*

Figure 51. *'R A' with vintner's crossed-spray above and below; probably a tavern bottle. A similar sign was once hung out above any premises licensed to sell wine and beer by retail, a practice stemming from the late medieval period. A large bottle somewhat difficult to date, but probably c.1700.*

Figure 52. *'Abraham/Frost/1701'. Excavated in London in 1975 during pipe laying operations.*

Figure 53. *Three bells, c.1705-10; almost certainly a tavern bottle. There are several seventeenth and eighteenth century seals with bells on them. Some of these seals have the addition of initials which are a little more helpful, without them the seal proves much more difficult to trace. Found during the digging of Shadwell Tunnel.*

Figure 54. *Crest of an elephant's head couped.* The English Glass Bottle, *the Truro Museum Exhibition Catalogue of 1976, records this crest as being that of Eliot of Port Eliot, St. Germans, Cornwall; c.1700-05.*

Sealed onion wine bottles, 1704-07

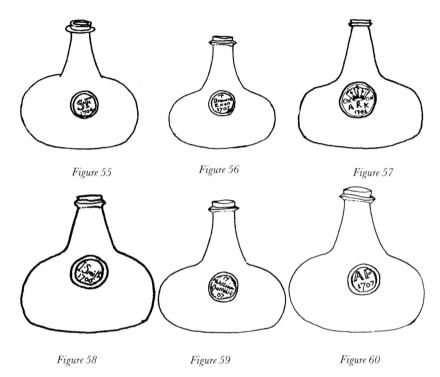

Figure 55

Figure 56

Figure 57

Figure 58

Figure 59

Figure 60

Figure 55. 'S·F/1704'; the true onion form. A badly cracked but very attractive bottle, found by a boy in the mud of the River Frome, Dorset.

Figure 56. 'T/Browne/Exon/1705'. Ruggles-Brise records this bottle as possibly belonging to Thomas Browne 1672-1710, a physician and literary gentleman who died at the age of thirty-eight by falling from his horse.

Figure 57. 'OXON/A K R/1706'; Alexander and Kathleen Richmond of the Crown Tavern, Oxford, 1706-31.

Figure 58. 'I·Smith/1706'. There are several claimants to this bottle none of which has yet been proved. There are also two or three complete bottles with the identical seal known.

Figure 59. 'William/Battishill/1707', the digits separated and positioned above and below the name. A bottle of West Country origin where the surname of Battishill is not infrequent today.

Figure 60. 'A·P/1707'.

Sealed onion wine bottles, 1707-09

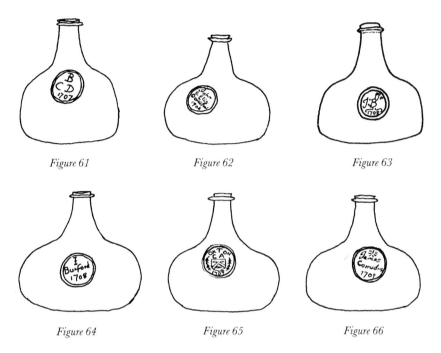

Figure 61   Figure 62   Figure 63

Figure 64   Figure 65   Figure 66

Figure 61. *'C D B' in large letters and date '1707' beneath; the pyramidal lettering sequence may not hold good here, and the initials could be 'B C D'. The bottle is surprisingly advanced in form for such an early date.*

Figure 62. *'John/& Eliz:/Dorrellpool/1708'; John and Elizabeth Dorrell (of) Poole, a curious but attractive form of seal.*

Figure 63. *'T:B:sson/1708'. Almost approaching the mallet form of bottle which is unusual at this early date.*

Figure 64. *'I/Burford/1708'; possibly an Oxford bottle, where a similar seal has been found.*

Figure 65. *'OXON/CAT/1709', a chevron and three tuns flanked on either side by a bunch of grapes; from the Three Tuns Tavern, Oxford. Licensees Culpepper and Anne Tomlinson, 1698-1712. As a widow, Anne Tomlinson continued at the tavern until her death in 1719.*

Figure 66. *'James/Carrudus/1709', and a fleuret above; one bottle and one detached seal known; apparently Scottish.*

Sealed onion wine bottles, 1710-13

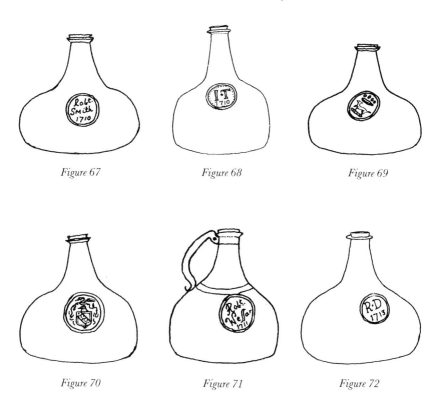

Figure 67   *Figure 68*   *Figure 69*

Figure 70   *Figure 71*   *Figure 72*

Figure 67. *Rob.ᵗ/Smith/1710'. There are many Smith seals as can well be imagined, and others are included in Appendix II.*
Figure 68. *'I·T/1710'; a straight-sided bottle, the initials possibly those of the Inner Temple, London.*
Figure 69. *A fox surmounted by a coronet; several of these bottles of c.1710 were excavated near the site of Tong Palace, Shropshire, and are thought to have belonged to the Pierpont family. Possibly related to the family was John Pierrepoint, a London vintner, who founded the school at Lucton, Herefordshire in 1708.*
Figure 70. *Coat-of-arms and crest of Cary; within a shield three roses, above this a knight's helm surmounted by a swan with wings displayed; c.1700-10. A very similar seal at first sight is that of Clarke of Suffolk.*
Figure 71. *'Rob.ᵗ/Wellar/1711', with the addition of a silver mount and handle by Albert Savory, London 1898. The seal is remarkably crisp and the letters beautifully delineated in script by the hand of a master engraver. Quite obviously a true gentleman's bottle.*
Figure 72. *'R·D/1713'.*

Sealed onion wine bottles, 1710-17

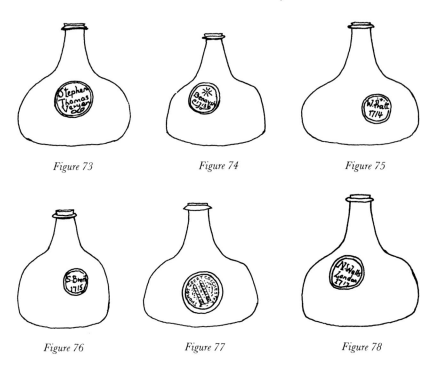

Figure 73

Figure 74

Figure 75

Figure 76

Figure 77

Figure 78

Figure 73. *'Stephen/Thomas/Veryan'; c.1710-15. Stephen Thomas lived at Veryan, Cornwall. The same family continued to seal their bottles well into the eighteenth century, as witnessed by two detached seals inscribed 'R Thomas Veryan 1765'.*
Figure 74. *'Benaysh/1713', fleuret above, and decorative scrolls below enclosing date.*
Figure 75. *'W.Pratt/1714', and a star above; besides two bottles in private hands, there is a magnum size with the same seal in Taunton Museum. Other bottles with the Pratt surname are known from this area.*
Figure 76. *'S·Brent/1715'; although an unusual form at this date there does exist a small group of bottles made in exactly the same manner (see figure 89). They may also have been made in order to improve capacity, for the squaring of the body is also accentuated by the increase of shoulder to base depth.*
Figure 77. *'THOMAS GREAT COLCHESTER', and two twisted posts in the centre. Belonged to Thomas Great of the Two Twisted Posts Tavern, Colchester, Essex. An almost similar seal was dug up in Virginia, and almost certainly belonged to the same publican. The intact bottle in Colchester Museum has been variously and almost certainly incorrectly dated as c.1720-25. Careful examination and comparison with other dated bottles renders it more likely to have originated c.1715.*
Figure 78. *'N·Wells/London 1717'; a straight-sided bottle in relatively pale green glass.*

Sealed onion wine bottles, 1717-21

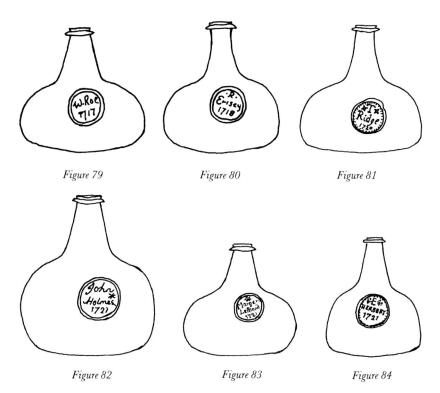

Figure 79   *Figure 80*   *Figure 81*

Figure 82   *Figure 83*   *Figure 84*

Figure 79. *'W·Roe/1717'.*
Figure 80. *'R/Erisey/1718'; the Erisey family from Erisey-in-Grade, Cornwall. The earliest seal, to the author's knowledge, relates to Richard Erisey and is dated '93, for 1693, seal only.*
Figure 81. *'T/Ridge/1720' with two six-pointed stars flanking the letter T; a pair of these bottles is known.*
Figure 82. *'John/Holmes/1721', and a star; magnum size. The seal carefully delineated in script.*
Figure 83. *'Marger(y)/Lethard/1721', star above; only a few bottles with a woman's name alone exist (another is Mary Rayes); c.1710-15.*
Figure 84. *'E/HERBERT/1721'; possibly Edmond Herbert, keeper of the Royal Forest at Whittlebury, Northants. Five or six of these bottles with the dates 1721 and 1724 are known to exist.*

Sealed onion wine bottles, 1723-27

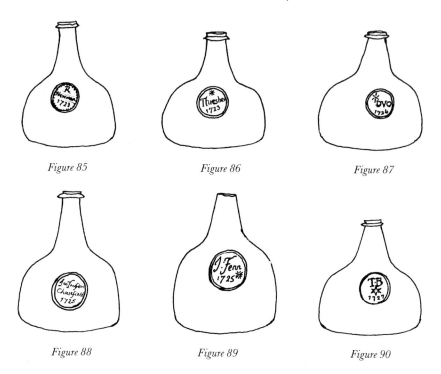

Figure 85

Figure 86

Figure 87

Figure 88

Figure 89

Figure 90

Figure 85. *'R/Newman/1723', within a decorative border. A good example of an early mallet bottle; recovered from Dartmouth Harbour. Originally belonged to Robert Newman, 1676-1739, see figure 42.*

Figure 86. *'Thresher/1723', star above within a decorative border.*

Figure 87. *'D V O/1724', and a decorative fleuret. We are now at the period where transitional forms linking the onion-mallet form exist; however, this bottle more nearly belongs to the latter category.*

Figure 88. *'Ino: Truston/Chasefield/1725'.*

Figure 89. *'J:Fenn/1725', flanked on the right by a star, written in script; a large capacity bottle, deep in the body. Found at Hastings, Sussex.*

Figure 90. *'T·B/1727', with a star between the initials and date.*

8. Bladder Onion Wine Bottles, c.1710-75

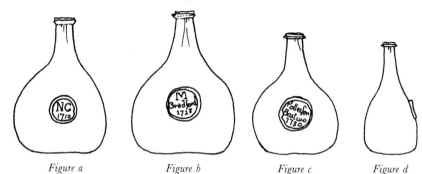

Figure a *Figure b* *Figure c* *Figure d*

Although not a true evolutionary bottle, the bladder onion must have had many adherents, as witnessed by its quite lengthy popularity. 'N C/1710' (figure a) represents the earliest dated example and the latest 'Iosh./Phillips/1775' (figure 102). The main period of manufacture, however, was c.1720-40, bottles both before and after this date being much scarcer. Strangely the percentage of actual dated seals is very high, seals of any other type on this category of bottle being an exception to the rule; I have examined very few bearing armorial crests, coats-of-arms or other pictorial devices.

The reasons for the bottle's inception seem obscure: the onion had already been in production for some fifteen to twenty years when the first bottle of this type appeared. Should the bladder onion have been purely a local variant or experimental form then probably it would have disappeared from the scene at a much earlier date. That the bottle's manufacture spanned a period of sixty-five years proves beyond doubt that many found it totally acceptable.

It is just possible that the bottle was a chance off-shoot of the onion finding favour with a large enough section of the buying public to warrant its continued production. Another suggestion is that this shape of bottle was used for certain types of wine.

The author's own hypothesis is simple, namely that it was a bottle developed with practicality in mind. It is easy to see that bottles of this form would occupy considerably less cellar space even when stored in the normal way. If we now examine the actual form of the bottle we shall find further evidence to support this theory. In actual fact there are two variants. The most frequent is evenly oval with the neck rather longer and more graceful, with the seal, when present, placed in the centre of the side (figures a, b, c, and side view d). The more uncommon form (figures e and side view f) has distinct 'flats' to the sides, a shorter neck, and the seal is placed upon the front. Examples which I have examined of this latter type often show distinct signs of scuffing to the sides and around the seal edge, consistent with bottles that had been stored horizontally, side by side, for the greater part of their life.

In other words the bladder onion was quite possibly an early attempt at a bottle suitable for binning. Even the ordinary form was capable of being laid flat on its side. Thus in both instances the liquid was kept permanently in contact with the cork. Such measures were essential in order to keep the wine in good condition (there is evidence to show that the early shaft and globe wines were laid down on a straw covered cellar floor, and the later onion wines stored upside-down, to ensure the contents were kept in contact with the cork).

Excavations at private household dumps have revealed that in one or two instances certain families used these bottles exclusively over a considerable period of time. Much of this evidence, and a large proportion of the bottles, emanate from the West Country. Indeed some collectors firmly believe that the form originated there and is peculiar to that region.

Almost certainly the Bristol bottle houses were engaged in their production, and the earlier examples found in the American colonies most

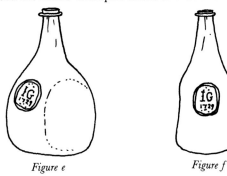

Figure e   *Figure f*

probably originated here. Certain later groups of 'chestnut' or 'kidney' bottles, as American collectors are apt to term them, possess discernibly different characteristics, and these probably represent the original productions of glass houses in that country.

Although space does not permit us to wander off on the path of American bottles, the subject has received thorough attention already, particularly by Ivor Noel Hume, see bibliography.

Plate   17.   *'Thos/Adams/Sen.*
1714'; one of the earliest dated
bladder onion wines in existence.
This bottle shows the more frequently
encountered type, evenly oval in form
with the seal placed upon the side.
Note the particularly prominent
'strain' in the neck.

Plate 18. *'C.Coker/1721'; a typical*
bladder bottle of the period. The bottles
varied considerably in the degree of
contraction to base, as these two bottles
illustrate.

Plate 19. *'L·S/1723'; the scarcer form with the seal on the front of the bottle and distinctly flattened sides. This small bottle is rendered all the more attractive by the bubbly nature of the metal employed and its overall good condition.*

Plate 20. *'I G/1729'. Points to note here are, firstly, the relatively crude draughtsmanship of the seal as evinced by the lettering itself and also by the stamp shape which proves the original die must have been (intentionally or not) far from circular in form; secondly, the presence of considerable 'scuffing' to the 'flats' of the bottle (reasons for which are given in the accompanying text).*

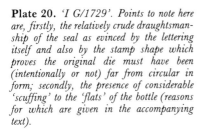

Sealed bladder onion wine bottles, c.1714-25

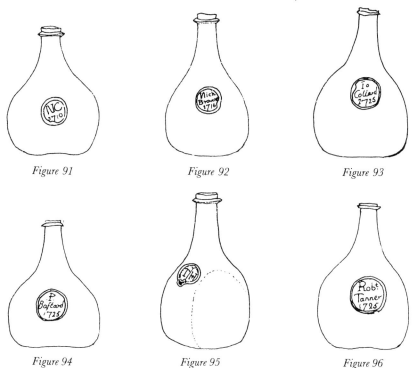

Figure 91   *Figure 92*   *Figure 93*

Figure 94   *Figure 95*   *Figure 96*

Figure 91. 'N C/1710'; *possibly the earliest dated bladder onion, followed by a bottle with the seal 'Thomas Adams Senr. 1714'.*

Figure 92. 'Nich:/Brown 1716', *with the 'N' reversed; found in the Olde Rummer Tavern in Cardiff, and now in the National Museum of Wales.*

Figure 93. 'Io/Collard/1725'.

Figure 94. 'P/Bastard/1725'; *the Bastard family, endemic to Devon and Dorset, favoured the bladder form of bottle over a long period of time, and a fair percentage of their sealed bottles have survived. For a while the frequency of Bastard bottles led to the term becoming synonymous with the form. Today we know of many families who favoured the use of these bottles. Other seals connected with the Bastard family are: 'Pollexfen Basturo 1730'; 'Thos Bastard, Exon 1709'; and the later cylinder wines of 'W Bastard 1753'. Of the oval form 'P Bastard 1725' or '1728' are the most frequently encountered.*

Figure 95. 'T H'; *seal letters stamped on separate matrices and seal placed on the front of the bottle as opposed to the side; c.1725.*

Figure 96. 'Robt/Tanner/1725'; *several broken bottles with the same seal have been excavated at a private household dump in the West Country.*

Sealed bladder onion wine bottles, c.1726-75

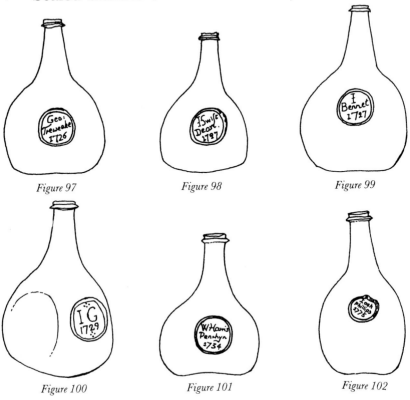

Figure 97

Figure 98

Figure 99

Figure 100

Figure 101

Figure 102

Figure 97. '*Geo:/Treweeke/1726*'; *probably belonged to George Treweeke of Camborne, who died in 1734; found near Helston, Cornwall.*

Figure 98. '*I Swift/Dean/1727*'; *Jonathan Swift 1667-1745, made Dean of St. Patrick's, Dublin in 1713 and a noted writer of his day.*

Figure 99. '*I/Bennet/1727*'; *double magnum; there are two bottles with this seal on them.*

Figure 100. '*I G/1729*'; *another bladder onion of the uncommon variety with flats to the sides, and seal set upon the front. Also unusual is the use of an oblong seal stamp.*

Figure 101. '*W Harris/Penrhyn/1734*'; *according to Ruggles-Brise (page 110) the place name on this seal is spelt as above, suggesting a Welsh origin for the bottle. However, even though the catalogue for the Wine Trade Loan Exhibition of Drinking Vessels, London, 1933, lists the bottle as 'W Harris Penrhyn 1734', reference to the illustration in that work appears to show the seal as 'W Harris Penryn 1734'; therefore, until the bottle can be examined once more, we seem to have the dual possibility of a Welsh or Cornish attribution.*

Figure 102. '*Iosh·/Phillips/1775*'; *the latest dated bladder onion known. Although this bottle is little more than skittle shaped than usual, it is none the less remarkably similar in most other respects to the much earlier oval-bodied bottles.*

9. Mallet Wine Bottles, c.1725-60

The transition from the onion to the mallet was a very gradual and natural one. The first mallets appeared a few years prior to 1725, were quite commonplace c.1730-40, and on the wane once more by 1750. The early mallet bottles were admittedly little different from the true onions; however, reference to figure a shows that even if the neck remained gracefully tapering, the body itself had begun to take on a more shouldered, square look. This bottle, dated 1723, is a truly transitional example.

By 1730 the true mallet shape was well advanced, even though many strange and odd shaped bottles remained; in fact, it is at this stage that bottles probably varied most of all. This is easy to understand; it was a period of great change, and most changes are only accepted slowly and with reluctance. The resultant range of quaint bottle shapes and forms possibly reflected the indecision of the glass houses as to which type was currently the best to produce (figure b).

The preference was undoubtedly for more upright bottles, and by 1750 these were the types most glass houses were striving to manufacture (figure c).

Mallets c.1725-30 often had large sag bases, with shoulders slightly narrower in diameter. Necks were fairly long and moderately tapering. As the period progressed, bottles c.1730-40 became truly square in the

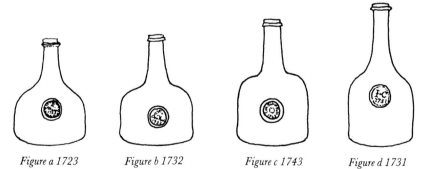

Figure a 1723   Figure b 1732   Figure c 1743   Figure d 1731

body, and had longer, wider and more parallel necks. Normally the neck length approximately equalled, or slightly exceeded, that of the bodies, but some very graceful long necked mallets were produced c.1730, in which the neck considerably exceeded these dimensions. In many respects these bottles were well ahead of their time and heralded the cylindrical form which would shortly follow (figure d).

Neck top formation on bottles, c.1725-45

c.1725   c.1735   c.1745

The kick-up on wine bottles reached its most exaggerated form in the mallet bottles of the 1730-40 era, resulting in a considerable hummock-shaped indent that reached up into the bottle to mid-body level.

Mention should also be made of the string-rim, which remained of neat bevelled construction throughout the period. On the later bottles it became, if anything, a little less ample and more deflexed. Furthermore, on several bottles we find a reversal of procedure to date; the string-rim being applied fractionally lower on the neck. Here again, reference to the illustrations above will help to clarify these remarks.

Although the great majority remained in dark glass, bottles were now available in a rather wider range of colours, and mallets of pale green and amber metal are known. In view of their comparative scarcity, one would assume that such bottles would be avidly sought after, but this is rarely the case, for most collectors seem to prefer the darker coloured glass.

Plate 21. *Early mallet wine bottle, c.1725. With the exception of the neck and string-rim there are few characteristics remaining to link this bottle with the later straight-sided onions. It is most closely similar to the sealed bottle 'R Newman/ 1723' in figure 85, and figure a on p.79.*

Plate 22. *'I Fogg/1734'. Typical mallet of square-shouldered form. Note the longer neck and prominent shoulders.*

Plate 23 *(left). 'Evan Jones/Llanellyd/1743'. Once again a form typical of the period; note slight increase in length of neck.*

Plate 24 *(right). 'BW/1758'. Late mallet bottle; the form here displays little change from the previous example, but many bottle houses had already produced more cylindrical forms, as the line drawn figures indicate.*

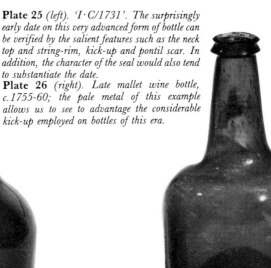

Plate 25 *(left). 'I·C/1731'. The surprisingly early date on this very advanced form of bottle can be verified by the salient features such as the neck top and string-rim, kick-up and pontil scar. In addition, the character of the seal would also tend to substantiate the date.*

Plate 26 *(right). Late mallet wine bottle, c.1755-60; the pale metal of this example allows us to see to advantage the considerable kick-up employed on bottles of this era.*

Sealed mallet wine bottles, 1729-33

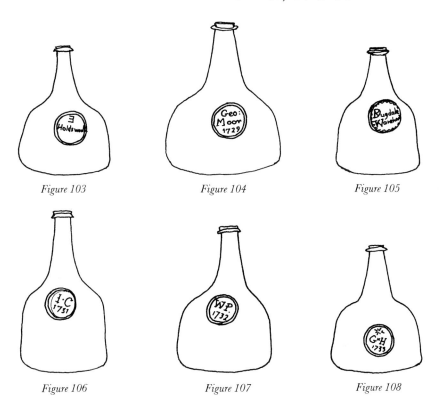

Figure 103   Figure 104   Figure 105

Figure 106   Figure 107   Figure 108

Figure 103. *'E/Holdsworth', the 'E' reversed, c.1730. Belonged to Elizabeth Holdsworth, 1674-1735, wife of Robert Holdsworth of Modbury, Devon. A prominent merchant family in Devonshire at the time, the Holdsworths have left us a considerable legacy of sealed bottles as witnessed by the following list. 'Arth:Holdsworth, Drtm. 1713'; 'Thomas Holdsworth, Dartmor.' (c.1725); 'E. Holdsworth' (c.1720); 'E Holdsworth' (c.1730); 'H Holdsworth 1807'; 'H J H' (Henry Joseph Holdsworth); 'R H 1765' (Robert Holdsworth) and similar dates; 'R Holdsworth 1820'; 'Rob. Holdsworth'. I have no doubt others will come to light.*
Figure 104. *'Geo:/Moor/1729'; there are several bottles known with the seal Moor or Moore, although this does seem to be the earliest dated example.*
Figure 105. *'R Dugdale/Wareham'; the 'R' and 'D' in monogram, the seal inner edge with dentil border. Robert Dugdale of Wareham, died 1766, seems a candidate for this bottle, c.1730-35.*
Figure 106. *'I C/1731'; an elegant long-necked bottle, not exactly typical of the period, being very advanced in form.*
Figure 107. *'W P./1732'.*
Figure 108. *'G H/1733' with fleuret above.*

Sealed mallet wine bottles, 1733-36

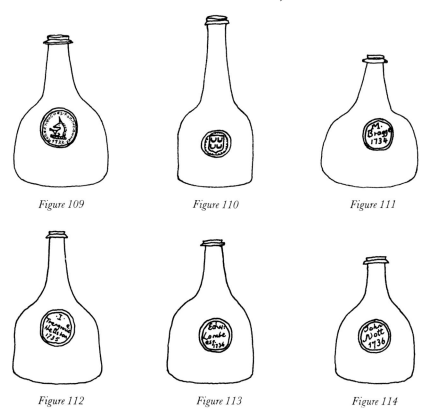

Figure 109

Figure 110

Figure 111

Figure 112

Figure 113

Figure 114

Figure 109. *A unicorn's head pierced by an arrow with, around the seal inner edge, the words* 'ROBERT HUGHES FOR THE OWNER 1733.'

Figure 110. *Four stirrups within a shield; a neat and elegantly proportioned bottle, c.1733-35.*

Figure 111. 'M./Bragge/1734.'

Figure 112. 'I/Trengrouse/Hellston/1735.' *Helston is an ancient stannary town near the Lizard peninsula. Another bottle from the same town is the bladder onion 'J Horner Helston 1758'; it is tempting to suggest that the two families were acquainted with one another.*

Figure 113. 'Edw:/Lombe/esq./1736'; *a well-known Norfolk family; this particular bottle belonged to Edward Lombe of Melton, who became High Sheriff of Norfolk in 1714.*

Figure 114. 'John/Nott/1736'; *apparently excavated in Barnstaple where a merchant of that name lived during the eighteenth century.*

Sealed mallet wine bottles, 1736-40

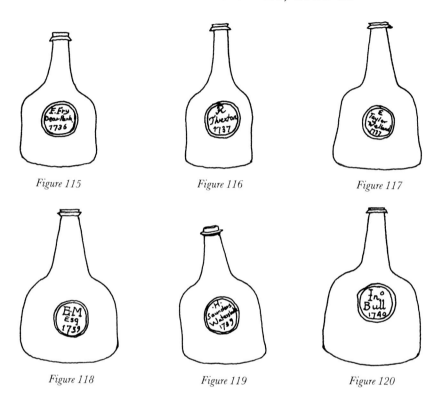

Figure 115

Figure 116

Figure 117

Figure 118

Figure 119

Figure 120

Figure 115. *'F. Fry/Dear Park./1736'; a badly cracked bottle, but with a very interesting seal; owner not traced.*
Figure 116. *'R/Threxton/1737', the seal beautifully executed in script. In many ways a very similar bottle to 'I C/1731' (figure 106). Both examples herald the cylindrical bottle.*
Figure 117. *'E/Taylor/Welland/1737'; two similar bottles are known. Welland is in Worcestershire, north-west of Tewkesbury.*
Figure 118. *'E M/Esq/1739'; bottles sealed with the addition of the word esquire are not common, and probably total no more than fifteen examples. Such a title carried much more distinction at this early date.*
Figure 119. *'H/Saunders/Waterslade/1738'. According to Ruggles-Brise Waterslade is at Taunton, Somerset, although the author has been unable to find a reference to the spot.*
Figure 120. *'In⁰/Bull/1740'.*

Sealed mallet wine bottles, 1740-50

Figure 121

Figure 122

Figure 123

Figure 124

Figure 125

Figure 126

Figure 121. *'Henry/Tucker/1740'; a bottle typical of the period. Other sealed bottles with the Tucker surname are 'Wm Tucker' and 'R Tucker, Street, 1778', the latter originating from the small shoe manufacturing town of Street in Somerset.*

Figure 122. *'R:L/1741', with a star above; a fairly frequent feature of mallet wines of the period is the inferior shoulder to base diameter; this example shows the point to advantage, but in a rather more exaggerated form than is usual.*

Figure 123. *'I:V/1742'; Ruggles-Brise gives Isaac Uppleby of Barrow-in-Humber as the original owner of this bottle.*

Figure 124. *'William/Hayne/1742'; in the Taunton Museum and almost certainly of local origin.*

Figure 125. *'A.F./Sampson/1746'; the increase in base to shoulder height is already evident in this example.*

Figure 126. *'R./Hamley/1750'; there are two bottles, one in Castle Museum, Norwich, the other in Nottingham Museum. Traditionally supposed to have been made in Nottingham. See Ruggles-Brise page 109.*

10. Octagonal Wine Bottles, c.1730-90

The middle of the eighteenth century was a period of experiment and invention particularly so in the glass houses of England. Around 1730 man's skill at moulding or part-moulding a bottle had resulted in the first of the cylindricals. Furthermore, at approximately the same time more complex moulds made possible the production of unusual bottle forms hitherto unseen. Pre-eminent amongst these was the octagonal bottle, a most distinctive and appealing wine container which instantly found favour in the eyes of many.

Three typical octagonal wines, c.1740-60

1741   c.1750   1760

Today these rare bottles are avidly sought by the collector, especially the sealed examples which are few in number. They are often called 'dip-moulded' bottles, a term which derives from their method of manufacture. A gather of glass was blown into a one-piece mould tapered slightly at one end to permit removal upon cooling, whereupon the pontil rod was attached to the base of the bottle and the neck and lip finished in the usual way. This was a considerable step forward for the glass makers who were now able to harness the blowing of bottles and produce vessels of a predetermined size or shape.

Fortunately for the collector the crudity of the first wooden and brass moulds ensured that the finished bottles retained virtually all their inherent character and charm. However, even though traditional means of production continued, the increasing use of moulds pointed inevitably towards the characterless bottles of today. Judging by examples in collections the octagonal wine bottle was available in unusual pale coloured metals, aqua, citron, and pale amber, in addition to the normal deep olive green and black.

Possibly the earliest known dated octagonal wine in existence is the 'Foote/Harwood/1731' bottle. This important seal was discovered when the bottle was brought by a member of the public to a meeting of the Cornwall Bottle Collectors' Society in July 1979 (figure a).

Figure a 1731

Figure b c.1750-70

Figure c c.1780-90

Figure d
The basal kick-up and
normal shape of most
octagonal wine bottles

Figure e
This form is rather
more uncommon but,
one would assume, cer-
tainly more stable in use

The octagonal was also to find favour in the field of medicine, where it continued in use long after its decline as a wine bottle. Its protracted use for medicinal purposes was due no doubt to its distinctive form which rendered the bottle instantly recognisable.

Octagonal half bottles for wine do exist although it may be safely assumed that the majority of 5-inch and under bottles were made for medicine. From the middle of the eighteenth century octagonals were increasingly produced in small sizes either in aqua or in clear flint glass. Such bottles were also favoured by the 'quack' or patent medicine peddlars. Plain bottles originally had paper labels, others were embossed from c.1750 onwards (figure b) and fewer still were sealed in the traditional wine bottle fashion (figure c).

Plate 27 *(left). Rare octagonal half bottle sealed 'POST/HOUSE/NEWARK', c.1770-80; unlikely to be a wine bottle, but unquestionably rare enough to be worthy of inclusion here. Compare this with figure c, opposite. A similar bottle is in Winchester Museum and bears the seal of the town hospital, see Appendix II, p. 321.*
Plate 28 *(right). Unsealed octagonal wine, c.1770. The great majority of octagonals are more rectangular in form than this example, see figures d and e.*

Sealed octagonal wine bottles, 1734-85

Figure 127

Figure 128

Figure 129

Figure 130

Figure 131

Figure 132

Figure 127. 'C E/1734.'; an unusual and rare aqua-coloured bottle.
Figure 128. 'R W/1739'; there seems to be some confusion as to whether this bottle is of hexagonal or octagonal form. Ruggles-Brise refers to the bottle as hexagonal, but the illustration of it in the Catalogue of the Wine Trade Loan Exhibition of Drinking clearly shows an octagonal bottle.
Figure 129. 'Wm/Vallis/1741', one of an interesting selection of mainly local bottles in Poole Museum.
Figure 130. 'Alex/Moss./Badwell Ash/1746'. Badwell Ash is a small village near Bury St. Edmunds, Suffolk.
Figure 131. 'Jno/Andrews/1770', with a small star above. Traditionally thought to have belonged to the historian and politician John Andrews, 1736-1809, although several seals examined with the Andrews surname have been West Country in origin.
Figure 132. 'A T/1785', with a star between the initials.

11. Squat Cylindrical Wine Bottles, c.1740-1830

Cylindrical wine bottles are known from as early as 1734-35 but are extremely rare at this early date (examples are 'Jno. Booker 1734' and 'James Oakes 1735', figure a, p.100).

In the natural course of events the first squat cylindricals developed directly from the mallet wine bottles, and bore strong resemblances to these at first. Comparison of the relative base, and shoulder to base measurements will show that mallet wine bottles have broad bases, considerably exceeding their body height (figure a). Conversely the squat cylindrical bottle invariably has a body height greater than its base diameter (figure b). These features enable the collector to distinguish between the two groups with reasonable accuracy.

Figure a 1746   *Figure b 1751*

There are exceptions to the rule, however; bottles of almost mallet dimensions can be traced as late as the 1780s, but their overall appearance differs considerably and with experience one is able to place even undated seals and unsealed examples with some accuracy.

Early squat cylindricals had a parallel or slightly tapering neck, very similar to the mallets they had superseded. During the middle of the period, however, in some instances as early as 1750, certain glass houses reverted to a fairly short tapering neck (as in figure b) almost onion-like in aspect. Dated seals testify that both forms were produced concurrently.

The squat cylindrical bottle was still far from suitable for binning, and as yet the stocky, sagged-base bottles had lost none of their inherent charm. That it was a popular bottle and much in demand is proved by its continued production over a period of at least a century, during which time it co-existed with bottles of the true cylindrical form.

However, between 1740-1830, subtle but important changes took place. The neck length remained a variable feature, but few really long-

Figure c 1744   Figure d 1773   Figure e 1794

necked examples were made after 1765; in general the neck was quite short and stumpy, especially towards the turn of the century, figure e.

As time progressed the body became a little less ample and although the shoulder-form varied from a right angle to a much less acute more rounded shape, the latter predominated, especially so post-1765; figures d and e.

Neck top formation, c.1740-1800

c.1740-60   c.1770-80   c.1790-1800

At the outset of the period the string-rim projected just below the bottle top, but gradually became more deflexed and band-like in appearance. By 1770 it was either distinctly deflexed, or the top itself was deflexed in order to form a double rim of glass, hence the term 'double string-rim'. The amount of flare to the neck top was minimal at first, increasing later to result in a double string-rim of almost equal proportions. Eventually the string-rim was relegated to reinforcing the neck, and the neck top itself now functioned as the string-rim.

As neck top formation coincided exactly on both squat and true cylindrical bottles the illustrations given here will serve both this and the following section.

The kick-up on most squat cylindrical bottles was wide and deep, but rarely as deep as on the mallets and not as acute as on the true cylindricals. Unlike this latter group of bottles very few squat cylindricals were manufactured in light-coloured glass.

Neck top formation, c.1800-20

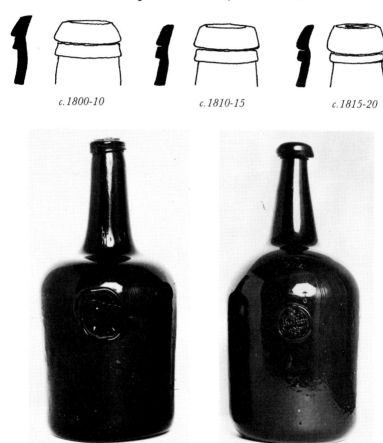

c.1800-10   *c.1810-15*   *c.1815-20*

Plate 29. *Left: 'I.W./1775'. This bottle in amber-coloured metal exhibits the earlier features to be found on squat cylindrical bottles, i.e. the fairly parallel-sided neck, and acute shoulders. Right: 'Thoˢ Rich/Over Stowey/1783'. The rounded, more gently sloping shoulders are now an almost constant feature of the squat cylindrical form.*

Plate 30. *Left: 'I:/Fleming/ Plymtree/1786'. The general form at this period is fairly constant, although the tooling of the string-rim quite naturally varies a little from bottle to bottle. Right: 'I. Elliott/Stonehouse/ 1794'. Considering the very rapid change in all types of packaging and containers today there is little if anything to note by way of change in these two bottles over a period of eight years.*

Plate 31. *Two undated squat cylindrical seal bottles. Left: 'W.B.L.'. Right: 'I. WATSON ESQr BILTON'; both c.1780-90.*

Sealed squat cylindrical wine bottles, 1743-48

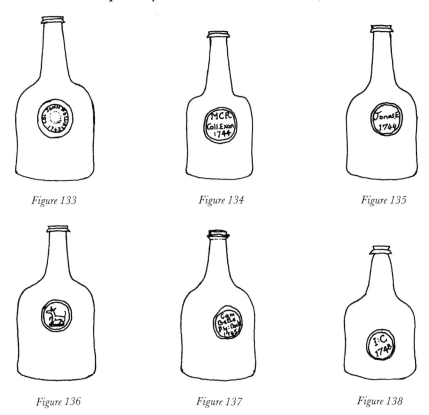

Figure 133   *Figure 134*   *Figure 135*

Figure 136   *Figure 137*   *Figure 138*

Figure 133. *'Col: John Folliott 1743'; an attractive amber-coloured bottle, also known with the date 1742; a further example has the seal twice repeated. Apparently a West Country bottle.*
Figure 134. *'M C R/Coll. Exon/1744'. Dated examples of college bottles are rare and the present example is, as far as the author knows, unique; originally made for use in the Common Room of Exeter College. It is uncertain whether the first initial M stands for 'Masters' or not. A similar bottle is sealed 'All: Souls College' and dated 1764.*
Figure 135. *'Jonas E/1744'; a good example of an early cylindrical bottle.*
Figure 136. *Dog standing upon a wreath, with sinister paw raised; unknown crest. The bottle is a good example of the forms linking mallet and squat cylinder wines, but is more accurately placed in the latter category, c.1745.*
Figure 137. *'Gam:/Betts/Ply: Dock/1745'; almost certainly belonged to Gamaliel Betts of Stoke Damerel, Devon.*
Figure 138. *'I:C/1748'; on body proportions alone this bottle is very close to a mallet.*

Sealed squat cylindrical wine bottles, 1749-55

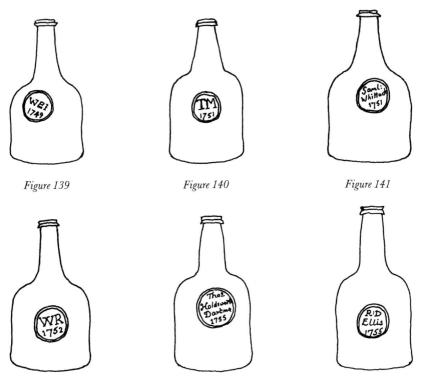

Figure 139   *Figure 140*   *Figure 141*

Figure 142   *Figure 143*   *Figure 144*

Figure 139. *'W E I/1749'. This bottle is in the Taunton Museum and is almost certainly of local origin.*
Figure 140. *'T M/1751'; one of the more frequent eighteenth century dated seals, of which there are several examples, most are squat cylindricals.*
Figure 141. *'Saml:/Whittuck/1751'.*
Figure 142. *'W R/1752'.*
Figure 143. *'Tho⁵/Holdsworth/Dartmᵠ/1755'. There are at least three of these bottles in existence, all sealed identically. Another 'Thos Holdsworth' bottle is a bladder onion, c.1725, but both bottles have the lettering 'Dartmᵠ' in abbreviation for Dartmouth.*
Figure 144. *'R:D/Ellis/1755'; other Ellis bottles are 'C Ellis', with dates 1793 and 1798, also 'H Ellis 1762 and H.Ellis 1780'. Nothing is known for certain about any of the bottles. 'H Ellis', however, was found in the West Country, from which a large percentage of sealed bottles still emanate.*

Sealed squat cylindrical wine bottles, 1756-62

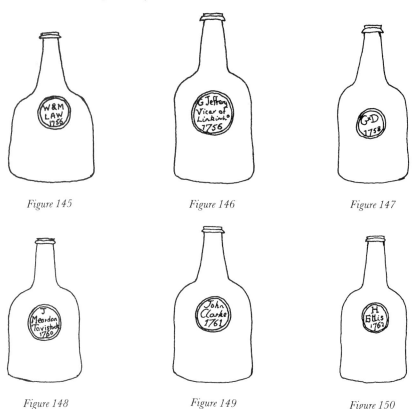

Figure 145

Figure 146

Figure 147

Figure 148

Figure 149

Figure 150

Figure 145. *'W & M/Law/1756'. A rather large, square-shouldered bottle.*
Figure 146. *'G Jeffery/Vicar of/Linkinhº/1756'; the Reverend George Jeffery, Vicar of Linkinhorne, Cornwall. Linkinhorne is about four miles from Callington and it is therefore quite possible that the Vicar knew a certain Mr. Calmady of that town, who has left us a bottle sealed 'S Calmady, Callington' of a very similar date.*
Figure 147. *'G D/1758'.*
Figure 148. *'J/Meardon/Tavistock/1760'; a further example is sealed 'J Meardon, Taviſtock, 1780'. Tavistock, Devon, was a prosperous wool town.*
Figure 149. *'John/Clarke/1761'.*
Figure 150. *'H/Ellis/1762'; see figures 144 and 183.*

Sealed squat cylindrical wine bottles, 1763-76

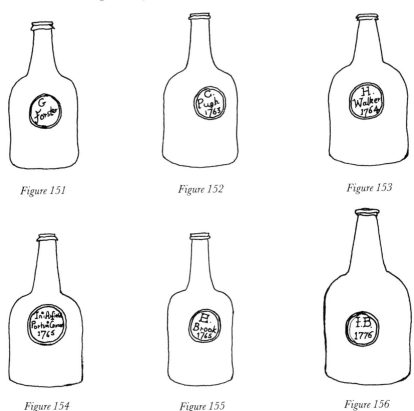

| Figure 151 | Figure 152 | Figure 153 |

| Figure 154 | Figure 155 | Figure 156 |

Figure 151. *'G/Forster'; undated, but c.1760-65; three examples known, at least two in magnum size.*
Figure 152. *'C./Pugh/1763'. Pugh is a name featuring frequently in seventeenth and eighteenth century Wales. Other eighteenth century seals with the name are 'C Pugh 1765', 'Chas: Pugh 1763', and 'John Pugh 1794'.*
Figure 153. *'H./Walker/1764'.*
Figure 154. *'Inº Arfield Portsmº Comon/1765'; present day maps show only Southsea Common, which may or may not be synonymous with Portsmouth Common, just south of the famous dockyard area.*
Figure 155. *'E./Brook/1765'; also known with the date 1768. A bottle of similar age is sealed 'W Brook, Lynton'. Lynton is in Devon, on the north-west border of Exmoor, and close to the coast.*
Figure 156. *'I.B./1776'.*

Sealed squat cylindrical wine bottles, c.1770-89

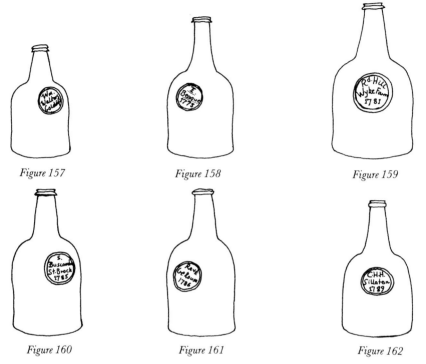

Figure 157

Figure 158

Figure 159

Figure 160

Figure 161

Figure 162

Figure 157. *'Wm./Walters/Goldrift', c.1770. A possible solution as to the whereabouts of Goldrift could be as follows: to the west of Helston in Cornwall is a village called Sithney and, further west still, we find Goldsithney. Drift occurs not far away to the west of Penzance, and it is just possible that Goldrift lies somewhere nearby.*

Figure 158. *'I./Beague/1773'; an almost identical bottle exists dated 1785. Forms such as these were still almost as frequent as the true cylindrical form.*

Figure 159. *'Rd. Hill/Wyke Farm/1781'; several examples of this bottle are known. Few bottles have the addition of the word farm on the seal, although it is known that many farmers had sealed bottles made for them. The bottle may have originated from Wyke-Champflower, Somerset, but there is also a Wyke in Wiltshire.*

Figure 160. *'S./Buscombe/St. Brock/1785'; an excellent example of a squat cylinder, with a large clearly defined seal. St. Breock (note the mis-spelling) is west of Wadebridge, Cornwall.*

Figure 161. *'Revᵈ Ino. Rouse/1786'. The Revd. Rouse was rector of Tetcott in Devonshire and later of St. Breock in Cornwall.*

Figure 162. *'C.H.H./Sillaton/1789'; a bottle of rather unusual form, with a flat band-like collar of glass for string-rim. This feature is not normally found on bottles until a much later date. The bottle comes from Sillaton Farm, at Pillaton, Cornwall.*

12. Cylindrical Wine Bottles, c.1735-1830

As we have seen in the previous chapter glass houses were experimenting with bottles of a cylindrical form as early as the second quarter of the eighteenth century. These early bottles were mostly 'squats' and it would be more exact to say that the true cylindrical evolved directly from these, making its first appearance c.1735.

By this time many bottles were blown into a simple type of mould as part of a process introduced in order to help standardise body size and shape, and hence capacity. Around 1755-60 most glass houses had produced the true cylindrical bottle which represented the culmination of the glass blowers' efforts to produce a standard bottle of sturdy form wholly suitable for binning.

However, the true cylindrical did not replace the squat and both forms were produced simultaneously, due no doubt to demand. Reluctance on the part of private individuals to alter their cellar arrangements may have been a contributory factor; whatever the cause, squat cylindrical bottles existed well into the three-part mould era.

Guidelines were given in the previous section on the division of late mallet and early squat cylindrical forms by means of comparison of the relative base and shoulder to base measurements. Once again in order to

Some early cylindrical wine bottles illustrating characteristics of the type

Figure a   Figure b   Figure c

Figure d   Figure e   Figure f

Figure a. *'Ino/Booker/1734' is typical of the first long-necked cylindricals.*
Figure b. *'Ionas·E/1744' follows on nicely, although most examples of this bottle appear to be nearer squat cylindrical in form.*
Figure c. *'W/Basterd/1753' is the form that most accurately typifies the true cylindrical wine bottle. Indeed, it was about this date that most, if not all, glass houses had finally succeeded in producing the true cylindrical form.*
Figure d. *'Magdalen/College/1760'; half bottle; the 'early' features can still be seen.*
Figure e. *An example of one of the commonest dated sealed wine bottles, '1770/James/Oakes/Bury'.*
Figure f. *'I:B/Columpton' with decorative scrolls beneath.*

Figure g   Figure h   Figure i

Figure g. *Example of a late eighteenth century bottle, c.1790, sealed with the solitary letter S. Similar examples are known sealed with the letter D.*
Figure h. *'Clapcott'; turn of the century sealed bottle, c.1800, of which several examples are known.*
Figure i. *'Wm. Rowe Newlands 1820'; an example of the tapering form.*

separate the closely allied squat cylindrical and cylindrical bottles the collector is urged to note the following criteria — in squat cylindrical wines the base to shoulder height is approximately 1⅓ times the base diameter whereas in the true cylindrical bottle the base to shoulder height is *at least* 1½ times the base diameter.

Characteristics of early cylindrical bottles lie in their inferior body height, with necks often long in comparison. Marked angular shoulders were also a feature. The neck length remained somewhat variable, but cylindricals became progressively taller, narrower in the body, and shorter in the neck. In general few long neck bottles existed after 1760, and by 1770 the form had settled down to a medium body and neck, with rather more rounded shoulders.

As late as 1760 the 'early' features are still discernible however; a half-bottle dated 1760 which the author recently examined shows this point to advantage (see figure d). These early college bottles are a good example of their type. Early dated cylinders are not common and difficult to acquire, especially the period of 1735-50, but enough exist to form a useful comparison to the later types.

String-rim formation was on a parallel with bottles in the previous section.

1770-80 saw little change in most cylindrical wine bottles except that some glass houses had, by the turn of the century, produced a narrower bodied form by heavily marvering the sides of the bottle and, a little later still, by actually mould-blowing the body section. This resulted in a tapering form with little or no sag to the base, a feature so characteristic of many bottles at the very close of the eighteenth century.

Reference to figure i will show an example of the latter type of bottle. Although the body section is quite obviously blown into a mould, there are no tell-tale mould seams to the shoulder or around the neck. The bottle is a transitional form just prior to the three-part mould era as the date on the seal suggests.

The kick-up on these bottles is normally neater, more shallow and a little more cone-shaped. The pontil scar, however, is still much in evidence, although the string-rim now bears some semblance to the neatly converging two-tier affair normally encountered on three-part mould bottles.

Plate 32. *Left: 'Mag: Col./C R.' The long parallel neck, projecting string-rim, and 'hard' shoulders to this Magdalen College bottle display all the features we should expect to find on early cylindrical bottles c.1735-65. Comparison should be made with figure d, p.101, a 1760 dated example. Examination of the wine accounts for the college could quite possibly prove whether or not the present undated example is prior to or later than this date. Right: Further useful comparison is provided by this c.1770 bottle sealed 'A S/C R' in script, for All Souls Common Room. The 'later' features are already discernible, in the somewhat longer body, more sloping shoulders, shorter neck and deflexed string-rim, which sits astride the actual bottle top.*

Plate 33. *'1770/James/Oakes/Bury'; the standard shape for this date. The only slightly unusual feature on this otherwise common seal bottle is the positioning of the date at the head of the seal.*

Plate 34. *Left: 'T.C.' within a shield with sinister hand appaumée see Appendix I under Thomas Carew; c.1780. Right: 'H.C.' and dexter hand appaumée. See Appendix I under Henry Carew; c.1790. The body of this bottle has quite obviously been blown into a mould, and the base has sagged a little.*

Plate 35 *(left). 'I/Taylor/1807'; a slightly more 'dumpy' bottle, but its proportions still render it a true cylindrical. Note the progression to what is now a distinctly double string-rim. The grooves on the neck, which are particularly evident in this photograph, are termed by collectors as 'strains' in the glass. They occur during manufacture when drawing and often inadvertently twisting the neck section to its correct shape and length.*
Plate 36 *(right). 'R H C/1815'; one of the more frequently encountered dated seal bottles; see Appendix II p.251.*

Plate 37. *Left: 'Geo./Willmott/Axminster'; the advanced form of string-rim, together with all its other features, dates this bottle to the opening years of the nineteenth century, probably c.1800-15. The speedy stamping of seals quite often resulted in the retention of a "rail" of glass upon the seal face, as seen in this particular example. Below: 'J. Wenfley/N.Taunton'; this undated seal is almost certainly of a very close date to the accompanying bottle.*

Plate 38. *Although basically a free blown bottle this unusual aqua example probably dates into the three-part mould era, c.1820-30. The string-rim is in its latest form prior to the adoption by most bottle houses of the more 'mechanical' cone-shaped affair. The low seal position is another late feature; the inclusion of an anchor with rope entwined would seem to suggest interesting maritime connections for this bottle.*

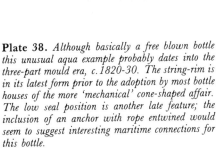

Sealed cylindrical wine bottles, 1753-64

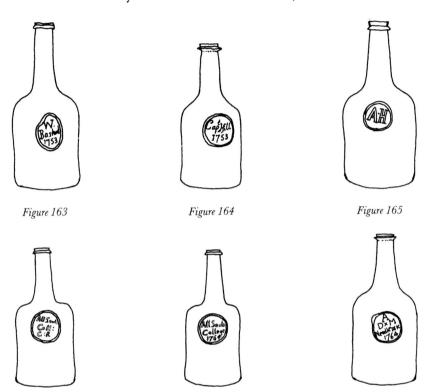

Figure 163

Figure 164

Figure 165

Figure 166

Figure 167

Figure 168

Figure 163. *'W./Basterd 1753'; probably William Bastard, 1689-1766, mason and architect of Blandford, Dorset.*
Figure 164. *'Capt/Hill/1753'; the addition of the word Captain makes this quite possibly a unique bottle. The reverse has the letters 'GIN' within an oval cartouche added in gilt.*
Figure 165. *'A.H', c.1760.*
Figure 166. *'All Souls/Coll:/C:R.' A total of almost twenty different seals from this college are known; the present bottle dates c.1760-63. Bottles quite possibly of squatter form were being ordered for the college from at least 1750, but the author has been unable to trace any earlier than the present example.*
Figure 167. *'All Souls/College/1764'; apparently the only dated bottle known from All Souls. Several of these have survived, and are sufficiently distinct from their contemporaries to suggest that not all early All Souls bottles came from the same source. Accounts show that a considerable supply came from the Stourbridge glass house, Gloucester, but on the dated bottles the books are unfortunately silent.*
Figure 168. *'A/D M/Needh^m MK/1764'; the abbreviation on the seal refers to Needham Market in Suffolk.*

Sealed cylindrical wine bottles, c.1768-73

Figure 169   *Figure 170*   *Figure 171*

Figure 172   *Figure 173*   *Figure 174*

Figure 169. *'Joseph/Batterham/1768'; Ruggles-Brise gives the owner of this bottle as a builder. An identical bottle dated 1770, and one sealed 'I Batterham' with a flower exist; all three are the property of the Wisbech Museum, Cambridge.*

Figure 170. *'Major/Grant/1769'; a well-documented bottle belonging to Major Jasper Grant of Fermoy, Co. Cork, who was Commander in Chief at the siege of Gibraltar. The bottle still remains in the family.*

Figure 171. *'1770/James/Oakes./Bury' (see Plate 33); James Oakes of Bury St. Edmunds is variously reputed to have been a banker and a wine merchant. This bottle, or variations of it, is one of the most frequently encountered dated eighteenth century seals. The present example with the date above the name is less common, and others dated indistinctly 1755 or 1765, with the name Okes, even less common. The latter bottles, and a single one sealed 'James Okes Bury 1735', may well have belonged to an earlier member of the family. Dates between the years 1770-95 are most frequent.*

Figure 172. *'T V/1771' encircled with vines, leaves and grapes. An involved and delicately executed seal. Found in the Helford river, Cornwall. According to* The English Glass Bottle, *the catalogue of the Truro Museum Exhibition, the one-time owner may have been Thomas Vyvyan of Trelowarren and later of Trewan.*

Figure 173. *'W/Stone/1772'.*

Figure 174. *'N/Bidgood/1773'.*

Sealed cylindrical wine bottles, c.1770-75

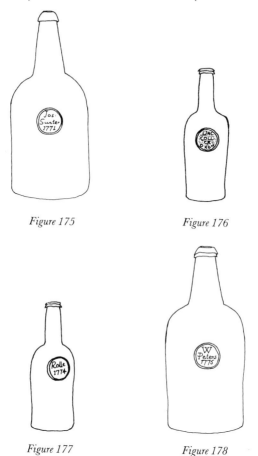

Figure 175

Figure 176

Figure 177

Figure 178

Figure 175. *'Jos:/Sunter/1771'; double magnum size.*
Figure 176. *'LINC/COLL/CR/OXON'; c.1770; a slightly later version had the same lettering written around the edge of the seal, but omitted the word Oxon. A less frequent type incorporates a set of antlers, the college crest.*
Figure 177. *'Rolle/1774'; the seal of Baron Rolle of Stevenstone. Seals with the letter R under a coronet are ascribed to the same person; several examples are known.*
Figure 178. *'W/Peters/1775'; probably the earliest of the Peters bottles and seals, all of which appear to be of West Country origin. Taunton Museum has 'F W Peters', and Launceston Museum 'Edward Peter North Hill'. North Hill is on the eastern edge of Bodmin Moor. Two detached seals are inscribed 'F Peter, St. Merryn', on the north Cornish coast, south-west of Padstow.*

Sealed cylindrical wine bottles, 1775-80

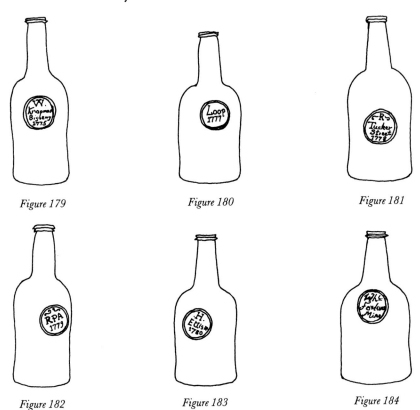

Figure 179

Figure 180

Figure 181

Figure 182

Figure 183

Figure 184

Figure 179. 'W./Knapman/Bigberry/1775'; one would assume this to be Bigbury, near Aveton Gifford, Devon.

Figure 180. 'Loop/1777'; a not uncommon seal bottle. One would assume Loop to be a place name, and if so there is a remote possibility it could be Loop Head on the western coast of Ireland — a long shot, but there may be some connection.

Figure 181. 'R/Tucker/Street/1778'; Street is a footwear manufacturing town in Somerset.

Figure 182. 'R P A/1779'.

Figure 183. 'H/Ellis/1780'; see figures 144 and 150.

Figure 184. 'Wh^l./Fortune/Mine'; c.1780. This possibly unique bottle was first purchased in Plymouth, and later sold at Sotheby's in October 1978. The Wheel of Fortune Mine, to which the seal relates was quite possibly that situated at Breage in Cornwall, and owned by the Earl of Godolphin.

Sealed cylindrical wine bottles, c.1780-90

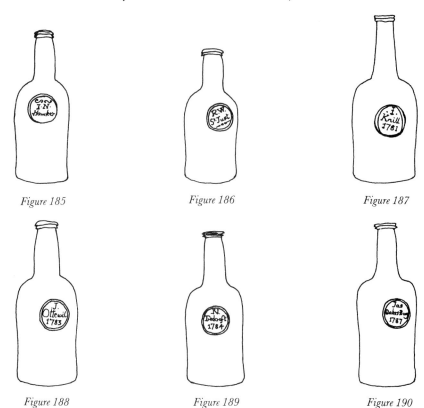

Figure 185

Figure 186

Figure 187

Figure 188

Figure 189

Figure 190

Figure 185. '*I·N·/Hawker*', *with decorative scrollwork above, c.1780-90. Two of these hitherto unrecorded seal bottles were excavated from a dump near Saltash, Cornwall, one incomplete, the other complete but unfortunately cracked. They apparently once belonged to Isobel Hawker, great-great-grandmother of Captain Hawker of Plymouth. The family were, and indeed still remain, noted wine merchants in the city.*

Figure 186. '*R.W./St Just*'. *The bottle may come from St. Just (otherwise known as St. Just in Penwith) on the west coast of Cornwall, or it may come from St. Just in Roseland. In the former locality there are ancient tin mines. The bottle dates c.1780-90.*

Figure 187. '*I/Knill/1781*'.

Figure 188. '*J./Ottewil/1783*'. *A pair of these bottles has been seen; they are made of a most attractive pale green metal, much paler in colour than is normal for a port bottle of the period.*

Figure 189. '*N/Tredcroft/1784*'.

Figure 190. '*Jas/Oakes Bury/1787*', *see figure 171.*

Sealed cylindrical wine bottles, 1788-94

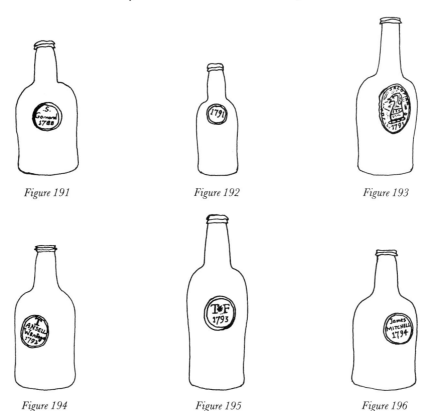

Figure 191   *Figure 192*   *Figure 193*

Figure 194   *Figure 195*   *Figure 196*

Figure 191. *'S/Gomond/1788'; a pair of these wine bottles originating from the Bristol area is known to be in existence.*

Figure 192. *'1791'; a large number of these half- and quarter-bottles, with nothing but the date on the seal, were found in London, and are now widely dispersed throughout collections.*

Figure 193. *'JUXTA SALOPIAM', a talbot's head, and beneath the date '1791'. This is the crest of Malvesyin, which John Chadwick assumed in 1791. Chadwick lived at Healey Hall, Staffordshire. Prior to this date, his bottles had been sealed with the Chadwick arms, and dated 1785 and 1788. Ruggles-Brise gives a very full account of the family and the variant bottle seals (see Appendix I, pages 212-214). There are several of these bottles in collections.*

Figure 194. *'T/ANSELL/Wantage/1792'. Wantage, Berkshire, is in the Vale of the White Horse. According to the Truro Museum Exhibition Catalogue, a 1791 directory of the town gives Thomas Ansell as a tanner.*

Figure 195. *'T F/1793', with large fleuret between the initials; magnum size.*

Figure 196. *'James/MITCHELL/1794'. Another bottle with the same surname, but quite possibly unrelated, is 'Mitchell Esq. Chiltern, 1785'.*

Sealed cylindrical wine bottles, 1795-c.1800

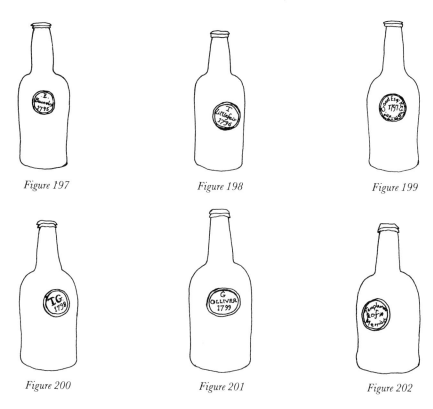

Figure 197

Figure 198

Figure 199

Figure 200

Figure 201

Figure 202

Figure 197. *'I/Barneby/1795'; four bottles, presumably belonging to the same person, were found together in a cellar in Staffordshire, in 1961. They included two examples of the above seal, plus one sealed 'I. Barnaby' and another 'Iohn Barneby'.*
Figure 198. *'T/Littlefair/1796'.*
Figure 199. *'Jnᵒ Croad Esq. Keyham: 1797'; the words are written around the seal edge with the date in the centre. A not uncommon seal bottle, although the locality and owner have not been traced.*
Figure 200. *'T.G./1798'; a similar bottle sealed 'T.G. 1801' in Hereford Museum is ascribed to a certain T. Godsell.*
Figure 201. *'G./OLLIVER/1799'; typical form for the period, but rather unusual in having the entire name in capital letters on an oval shaped seal.*
Figure 202. *'Templeman/of/Merriot'; c.1800. Merriot is in Somerset. Another bottle (of double magnum size) from the same locality is 'R. Cris, Merriott 1803'.*

Sealed cylindrical wine bottles, 1800-14

Figure 203

Figure 204

Figure 205

Figure 206

Figure 207

Figure 208

Figure 203. *'Wm Hodge: Lambourn 1800'; the date is written between the name and locality. The catalogue of the Truro Museum Exhibition gives William Hodge of Callestock, and later of Lambourne, Cornwall. However, if the seal engraver was word perfect in this instance, then we should have to consider the downland village of Lambourn in Berkshire.*

Figure 204. *'Ino/Wakefield/1802'; from the same family are 'John Wakefield 1802' and 'J. Wakefield, Sedgwick'. The family were bankers who resided in Sedgwick and Kendal in Westmorland.*

Figure 205. *'R.M.B./Flexbury'; c.1800. Belonged to Richard Martyn Braddon of Flexbury, Cornwall.*

Figure 206. *'R C./1811'.*

Figure 207. *'T Grose/, St Kew/1814'; also recorded as a detached seal with the later date of 1820. St. Kew is in Cornwall, just a little to the north of St. Kew Highway; the church there is noted for its fifteenth century stained glass.*

Figure 208. *'Ino/Williams/Ruan./1815.'*

13. Three-piece Mould Cylindrical Wine Bottles, c.1811-1900

Once an almost totally suitable and acceptable wine bottle form had been produced, all that now remained was to make this as quickly and efficiently as possible to meet the ever-increasing demand.

To this end, One Henry Ricketts of Bristol produced a three-piece mould c.1821, and so successful did this prove that within ten years most, if not all, of the glass houses in England had adopted this means of production. A few three-piece (or three-part) mould bottles exist c.1810-11 but have no base markings to indicate their place of manufacture. It is thought, however, that they were early Ricketts bottles made before the advent of the company's policy of mould-marking the base.

Production was speeded up considerably, and bottles now left the factory with guaranteed measure and in dependable quality. The vagaries inevitably associated with free-blown bottles were gone, and so too had much of the charm and character of these earlier items. But mechanisation had not entirely taken over, bottles were still manually blown into the mould and when cool lifted on the pontil rod in order to hand finish the lip and rim. Fewer bottles were sealed, but those that were were finished in the traditional fashion. The mould seams on bottles were plainly visible, and many examples carried embossing around the circumference of the base. Examples of this lettering are 'H. RICKETTS & CO GLASSWORKS BRISTOL'; 'H.R. BRISTOL'; and later, following the amalgamation of the company, 'P.R. & F. BRISTOL', standing for Powell, Ricketts and Filer. A scarcer much less frequently

Neck top formation, 1820-50

c.1820-30   c.1830-40   c.1850

seen mark is 'WEAR GLASS BO. CO. DEPTFORD.' Embossing was also to be found on the shoulders of certain bottles, the two examples known being 'PATENT' and 'IMPERIAL PATENT'.

The string-rim had altered drastically and was now a neat cone-shaped two-tier affair which altered just a little over the next three decades or so, as reference to the illustrations on p.115 and below will show. It remained however a separate applied collar of glass and was not moulded integrally with the bottle top until 1900 or thereabouts.

Three-piece mould wine bottles dated '1821', '1846' and '1887' respectively. Note on the bottle on the right the change in string-rim formation, entasis to the neck, and the particularly narrow, somewhat attenuated base. The slightly oval seal stamp and its low position are also late features.

Note on the base of the Ricketts bottle on the left the continued presence of the pontil scar as opposed to the 'pimple base' of the later example on the right, from the same firm.

About 1840 the use of tapered moulds and the 'snap' alleviated the need for the pontil rod and, for the first time in the history of the wine bottle, the associated pontil scar had disappeared. Furthermore the practice of sealing bottles rapidly declined after the middle of the nineteenth century, particularly so with private individuals' bottles.

Seals enjoyed a partial renaissance during the latter part of the nineteenth century when wine and liquor merchants readopted the habit mainly as a way of promoting their wares.

Suffice it to say, by 1920 completely mechanised bottle-making machines existed, a new era of mass production had begun and a long tradition was finally at an end.

Plate 39 *(left). 'I.B. Smith/Dartmouth'; the slight entasis of the neck, unevenness of the base, together with characteristics of seal and kick-up, etc., place this bottle at the beginning of the three-piece mould era; c.1820.*

Plate 40 *(centre). 'I/Risdon'; embossed 'IMPERIAL' and 'PATENT' on shoulder, and 'H. RICKETTS & CO, GLASSWORKS, BRISTOL' beneath base. The embossing here varies and can, of course, help in dating the bottle. Post-1826 in date, when Imperial measure was introduced and replaced the old English Wine Standard. The consistency of the string-rim construction, c.1820-50, is also seen to advantage in plates 39-43.*

Plate 41 *(right). 'DONERAILLE HOUSE', c.1830; this Ricketts bottle now lacks the addition of IMPERIAL to the shoulder and it would be useful to know for dating purposes at what point this was discontinued. If the assumed date for this bottle is correct, it could for instance lead to a possible dating of c.1824-30 for those with the addition of IMPERIAL, and post-1830 for those without.*

Plate 42. *'J·H', c.1830-40; considering the rapidity with which the form originally evolved, the change in bottle construction c.1820-80 was negligible*

Plate 43 *(below). Two squat three-piece mould bottles. Left: 'BRANDY', c.1830, and right: 'T. ROGERS·HOTEL·WESTON SUPER MARE', c.1850-60. The squat form of a three-piece mould bottle was almost as frequent as the cylindrical. The number of bottles in pale-coloured glass increased from the mid-nineteenth century particularly. Both the bottles are examples of 'commercial' seals. Note the later bottle has an oval seal stamp, pronounced mould seams and distinctly projecting lower collar to string-rim.*

Seals which refer to the bottle's contents are more a nineteenth century innovation; in the eighteenth century bottles would be gilded or have specially engraved silver wine labels.

Plate 44. *'Rousden/Jubilee/1887'; one of the last of the three-piece mould bottles. The narrowness of form, slight swelling to the neck and change in string-rim shape are characteristic.*

Sealed three-piece mould cylindrical wine bottles, 1820-87

Figure 209

Figure 210

Figure 211

Figure 212

Figure 213

Figure 214

Figure 209. *'Wm Rowe/NEWLANDS/1820'; the lettering runs around the seal edge, with the date in the centre. Newlands stands on the edge of the Forest of Dean in Gloucester, but there are also Newlands in Cornwall.*

Figure 210. *'I RISDON'; thought to be a Devonshire family, there are a number of Risdon bottles in existence including 'G.S. Risdon', 'Jos. Risdon 1818' and 'Josh. Risdon 1821'.*

Figure 211. *'Jo^s/H. Arlett./1822'.*

Figure 212. *'W W' beneath a lion's head erased, the crest of Wadham-Wyndham of Dinton House, Salisbury, Wiltshire, c.1830.*

Figure 213. *'H W C'; c.1840; several half and quarter bottles carrying this seal are known.*

Figure 214. *'Rousden/Jubilee/1887'; a very common bottle made to commemorate Queen Victoria's Golden Jubilee.*

14. Decanter Wine Bottles

Shaft and globe, onion, and mallet wine bottles with applied glass handles, originally intended as true serving bottles, are exceptionally rare. The number of sealed examples can virtually be counted on the fingers of one hand. In a sense, all early bottles were serving-bottles, but the addition of neatly formed glass handles left no doubt in the matter, added considerable prestige, and rendered the bottle wholly suitable for the table. These considerations alone, with the exception of the long-necked seventeenth century bottles, the practical addition of a glass handle to the later short-necked varieties seems a logical move. Considering just how difficult some were to hold safely it is truly surprising that more bottles were not fashioned in this manner. However, we must not lose sight of the fact that as early as 1670 clear glass decanters became available, and many of the more important households must have used them. These early decanters were still known as bottles, and many were of Venetian origin. Slightly later, London's Savoy glass house produced such examples under the direction of George Ravenscroft whose clear 'Glass of Lead' was initially to prove quite expensive.

Obviously with the advent of decanters not all individuals relegated their wine bottles to the secondary status of mere storage vessels, and indeed the few true decanter bottles that do exist prove otherwise. Most, when closely examined beneath, show considerable wear, the result of long and protracted use. Furthermore these decanter bottles were held in high esteem by their owners. Both these factors undoubtedly contributed to the bottles' chances of survival.

Like their early pottery counterparts, glass wine bottles were also adapted and made suitable for the table as decanters by the addition of either silver or pewter mounts. Some such mounts covered only the very top of the vessel and were fitted purely as decoration. Others were more complete; in some cases bottles were entirely 'converted'. When a handle was added it was normal practice to encircle the bottle just above shoulder level (figure c). However, by making the top mount more ample, it was occasionally possible to leave the handle unattached at this point (figure b). In many instances, bottles were mounted simply to cover up damage.

Where the all-vulnerable string-rim had suffered extensive chipping a neat silver mount could be added, and the bottle made serviceable again. To accomplish this, however, the remaining sharp projections were often ground flush. It is difficult to assess what damage if any a mount may conceal, but the width of the mount is obviously a good indication as far as the string-rim is concerned. Although some mounts are contemporary with the bottles on which they are found, many more have been added at a later date as the hall-marks on silver examples often testify. Approximate dates can also be deduced for certain of the pewter touch-marks.

It has been very difficult to trace many examples of decanter bottles; none the less, it is interesting to note that in construction glass-handled examples follow the same design.

Decanter wine bottles

Figure a *Figure b* *Figure c*

Figure a. *Late sealed onion decanter, c.1695. Sealed with a phoenix issuant from a coronet.*
Figure b. *Wine bottle c.1680 with elaborate silver mount, the seal 'I.C.' and three tuns. Note also the silver capped cork and ring pull, a feature of many wine bottles intended for personal use whether mounted or not. The mount on this example is not contemporary and of a much later date than the bottle.*
Figure c. *Pale green rather straight-sided onion bottle with the seal of Robert Wellar, 1711. The rather elaborate silver mount carries a Victorian hall-mark.*

Plate 45. *Rare decanter onion of Sir James Tillie of Pentillie, near Saltash, Cornwall. Mint condition; a highly desirable item; c.1700-10. See also figure 217.*

Sealed decanter wine bottles, c.1670-1821

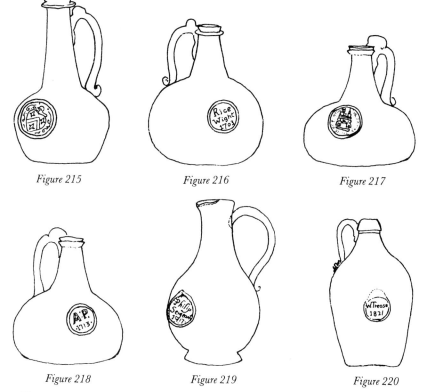

Figure 215

Figure 216

Figure 217

Figure 218

Figure 219

Figure 220

Figure 215. *Arms of Chetwynd, a chevron between three mullets. Not an easy bottle to date, but certainly seventeenth century, probably c.1670.*

Figure 216. *'Rice/Wight/1703'; a large clearly sealed decanter bottle. As there is no punctuation, one assumes this to be the gentleman's full name.*

Figure 217. *'Sir James Tillie of Pentillie', and the boat-house gateway and lodge entrance in seal centre; c.1700. Sir James Tillie, self-styled gentleman of Pentillie 'Castle', situated on the Coryton Estate in Cornwall, on the banks of the River Tamar north of Saltash. It is said that when he died he was seated, on his own request, upright in his chair for upwards of a week.*

Figure 218. *'A:P./1713'.*

Figure 219. *'Philip/Sergeant/1717'; a unique pale green glass jug with applied handle in identical manner to decanter bottles of the period; in the Victoria and Albert Museum, London.*

Figure 220. *'W. Trease/1821'; a handled flagon. A squat cylindrical bottle with the same surname is 'Thomas Trease, St. Ginnis 1815'. St. Ginnis is in Cornwall.*

15. Nailsea Wine Bottles

From an advertisement in a Bristol journal, it is known that the Nailsea Works at Bristol were operative in 1788. This factory produced the characteristic flasks, jugs and bottles with white enamel decoration in the form of spotting, splashing and flecking on the surface. Wine bottles represented a small percentage of the products of this factory, originally set up by one John Robert Lucas, a Bristol bottle maker. Many of the vessels made were intended for the country market and, by adhering to the use of bottle glass, Lucas benefited from the lower rates of excise duty payable.

It is known that similar wares were made elsewhere in Britain, both in the Midlands near Birmingham, and as far north as Perth. However, ascribing such pieces to individual factories is more difficult, and at present most collectors refer to all these items as 'Nailsea'.

As yet I have not been fortunate enough to examine any dated eighteenth century examples, if in fact they do exist. Sealed and dated Nailsea wine bottles are scarce, the few that have come to light bearing dates from the early to mid-nineteenth century.

Scarce though they are, not all collectors find the Nailsea bottles appealing, and the bottles do not represent a distinct evolutionary link as far as wine containers are concerned. Their bulbous form, coupled with a

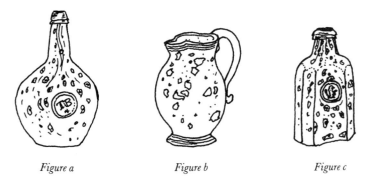

Figure a   *Figure b*   *Figure c*

Figure a. *A somewhat peculiar but characteristic Nailsea bottle form sealed with the initials 'T.B.'; c.1830.*
Figure b. *Typical Nailsea ale or water jug with narrow glass 'trails' around neck top and foot; 1800.*
Figure c. *Rare sealed octagonal bottle, c.1820.*
All three examples carry distinct pontil scars.

typical Ricketts neck and top, leave them very much isolated from the traditional wine bottle of the period. Nor were they intended to rival that market. The manufacturers' main aim was to produce country wares for domestic use, and it so happened that this range of vessels included wine bottles.

As the bottles were free-blown, and the white enamel markings rolled or marvered on to the bodies, they certainly could not be produced anywhere near as quickly as the moulded bottles of the day. This reversal to earlier and more skilled means of manufacture came at a time when in most factories speed was the essence of the day, and quantity not quality the important factor.

As a wine bottle the Nailsea bottle provided a most colourful and decorative alternative to the otherwise sombre products of the period. Today they are understandably scarce, simply because large amounts were never made; and those that were may well have been produced to special order.

Plate 46. *Although a plain bottle this could represent one of the earlier Nailsea productions. If it is Nailsea, then the earliest date we can ascribe to this example is the close of the eighteenth century. It is interesting to note, however, that the form, even if copied, is more nearly early eighteenth century.*

Plate 47. *Although not necessarily used for wine, these Nailsea jugs are sufficiently rare and interesting to include here. The construction of the string-rim conforms almost perfectly to normal wine bottles of the same period and, with the neck top alone, we could quite confidently ascribe a date of c.1800-15 for these.*

Nailsea wine bottles, 1820-34

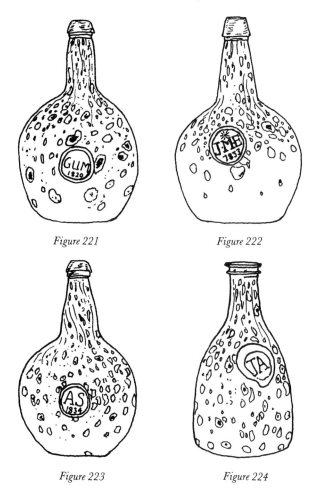

Figure 221

Figure 222

Figure 223

Figure 224

Figure 221. 'G U M/1820'; the first letter is a little poorly struck and could quite conceivably be a 'C'. Like the other drawings here it is a typical form for the Nailsea works.
Figure 222. 'J M E/1833' with fleuret above.
Figure 223. 'A S/1834'.
Figure 224. 'J A'; a decanter of types, early nineteenth century; trailed glass around rim, no stopper.

16. European Wine Bottles

Due to our once prolific trade with European countries, one further difficulty the collector faces is separating English and European wine bottles.

Countries such as France, Spain and Portugal all exported wines to this country, often in prodigious quantities. Many of their bottles were very similar to our own and, as bottle production in these countries was not known to be markedly different, an obvious difficulty in identification arises. As far as we know, no single method was employed which would instantly identify all such vessels. A few forms of bottle, however, appear to have no exact parallel in England, and these at least form a basis for much needed further research.

The Dutch onions of the 1720-50 period are certainly characteristic, and a case in point. The Dutch continued the production of these bottles long after the English had ceased to do so. Sound documentary evidence for this is amply provided by the numerous wreck artifacts recovered from various sites around Britain. Amongst these wine bottles are often predominant. Bottles from the *Hollandia,* which sank off the Scillies in 1743 (figure a), and the *Amsterdam* which foundered off St. Leonards in 1747 (figure b) are shown. They are characteristic in shape, with squat dome-shaped bodies, long evenly-tapering necks, and flattened collar-like string-rims. Here at least we have no exact English counterpart. These Dutch onions are also lighter both in weight and colour; furthermore the basal kick is cone-shaped and the pontil scar smaller and less irregular than in English bottles.

Unfortunately our knowledge of seventeenth century European wine bottles is even more scanty. For useful comparison however I have

Figure a Hollandia, *1743*   *Figure b* Amsterdam, *1747*   *Figure c* c.*1690*

included one further example of a Dutch bottle which I tentatively date as late seventeenth century figure c (a section through the base with attendant kick-up and hollow pontil scar can be seen at figure j).

Figure d c.1750   *Figure e c.1770*   *Figure f c.1820*

Some Dutch mallet and cylinder bottles are also different from our own, as figures d, e and f show. As can be seen, the c.1750 Dutch mallet bottle is quite distinctive, as is the strange looking cylinder wine c.1770. The French made a very similar bottle with a fairly small body and disproportionately long and attenuated neck. The neck became so drawn in many instances as to be narrower at a point well removed from the bottle's top. In the French form, however, the string-rim was a more protruding affair, far less flattened, and set at some distance from the top. Later cylindrical wines differed very little from our own.

Having established some useful criteria for distinguishing European wine bottles, it was a little confusing to find some very typically English looking examples in a selection of *Hollandia* bottles auctioned by Christie's in 1977. To add to the confusion the bottles ranged in date from c.1690-1740 and included both onion and mallet wines (figures g, h and i). The presence of these early bottles can be explained by their continued use over a long period of time. The early onions and mallets looked unmistakably English and, if they are English, their source remains a little more problematical, especially as the ship was on her maiden voyage; unless, of course we accept that many an 'English' bottle is in reality European. This is not as impossible as it may sound, for the bottles produced by individual glass houses are virtually unknown in England, let alone the Continent.

As there are too many pitfalls involved, it would be imprudent to be dogmatic about the origins of the *Hollandia* cargo, or any other for that matter. The bases of wine bottles often bear witness to hard and protracted use. As mere cargo many hundreds of unsealed bottles spent

Figure g c.1690   *Figure h c.1690*   *Figure i c.1740*

their lives transporting wine from one country to another, and there is no reason to suppose that such bottles were discarded until severely damaged or quite simply broken.

Such trading activities eventually resulted in the widespread dispersal of various bottle types not only in Europe but throughout the colonies.

Another pertinent factor is the export of English wine bottles which began as early as the middle of the seventeenth century. Obviously it is not hard to see that English and European bottles soon became totally integrated.

Furthermore what effect if any did the productions of other countries have on our own glass houses? Initially we must have copied, or at least been inspired by, the French on whom we were heavily reliant for imported bottles well before our own glass houses had started production. These imported bottles were of the shaft and globe variety, but how closely our first efforts at a similar bottle resembled these is uncertain. Unfortunately none of the French bottles can be identified today with any certainty; evidence for the early part of the seventeenth century is sadly lacking.

Later in the seventeenth and eighteenth centuries the use of different methods and materials allows us to ascribe an English or European attribution with more confidence and accuracy. Careful examination of any wine bottle will soon reveal the techniques used in its construction, though it is only fair to say that not all methods are immediately definitive of a bottle's true origin.

A variety of tools was used to form the basal kick-up on wine bottles; empontilling techniques varied too. At least by investigating these some generalisations can be made. In the seventeenth and eighteenth centuries the British favoured an iron, glass-dipped pontil rod and, with the exception of the earlier part of the seventeenth century, a normally generous and hummock-shaped push-up. Many Continental bottles of this period, however, show evidence of a narrower, cone-shaped kick-up, and frequent use of the actual glass blowpipe itself as a pontil rod. The latter method leaves a distinct core of glass adhering to the base as in Figures l and n.

In a similar vein are bare-iron pontil marks, where the detachment of the bare-iron rod has resulted in a residue of red or blackish deposits, often of a scale-like character. This method was in vogue in various countries, mainly from the late eighteenth to the mid-nineteenth century.

However it is quite possible for much earlier bottles to show marks of a similar type, simply because a pontil rod which had been insufficiently coated in glass may well have adhered to the bottle itself.

The final stage, the formation of the kick-up during the actual mould blowing of the bottle, occured in England around 1820, or perhaps a little

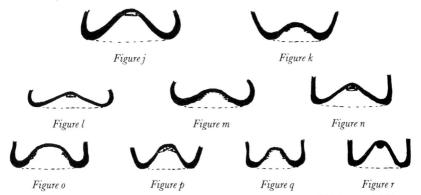

Figure j

Figure k

Figure l

Figure m

Figure n

Figure o

Figure p

Figure q

Figure r

Figure j. *Late seventeenth century Dutch onion bottle with cone-shaped kick-up and hollow pontil scar.*
Figure k. *English bottle c.1690 with normal 'open' pontil scar.*
Figure l. *Dutch onion c.1720. Shallow cone-shaped kick-up and hollow pontil scar.*
Figure m. *English onion bottle c.1710-15. Medium depth kick-up and normal pontil scar.*
Figure n. *Dutch mallet bottle c.1735-40. Fairly acute cone-shaped kick-up and hollow pontil scar.*
Figure o. *English mallet bottle c.1735-40 with generous hummock-shaped kick-up.*
Figure p. *French 'flowerpot-shaped' wine c.1760-70. Fairly acute kick-up with prominent pontil scar in apex (similar bottles are also to be found with the hollow pontil scar).*
Figure q. *Typical English wine bottle c.1760-70 — deep kick-up with 'open' pontil scar.*
Figure r. *French mould-formed bottle c.1800-20. Kick-up deep and acute with large central boss in apex. Bottles of this particular shape and form (see Miscellaneous Forms, figures r and 229) do occasionally carry a heavy pontil scar, and some at least are thought to be eighteenth century in date.*

earlier (figure s). Continental bottles followed suit at a slightly later date (figure t). At first the pontil rod continued in use, but the introduction of bottle cradling devices such as the snap and the sabot soon led to the disappearance of this device. None the less, some mould formed bottle bases still retain a pontil scar as late as the mid-nineteenth century (figure v).

Much has been written of the sand pontil mark, which is quite simply a normal iron pontil rod dipped in glass and then given a further light coating of fine sand prior to its attachment to the base of the bottle. The application of the sand ensured the not too firm adhesion of the rod, and its subsequent easy removal. Unfortunately this method is not definitive of any particular country, although its use was certainly widespread throughout England during much of the eighteenth century. Some early nineteenth century bottles also display this feature, even though the base is mould formed. A pimpled or peppered surface results from this method with occasional particles of sand still *in situ* (figure w).

A further Continental feature is the use of a four-pronged tool in order to form the kick-up; the resultant marks on the bottle base being quite distinct. I have not seen the blowpipe pontil rod used in conjunction with

| *Figure s* | *Figure t* | *Figure u* | *Figure v* |

Figure s. *English three-part mould bottle c.1820. The shallow mould-formed kick-up will occasionally carry embossed lettering on its outer edge and the pimple in the centre of the base is typical of many examples. Earlier examples often pontilled but this feature persisted in some cases until the mid-nineteenth century.*

Figure t. *Late nineteenth century French wine bottle. The enormously exaggerated mould-formed kick-up was a feature which persisted well into the twentieth century.*

Figure u. *The later nineteenth century English moulded bottles taper somewhat to the base and some minor differences are observable compared with figure s. Simplified embossing and total lack of a pontil scar are features of this late period.*

Figure v. *English bottle c.1860 showing a late occurrence of the pontil scar.*

this particular method, which is reasonably frequent on French wine bottles c.1720-60 (figure x).

Very narrow rods were used on smaller bottles to form the characteristic pinnacle shaped kick-ups associated with this method (figure y). Although common to many English and European bottles wine bottles were not treated in this manner.

The formation of the string-rim also affords us means of separating English and European wine bottles, and a reasonable cross section of various types with approximate dates are given on p.134.

Techniques varied tremendously, and it is only fair to say that many European examples had English counterparts. Once again, in the seventeenth century a paucity of evidence is noticeable. However, the c.1660 German bottle is interesting with a pincered collar of glass in place

Figure w

Figure x

Figure y

Figure w. *English bottle c.1770 with the peppered effect resulting from use of the pontil rod dipped in glass and then lightly coated with sand prior to its attachment to the bottle base.*
Figure x. *French bottle c.1740 with four-pronged indent on the base and 'open' pontil scar.*
Figure y. *The acute pinnacle-shaped kick-up seen here is normally only to be found on pharmaceutical bottles, but its use on smaller bottles and phials, even in this country, probably dates from at least the sixteenth century. English, c.1720.*

Two Continental wine bottles, late eighteenth century and early nineteenth century respectively. Note the cone-shaped kick-ups, particularly on the larger bottle. The use of the blowpipe, or any other hollow glass pontil rod, results in a neat symmetrical scar of smaller diameter than on most English wines, and leaves the very centre of the kick-up quite untouched.

of the normal string-rim; this isolated example obviously cannot be taken as typical for German bottles of the period, but it is unusual, and worthy of inclusion.

Later German bottle-tops somewhat resembled those of the French, with quite ample coil-like rims of glass. In the French examples the string-rim was often poorly tooled, uneven, and therefore lacking in uniformity.

The Dutch certainly employed distinctive techniques, and the tightly fitting almost flat collars of glass applied to their onion and mallet bottles of the 1700-60 period are instantly recognisable. The English equivalent of the same period was a neatly bevelled, much more protruding affair.

A smaller percentage of the Dutch bottles had a much more ample mushroom-shaped string-rim, set upon and entirely encompassing the neck top. By the late nineteenth century production closely resembled our own.

One definite Continental tendency on nineteenth century wines was the formation of a flat band-like collar of glass to serve as the string-rim; this method appeared towards the middle of the nineteenth century and

French	Dutch	German	American
1730	1720	1660	1790
1740	1730	1750	1820
1760	1740	1790	1870
1850	1760	1840	**Spanish**
1870	1880	1900	1800
			1820

persisted well into the first half of the present century. Even today Continental wines have a very similar neck top, although these are now totally mould formed.

A few remarks may be made as to the type of 'metal' used by the European glass houses, a metal held by many to be of rather inferior quality to our own; one author actually states that in his opinion the inferiority of the glass is manifest in the often very poor condition of dug and excavated bottles.

It is beyond dispute that certain differences do exist; many European bottles are lighter both in weight and colour, often have a considerably larger amount of bubbles in the glass as well as other marks indicative of impurities. The exact hue of the metal often differs from that of English wine bottles; an unusual sea-green or emerald tinted bottle, for instance, invariably denotes European parentage. English bottles tend to be of more sombre natural colours — light green to almost black. Continental

134

bottles of the seventeenth century often have a turquoise or bluish cast to the metal, a colour certainly not employed on English wine bottles of the seventeenth and eighteenth century.

Amber and reddish amber glass was often favoured by the Continental glass houses in the nineteenth century, whereas in England such colours were normally reserved for beer bottles.

'Black glass', strictly speaking a misnomer as far as wine bottles are concerned, is, however, the term more usually applied to English bottles many of which are certainly almost black, except in transmitted light. In general far fewer Continental bottles are of this really deep shade of metal.

Unusual colours such as aqua, pale green and citron occasionally appeared both here and abroad, but were rarer prior to the advent of the nineteenth century. Rare though they are, sealed wine bottles in aqua and clear glass are known in England, and even these no doubt had their Continental equivalents. Onion, octagonal and bladder onion bottles readily spring to mind, but such rare, perhaps unique bottles, are well out of the normal run of wine bottle production, and were no doubt made to special order.

In conclusion, the further investigation of European wine bottles is much needed; for the present the author has tried to bring together all those criteria that are known and currently accepted, at the same time providing useful comparisons wherever possible.

If too many generalisations have been made and even fewer conclusions reached it only serves to emphasise the need for more research.

For the embryo collector at least the pursuit of Continental wine bottles could well prove a most fruitful and informative venture.

Today it is increasingly difficult to find a worthwhile field of unexplored antiques, and avoid the keen competition of other collectors. In this country at least Continental wine bottles provide this opportunity simply because at this moment there appears to be little or no vogue for collecting them. Hence prices are curiously depressed, often perhaps half or even less than half of their English counterparts.

Those most frequently found are Dutch eighteenth century bottles, of cylindrical, mallet and onion form. Many of these have been recovered from canal sites and imported into this country by antique dealers. Prices several years ago were very respectable, but collectors soon realised the supply was for from limited, more and more appeared and their value dropped dramatically.

It would appear little has changed and unsealed Continental bottles of whatever nationality normally sell quite cheaply. Sealed wines rarely appear for sale in this country; except, of course, for the later nineteenth century bottles which abound, and consequently have little or no value.

Should an early dated Continental bottle appear at auction the reverse could well be the case; these appear to be far from common, but how sought after remains to be seen.

Plate 48. *A pair of typical Dutch onion wine bottles of the period 1720-40, the long-necked example being the earlier of the two. For an earlier example still see figure c in this section.*

Plate 49. *The European 'boot' bottle, a not uncommon bottle but one about which very little is known. Possibly Dutch in origin, but see also remarks on page 142. The bottle, in modified form, is known in England as early as c.1680-90.*

Plate 50. *A pair of Dutch long-necked cylinder bottles of characteristic form, used for Constantia wine, c.1760-80. This particular bottle form continued to evolve with a shortening of the neck, and gradual sloping away of the shoulders. Some later bottles were sealed; see figure q on page 143. Note the variation in width of the typically Continental flat, band-like string-rim. The example on the right has a multitude of bubbles or 'tears' in the glass; this too, is a Continental tendency said to be due to poor quality metal.*

Plate 51. *Left: French wine c.1780; a surprisingly neat and well advanced form for its age. Considering the care taken in its making, the poorly tooled string-rim is a distinct anomaly. Both the Dutch and French used these bottles and a slightly more squat shouldered form c.1820 can be seen in figure f in this section. Right: Later, as the nineteenth century progressed, the form developed into a narrower bottle with band-like string-rim, c.1890-1900. Many such bottles of this form were used in Germany specifically for hock.*

Plate 52. *Left: French sealed three-part mould bottle with exceptionally wide collar-like string-rim; late nineteenth century. Right: French cognac bottle of two-piece mould construction; early twentieth century. This is a good example of a 'turn' or 'spun-moulded' bottle (see pages 149 and 150) while the pale-coloured metal allows us to trace the resulting striations in the glass with ease.*

Plate 53. *Two early twentieth century Italian wine bottles. The pale-coloured glass used allows us to see the kick-up profile with ease. These inverted basin-shaped kick-ups are distinctive, always mould-formed, and late in date. The double mould-formed string-rim is unusual.*

17. Miscellaneous Forms

Having concluded our investigation of the various basic types of English and European wine bottle, a few additional remarks concerning certain miscellaneous forms may not go amiss. These include many unsealed bottles which, because of their unusual shape or construction, pose the difficult questions of date and provenance.

Figure a shows a most unusual bottle of which very few examples are known indeed. It is a triangular Mason's bottle, and carries on its seal the symbolic square and compass. Judging from its construction it is of late eighteenth century date. Figure b shows an almost equally rare bottle, the hexagonal 'R W/1739.'; fewer than a dozen of this type are thought to be in existence. A very early two-part mould octagonal is shown in figure c which, with its flat collar-like string-rim, is thought to be of Dutch extraction. The bottle is rather tentatively dated at c.1770-80, but by its extreme crudity could be much earlier. It was dug up from a much later Victorian site at Tunbridge Wells in Kent.

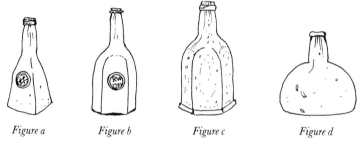

Figure a   *Figure b*   *Figure c*   *Figure d*

Another very strange bottle, and again possibly of Dutch origin, is shown in figure d. The bottle does not conform with any of the usual types and can only be loosely termed as of 'onion character'. The clues to be gained by careful examination of this vessel prove somewhat contradictory; the kick-up is shallow and the pontil scar wide in diameter, features pointing to an English place of manufacture. Conversely, the colour of the metal inclines a little to amber, and the string-rim bears no comparison to those normally found on English wines. Taking everything into account a date in the 1730s could be given to this bottle which corresponds rather well with what appears to be a very similar one featured in one of the famous Hogarth engravings of 1732.

Another problematical bottle is shown in figure e. If this is an English bottle then the shape, although a little broad, is reminiscent of the late seventeenth century; the kick-up is a little too large, however, and once again the string-rim does not conform. In figure f we have an apparently typical English mallet, yet upon closer examination this bottle proves to be almost assuredly European. The kick-up is cone shaped and the associated pontil scar small and hollow. Furthermore the metal is of an unusual sea green tint. The form is not unusual for an English mallet, but the bottle has all the characteristics we have come to accept as undoubtedly European. One wonders, since the study of wine bottles is still somewhat in its infancy, whether or not we can afford to be so dogmatic; only time will tell. The bottle dates c.1725.

Figure g, a rather stocky, rotund onion, has enough unusual characteristics to merit its inclusion here. The author has now encountered three of these bottles which must date somwhere in the 1700-25 region. They differ from the typical onion wines of the period in their distinctive shape, extremely narrow and neatly bevelled string-rim, and light amber coloured metal. The mouth of the bottle is also decidedly wider than in most vessels of this age. They certainly appear to be English but, as the author has been unable to find their exact parallel in a sealed and dated example, their true provenance remains debatable.

Figure h shows a truly remarkable bottle form known affectionately to the bottle collecting fraternity as the 'boot' bottle or Rugby ball. Certain authors consider these bottles to be American in origin, but as the self-

| *Figure e* | *Figure f* | *Figure g* | *Figure h* |

same forms have been found in several areas of Europe, including England, one supposes their manufacture was more widespread. As will be seen in the following figures, bottles of very similar form with typically English characteristics occur as early as the seventeenth century. Figure i shows an embossed leather bottle sealed 'S T L/1600' for Sir Thomas Leigh. Its similarity in shape to the later 'boot' bottle suggests the form was resurrected. It should be stated, however, that the author has yet to see the exact form illustrated in figure h with typically English string-rim and neck top, nor has he been able to examine a single sealed example. In consequence little is known about the set purpose of these bottles, if indeed there was any.

The same comments apply to the bottles illustrated in figures j and k. With these, however, we have all the characteristics of a typical English wine bottle, except of course for the shape. Figure j, c.1680, is a rare bottle, and few examples of this quaint flat-sided form are known at this early date. Figure k, another English bottle, follows on very nicely in every respect from the previous one and dates c.1710-15.

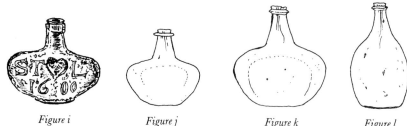

Figure i   *Figure j*   *Figure k*   *Figure l*

A bottle with no known duplicate is illustrated in figure l; the only sealed bottle even remotely like it being 'R. Hughes 1733', and after careful examination a date very close to this would seem appropriate. From the sketch the bottle may well appear somewhat bladder-shaped, but it is in fact only very slightly oval and considerably deeper in the body.

Figure m is a rather unusual octagonal bottle, sealed 'W. Walker/York', with the Prince of Wales' feathers. The bottle is rather flask-like in character and almost totally lacks a string-rim of any kind. Although difficult to date, it is probably late eighteenth or early nineteenth century.

'W/Wrather/1776', figure n, is unusual by way of its wide neck and mouth. The seal too is placed in a very low body position. Like the following bottle (figure o) it may not have been used for wine; other writers have suggested, quite feasibly, the storage of preserves and such like. Whatever the case, both types are sufficiently rare to be worth noting.

Figures p and q show two Dutch bottles of the type used for Constantia wine. The earlier of the two is distinctive by way of its curious spindle-

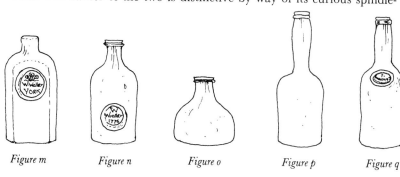

Figure m   *Figure n*   *Figure o*   *Figure p*   *Figure q*

shaped neck which is almost as long as the body. The sealed example has
the name 'Constance' inverted on the seal and dates c.1800. The earlier
bottle is c.1760-80. Both types are quite commonly found in England, and
frequently turn up at old dump sites.

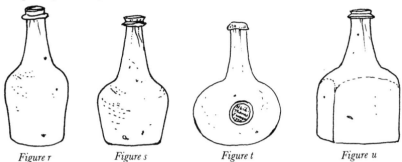

| Figure r | Figure s | Figure t | Figure u |

Figures r and s show two distinctive French wine bottles, c.1740-50,
and c.1760-70. The later bottle recalls certain seventeenth century forms,
but careful examination soon dispels this. The body is heavily marvered,
the kick-up deep and conical, and the string-rim neatly bevelled. Note the
much less uniform and more coil like string-rim on the earlier bottle.
Later specimens are not uncommon and often occur in collections labelled
as English. The earlier examples c.1730-40 are scarcer, and provide an
interesting contrast to other forms of the same era.

A most unusual eighteenth century bottle of 'onion' shape is sealed
'Htid/Thomas/Swansea/1770' (figure t). It is not dissimilar to the Nailsea
bottles of the early nineteenth century, and one assumes it was made to
special order.

In figure u is a scarce bottle type c.1710-15. The author has been
fortunate enough to examine two complete examples of this square form,
both of which were of English manufacture. Like the bottles specifically
designed to hold gin, one assumes these were similarly mould-blown in
order to accommodate them in wooden crates as part of a ship's cargo.

In typical dark olive green almost 'black' bottle glass, the bottles have a
typical onion neck, top and string-rim. Here, one supposes, we have an
English 'case wine' bottle as opposed to the much commoner case gin
already alluded to. It seems strange, however, that if merely intended as
cargo vessels the bottles have not survived in larger numbers.

Plate 54. *Surely one of the most extraordinary bottles for its age is this Welsh bottle sealed 'Htid/Thomas/Swansea/1770'. It conforms in virtually no way to normal bottles of the period, and even the string-rim is far from typical. See figure t in this section.*

Plate 55. *Probably intended for purposes other than wine. These wide-mouthed octagonals are rare, and date from the middle of the eighteenth century. A round bodied bottle, of otherwise similar purpose and age, is shown in figure 226.*

The kick-up and pontil scar on the bottle. Note the considerable wear-ring on the base.

Plates 56. *The Rugby ball or boot bottle. It is debatable whether this form was actually produced in England, and the exact date of manufacture is uncertain too. There are surprising similarities between this form and certain types of leather bottle known to have been made during the early part of the seventeenth century. An uncanny resemblance occurs in the characteristic shape of this bottle to an embossed leather bottle presented to the City of London by Sir Thomas Leigh in 1600, see figure i in this section. These similarities can only be the result of a form either wittingly or unwittingly resurrected at a later date.*

Miscellaneous forms c.1710-1850

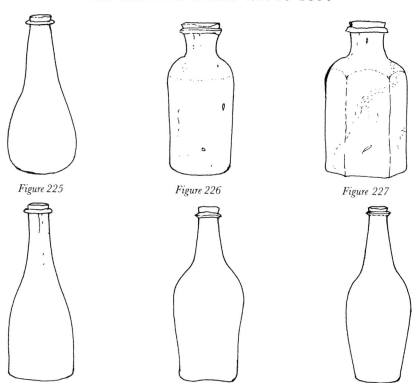

Figure 225   Figure 226   Figure 227

Figure 228   Figure 229   Figure 230

Figure 225. *Cook's culinary bottle, c.1710-20; dregs from the decanters were often transferred to a vessel such as this to enable the cook to make wine sauces, etc., when the occasion arose. A quaint but now very rare bottle.*

Figure 226. *A preserve bottle with wide mouth and narrow string-rim; about the middle of the eighteenth century.*

Figure 227. *Crudely moulded octagonal bottle of a very similar age to the previous example, and possibly used for the same purpose. A scarce bottle, especially with the wide mouth.*

Figure 228. *Wine bottle of French origin; the surprisingly neat form can be deceptively early in date. Evidence from the Yorktown harbour recoveries, and Yorktown itself, suggests that although mould-blown and often possessing no pontil scar, these champagne-shaped bottles could date as early as the 1780s.*

Figure 229. *Late French wine bottle, c.1760-70, of narrow flower-pot form. This bottle is a later development of the form illustrated in figure s in this section.*

Figure 230. *A further development of the previous bottle; this form with much attenuated base is often referred to as a skittle. French, c.1790-1800.*

18. Wine Bottles after 1900

The novice collector who, having read this book, would go out and search for his first wine bottle, should have no difficulty in acquiring an example from virtually any overgrown hedgerow. But what will enable him to recognise the much later bottles he is likely to find?

Firstly it must be remembered that the role of the later wine bottle had altered drastically. No longer was it expected to double as a storage vessel, serving vessel and decanter. After 1900 far more wines were shipped to this country direct in the bottle, and large amounts of English wine bottles were no longer a necessity. In this country the bottle houses concentrated their efforts from the closing years of the nineteenth century on the further development of beer, ale and porter bottles. In this closely related field we did develop our own characteristic bottles, as reference to figures a and b shows. Embossing became the means of identifying such bottles, and special closures were developed including the internal screw (Henry Barrett, 1872) and the crown cork (William Painter, 1892). A further variation, which appeared in 1875, was the swing stopper. The familiar crown cork, with its crimped metal cap, has of course survived to the present day. Wine bottles, however, continued to be cork stoppered and rarely ever embossed. It follows, therefore, that, with a few exceptions, the majority of wine bottles found in this country after 1900 are likely to be of Continental origin.

Figure a. *Typical embossed beer bottle with screw-threaded top, c.1890.*
Figure b. *A paper labelled, blob-top stout bottle, cork stoppered, c.1880-1900. After this date, labelling became the usual method of marking beers, ales and wines.*

Figure a   *Figure b*

To recap, the three-piece moulded bottles developed c.1811 faded from the scene around 1900, and as early as 1840-50 the pontil scar had disappeared from the base of most wine bottles. We also saw how this area of the bottle, now devoid of an ugly scar, was usefully employed for embossing with the company's name, etc. Further change, the result of almost complete automation, led to the making of bottles in two-piece moulds c.1900. Gone now was the third seam encircling the bottle at shoulder level. As figures c, d and e show the neck tops had undergone change too. Three-piece and two-piece moulds initially had separately applied tops, but in the latter case they were of short duration, and by 1920 the entire bottle was moulded in a single operation. It is worth bearing in mind, however, that not all glass houses adopted these techniques at the same time.

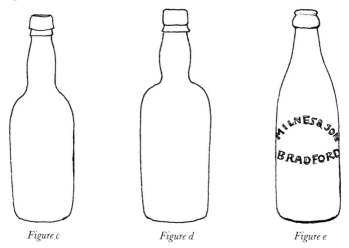

Figure c   *Figure d*   *Figure e*

Figure c. *Early two-piece mould wine of narrow cylindrical form, c.1899. This bottle too may have originally had a paper label.*
Figure d. *Port bottle, c.1900; note the distinctive neck-top.*
Figure e. *A two-piece mould crown cap beer bottle c.1920, with the usual embossing.*

So, just how do Continental wine bottles differ from those made in this country at the close of the nineteenth century? Firstly there was an increasing tendency to manufacture them in somewhat pale coloured glass — pale green, sea green and citron were not unusual, and amber on occasion. The metal was of much better quality, with fewer bubbles, tears, and imperfections. Also worth noting is the Continental tendency during the manufacture to turn the bottle within the mould, before removal. This helped to eradicate unsightly seam marks and is traceable by the wrythen markings running in an oblique direction around the bottle. Such bottles are termed by collectors 'turn', or 'spun' moulded. This feature can also be detected on a smaller percentage of English bottles towards the latter part of the nineteenth century, but is of common occurence on Continental examples until well into the twentieth century (see plate 52).

Even taking into account these minor differences, it is the overall form of the Continental bottles that renders them so very different from our own, as reference to figures f, g and h show. They are taller, neater and more slender in general, with a flattened band-like collar of glass to serve as a string-rim, this being moulded together with the bottle in modern examples.

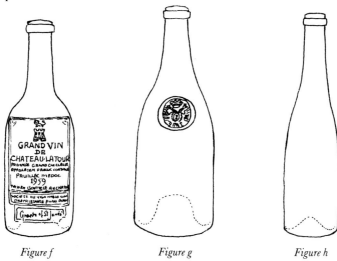

| Figure f | Figure g | Figure h |

Figure f. *Typical Continental wine bottle with paper label dated 1959; for obvious reasons no great reliance can be placed on bottles 'dated' by this means and, as in this instance, the bottle may well be a little earlier than the label suggests.*

Figure g. *Austrian wine bottle with double-headed eagle seal. Common to Continental wine bottles of the early to mid-twentieth century are the oval seals placed high up on the body, the band-like string-rim, and the high, mould-formed kick-up.*

Figure h. *Continental hock bottle in reddish-amber glass, probably German, but the form was widespread in Europe during the early twentieth century. Indeed almost identical bottles are still made today.*

By the opening years of the twentieth century the main wine-producing nations of the world, France, Spain and Portugal, had developed special types of bottle to suit specific wines, although it does not seem that each type and its respective contents were rigidly adhered to. None the less, the so-called hock, burgundy and claret bottles remain with us today in virtually unaltered form.

Since the mid-twentieth century little change has taken place in the construction of the wine bottle; the glass is now near perfect, the sombre tones of the old bottle glass have given way to bright startling greens, and other equally unnatural colours. But considering the lapse of time, and the speed with which the form originally developed in the seventeenth and eighteenth centuries, the 'modern' wine bottle has changed very little indeed over the last hundred years. The bottle that now graces your dining room table is not so very different from those made around the year 1800, and furthermore the great majority will be of Continental origin.

In recent years, there has been a small but somewhat pathetic revival of the old practice of sealing bottles but since the seal is moulded with the rest of the vessel, and not separately applied, the effect is not convincing. In the case of port bottles, certain companies have sought to recapture the traditional shape and colour of the earlier bottles; unquestionably a more successful venture than the imitation of the noble seal bottles of the seventeenth and eighteenth centuries.

However, we are constantly reminded that the antiques of tomorrow are in the making today, so perhaps we should keep an open mind on the subject.

19. Seals Discussed

Without the information derived from seals the study of wine bottles could well have progressed only slowly. Fortunately several authors cognisant of the fact have already published their findings, pre-eminent amongst them E.T. Leeds, whose careful study of the Oxford tavern bottles amply illustrates how even undated seals could be placed quite accurately to within a year or so of their date of manufacture.

Such research meant that unsealed bottles, the silent majority, were more precisely datable than was previously thought possible. As a result 'bottles', which had long remained a much neglected by-way of antique glass, received the full attention they deserved. The publication of *Sealed Bottles* by Sheelagh Ruggles-Brise in 1949, added a further stimulus to the hobby.

From at least the middle of the seventeenth century a certain percentage of wine bottles had the addition of a glass seal placed on the body, thus enabling the owner instantly to identify any particular vessel as his property. The seal itself was merely a blob of glass placed in the desired location while the newly finished bottle was still warm and malleable. This pad of glass was then stamped with a metal die upon which the owner's personal 'marks' had been engraved.

No doubt considerable prestige attached to owning such bottles; marked with the owner's name, crest, cipher or coat-of-arms, they were an open declaration of independence, often coupled with rank, position and wealth.

At first few bottles were sealed, due partly, no doubt, to the extra cost involved. 'Marked' bottles, as they are often referred to in the wine accounts of the period, could easily cost as much as 1s. (5p) a dozen extra, and this as early as 1680. The cost of plain quart sized bottles varied from 3s. 6d. to 5s. a dozen. The same account books refer unequivocally to seals, with orders ending in 'with my Lords Coat on yem at 5s p doz', or similar such phrases.

At this early stage it appears that wine bottles were available from a number of sources; in addition to the glass houses, independent glass carriers supplied them as well as beer and wine merchants. In short there were as yet few restrictions on the trade.

Although undated, the earliest seals appear to have been made for private individuals, but the trend rapidly found favour with the gentry and vintners alike.

When exactly the practice of marking bottles began is unknown, and the sealed bottle 'C.B.K. 1562', recorded as unearthed in Chester in 1939, cannot now be traced. This is all the more unfortunate, as a considerable number of years separates this bottle and the first undoubted seal, 'John Jefferson 1652', which survives as a seal only (The Museum of London). 'R.P.M. 1657' remains as the first intact dated seal bottle (Northampton Museum).

   Where a number of sealed bottles exist for a single household or tavern, it often follows that several variations in the seal occur, and such minor differences will often assist the collector in dating bottles of this type. To illustrate the point the R.E.P. tavern seals of Richard and Elizabeth Pont, sub-licensees of the Three Tuns in Oxford from 1666-87, are shown.

Seals of the Three Tuns Tavern 1666-87

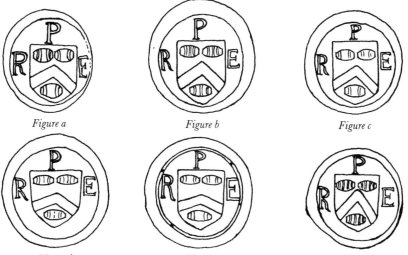

Figure a   Figure b   Figure c

Figure d   Figure e   Figure f

Figures a, b and c, and in all probability d, belong to the joint tenancy period at the Three Tuns, Oxford, of Richard and Elizabeth Pont, 1666-71. Figures e and f relate to Elizabeth's sole tenancy following the death of her husband, and date 1671-87. The seals are illustrated in their correct order of ascendancy. Several minor differences are observable in the lettering on the seals; the formation of the letter 'R' should be noted, but the more obvious alterations are as follows:

Figure a. *Broad 'tuns', shield with blunt, almost rounded base.*
Figure b. *Narrower 'tuns', shield with triangular base.*
Figure c. *Shield taller, chevron distinctly narrower.*
Figure d. *Shield broad, base bluntly triangular, chevron widely arched.*
Figure e. *'Waved' base to shield, chevron even more widely splayed, 'frame' to inner seal edge.*
Figure f. *Shield smaller, chevron very steeply arched.*

Comparison of closely similar seals can reveal far more then their age, however; an addition or subtraction to the design of a seal will often indicate a family union, marriage or death; sometimes the amalgamation or division of a large estate. For these reasons some seals were radically altered over a period of years. While considerable importance can therefore be attached to such alterations, it is only fair to say that on occasions certain very minor modifications were nothing more than the whim of the owner, the result of a fresh batch of bottles, a new engraver, or even a different glass house (see plate 57).

The character of seals varies tremendously. Most frequent on earlier bottles are solitary names, sets of initials, emblems, and coats-of-arms. Initially bottles with the addition of a date were in a minority. Various categories of seals can be identified, including those of private individuals, tavern keepers and merchants, and each type is normally distinct in its design; examples of all three are given below.

| Category A | Category B | Category C |

Category A is obviously the most variable. Pictorial devices in Category B are often self-explanatory; the pyramidal form of lettering invariably denotes a husband and wife partnership, here for instance Ralph and Joan Flexney of the Bear Inn, Oxford. Category C is of the utmost rarity, in fact the example illustrated is thought to be the only dated one found in this country. However, several have been excavated from the early English settlements in Jamestown, Virginia, although evidence suggests that many of these were made to order in English glass houses. Merchants' marks were a further way of identifying the ownership of goods, and were favoured by the larger guilds and corporations in the more important trading centres of the world. Various merchandise was treated in this manner, especially textiles, fabrics and metalware and, to a much lesser extent, silver, glass and pottery.

Merchants' marks appear on wine bottles c.1660-1760, although their usage in general stems from at least the early sixteenth century. The intriguing symbols and insignia employed are not easily traceable and no work to date appears to explain them fully. Few good condition wine bottles with these seals exist and their use does not appear to have been exactly commonplace. Most merchant-mark seals fall in the 1680-1730 period, and detached seals are the most frequent; dated examples are rare.

As time progressed seals with the person's name, locality and date became more frequent, and ultimately the types encountered were virtually endless. In fineness of execution seals were equally variable; much depended on the ability of the engraver and, no doubt, the purse of the customer. It is interesting to note that certain seals were quite obviously entrusted to the care of a master engraver, for they are perfect in every detail. Furthermore such finesse was no late development in the history of sealing wine bottles, as many seventeenth century seals display considerable skill in their workmanship. On a 1674 bottle in the author's collection even the engraver's guide lines for the name and date are easily traced upon the seal (see plate 58).

On the other hand, spelling was not always a strong point with the engravers as the seals below illustrate:

| Figure g | Figure h | Figure i |

Figure g has Woodbridge rendered 'Wodbrig', while figure h has the delightful 'John & Eliz: Dorrellpooll', a seemingly strange surname until one realises what was intended: John & Eliz. Dorrell (of) Poole. Figure i has the seal inscribed 'H. Browse, Yalberton', which one assumes is intended to be Yelverton.

Where such rustic orthography occurs it is almost certain to enhance the value of the bottle, giving it extra character and an imbued depth of curiosity. Other seals with strange abbreviations or total lack of punctuation come into the same category.

Seal positions 1650-1850

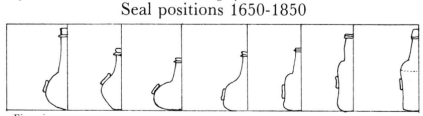

Figure j

Figure j shows how the seal's position in relation to the bottle altered with the changing shape of the vessel. From about 1650-70 the seal was at or close to the centre of the body; c.1680-1700 it was on the shoulder, often almost against the neck; c.1700-25 on or just below the shoulder, and finally c.1730-1850 it had reverted back to a central body position, where it remained till the practice of sealing bottles ceased.

Examination of bottle seals c.1650-1850 will occasionally reveal slight differences in the method of application, and such subtleties can often assist in dating a seal, even when the seal has long since parted company with the original bottle.

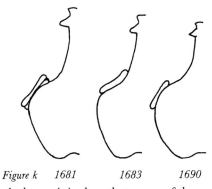

Figure k   *1681*   *1683*   *1690*

As figure k shows, it is clear that many of the early bottles c.1680 had a small 'cushion' of glass laid on the bottle before the main seal was applied. This separate layer of glass was carefully placed so as to assist in setting the seal squarely upon the body, and therefore obviated the difficulty of accommodating a seal on an otherwise awkward shoulder angle. Such a move was also practical; the pressure necessary in stamping a seal so that it should conform to the exact bottle profile would quite often result in some collapse or distortion at this point. Indeed some bottle houses are known to have used a specific tool to support the inside of the bottle during this operation. Not all seventeenth century bottles were sealed with such care, but a fair percentage of the 1670-85 bottles appear to have this feature, due no doubt to the pronounced shoulder angle current at this period. However some glass houses overcame the problem simply by setting the seal tight in against the neck as in the 1683 example shown. In the 1690 bottle the seal is applied and positioned in the normal way for its date.

In size seals ranged from 1in. to 1¾ins. in diameter and, considering the vast array that once existed, it is surprising how few of the original brass dies have come to light. One supposes that a large proportion of them were melted down for reuse. These dies were normally circular in shape, very rarely square, oblong or oval, and mounted by way of the shank into a wooden handle. One variation of the stamp, which did not involve the making of a specific die, was the use of interchangeable letter heads, which could be set up in any desired combination and stamped accordingly. This method resulted in a distinct oblong impression, with the division between the separate letters often plainly visible (see centre example in figure l). Although possibly a cheaper way of sealing one's bottles its popularity was limited, and its use was confined chiefly to the seventeenth and early eighteenth centuries.

Oval seal stamps are more a feature of the nineteenth century and often occur on wine or beer merchants' bottles. By then, stamps were more of an advertisement and far less a means of personalising a vessel (see left hand example in figure l and plate 62).

Some small tavern bottles appear with coin-like 'medallions', an allusion to the almost total lack of a pronounced flange and its replacement by a milled edge, figure m. In early literature, seals were often referred to as medallions, stamps, buttons and lozenges.

Figure l Oval, oblong and square seal stamps

Figure m

Plate 57. *Detached seals belonging to the Carew family of Devonshire; see Appendix I, p.211. Note the minor modifications. Above: detached seals from onion wines of the late seventeenth and early eighteenth century. Below: seal on cylinder wine bottle c.1800.*

Plate 58 *(top left). Considerable effort has been made by the engraver in this early seal dated 1674. Note the engraver's guide lines are perfectly traceable in the glass. In order to obtain a clear and accurate stamping, the careful application of the glass blob and its stamping at the critical moment during cooling were essential.*

Plate 59 *(top right). This onion seal initialled 'W W', c.1700, was probably stamped while the glass was just a little too 'plastic'. On removal of the die the glass has continued to move and settle, resulting in a poor impression.*

Plate 60 *(below). The use of just two digits to indicate the year was more a feature of the seventeenth century, as in this early seal dated 8 and 1 for 1681. More often the two latter digits of the year occurred side by side, e.g. 91 for 1691. See also figures 31, 45 and 46; 'N.N.' p.227 and Crest of Warre p.231.*

Plate 61. *Three seals incorporating the name of the establishment in which they were used. Top to bottom: 'T. ROGERS/HOTEL/WESTON/SUPER MARE'; 'POST/HOUSE/ NEWARK'; and 'GENERAL/HOSPITAL/Bristol'.*

Plate 62. *Three late merchants' seals; the lower seal merely indicating the bottle's contents. All are nineteenth century.*

Plate 63. *The maritime connections for this seal seem obvious, though it may not have been used on board ship. Naval colleges may have had bottles, and there is always the possibility that the seal refers to an Anchor public house. See also* The English Glass Bottle, *Exhibition Catalogue, Truro Museum, 1976, item 287.*

Plate 64 *(right). 'W. Leman/Chard./1771'. There are obvious anomalies here; this three-part mould Ricketts bottle, post-1821, bears an eighteenth century date as a commemoration of some event or other; not as its date of manufacture. It is as well to remember that the construction of the bottle provides the vital pointers as the date can be misleading.*

Plate 65 *(far right). Judging by the number of Cornish mines in operation at this period there must be other 'mine' bottles in existence. None the less this bottle from the Wheel of Fortune Mine is rare and interesting; c.1780-90. See also figure 184.*

20. Bottle Seals Illustrated

The seals illustrated in this section have been chosen in order to show the various types discussed in the previous section. Quite obviously the desirability of a sealed bottle is greatly enhanced by the attractiveness of the seal itself. Collectors soon learn to appreciate the subtle differences, which in addition to providing useful dating aids are often far more significant in determining value, than either age, condition or rarity.

Most bottles with a full name, date and locality are eagerly sought after, although the great majority stem from the eighteenth and nineteenth century. Seventeenth century examples are scarcer but often delightful; take for example the 'R. How at Chedworth, 1683' seal and, in a similar vein, 'ANTHONY HALL IN OXFORD, 1685.' Such bottles as these are at a premium, and much in demand.

None the less, for those collectors prepared to research their bottles tirelessly, even those with obscure family crests and coats-of-arms will often provide all the information needed to allow fairly close dating. Only where a bottle bears a solitary name, or set of initials does life become more difficult. It is only fair to say that in many such cases, short of an unimpeachable provenance, there is little that can be done in order to establish the former owner, but at least the date of the bottle can be arrived at by assessing form, construction, etc.

In the plates that follow the reader can compare at random the various seal types used throughout the seventeenth, eighteenth and nineteenth centuries, noting at the same time the differences between private household or 'gentleman's' seals, and those employed by the numerous inns, taverns and hostelries of the period.

Seals provide an important link with the past, and the discovery of even fragmentary bottles or detached seals should always be carefully noted; for the collector it soon becomes obvious that the whole study of antique wine bottles revolves around the all-important seal.

Plate 66 *(left to right, top to bottom). 'B' under a foreign crown; 'William/Battishill/1701';*
coat-of-arms: a shield with three fleur-de-lis and a chevron charged in its apex a shield with
sinister hand appaumée; coat-of-arms: within a shield three bulls' heads caboshed, crest: a
bull's head upon a knight's helm to dexter.

Plate 67 *(left to right, top to bottom). 'O/Kingdon/1786'; 'R.N/1691'; 'R H C/1815'; 'Jos./Sunter/1771'.*

Plate 68 *(left to right, top to bottom). 'Doneraile House'; 'W-B./L'; 'Evan Iones/Llanellyd/1743'; 'R.R.' in monogram.*

Plate 69 *(left to right, top to bottom). 'J. Wenfley/N. Tawton'; 'I/Taylor/1807';*
'B W/1758'; 'J/H.'

Plate 70 *(left to right, top to bottom). Crest: a greyhound's head erased beneath a baron's coronet; 'I.W/1775'; 'Tho. Rich/Over Stowey/1783'; 'John/Garneys/1724'.*

Plate 71 *(left to right, top to bottom). 'E.L.'; 'I/Fogg/1734'; 'I. Elliott/Stonehouse/1794'; 'Geo/Willmott/Axminster'.*

Plate 72 (*left to right, top to bottom*). 'H' under a viscount's coronet; 'T. Hesketh';
'I.H/1764'; 'N I D/1715'.

Plate 73 *(left to right, top to bottom). 'KENTRAUGH'; crest: a castle tower aflame;*
'HAMILTON/APLIN & CO./26/BUCKLERSBURY'; 'R./Gaskell/1761'.

Plate 74 *(left to right, top to bottom). 'I. Smith/1706'; 'Wingerworth 1711' and a cockatrice crest; 'P' under an earl's coronet; 'I. Watson/Esqr./Bilton'.*

173

Plate 75 *(left to right, top to bottom). 'R W/1690' and a king's head; 'R E W/1699' and a king's head; 'Rousdon/Jubilee/1887'; 'I.C/1731'.*

Plate 76 *(left to right, top to bottom). 'Sam!./Whittuck/1751'; 'Sir Wm Wynne/Sandown Fort/I of Wight'; 'A.S/C.R.'; 'A S/C R' in script.*

Plate 77 *(left to right, top to bottom).* *'1770/James/Oakes/Bury'; 'I:/Fleming/Plymtree/ 1786'; 'T.C.' and sinister hand appaumée; 'H.C.' and dexter hand appaumée.*

Plate 78 *(top to bottom). Cipher of William and Anne Morrell, a crown, 'OXON' and '1684' (this is an addition for the Morrell series); 'W.H.P.' and the King's arms. See Appendix II where Ruggles-Brise includes it incorrectly under 'W.P.H.'*

21. Thames-side Seal Recoveries

Probably no other river in this country has received so much attention from collectors, archaeologists and curio hunters, as the Thames.

For the mud-lark of today the pickings are much leaner, but even so the river does continue to yield important artifacts from the time to time. It is these that have enabled present day historians to gather together the history of the metropolis, or fit one further piece into the colourful jigsaw that was once the past.

The river yields few complete wine bottles, but the all important seals survive relatively well, and few artifacts from the Thames are as informative as these. The discovery over the years of interesting and important seals has largely gone unnoticed and unpublished and, although this is unfortunately not the place to rectify the situation entirely, it was possible to show at least some of those recovered in more recent years. It was quite evident from the start that a large number of the seals were hitherto unrecorded, many of them dating to the seventeenth and early eighteenth centuries, and together they form a most welcome and valuable addition to the book.

Plate 79. *A sun full face. A similar detached seal is 'T P' and a sun full face which belonged to Thomas Padnoll of the Sun Tavern, London. Both seals are of seventeenth century date.*

Plate 80

Plate 81   *Plate 82*

Plate 80. *Note the variations in the style of the two mitres and the beaded border to one of the seals. There are further variations of this seal with the same initials ('W P'), and it now seems unlikely that any of the seals actually belonged to a bishop. Evidence has since shown that both William Proctor and William Pagett are more likely candidates for the ownership of these seals. Both were licensees of Mitre Taverns in the mid-seventeenth century and thus the bottles are very likely to stem from these establishments. See also Appendix II.*

Plate 81. *Coat-of-arms: 'P H' and a sun; crest: a pegasus courant.*

Plate 82. *'R E P', a chevron and three tuns; see Appendix II, also figures a-f, p.153. This seal could represent yet another variation in the 'R E P' series if the waved apex of the shield is to be believed, but the detrition of this example leaves this open to some doubt. Otherwise it is closely comparable to figure f on p.153.*

Plate 83

Plate 84

Plate 85

Plate 86

Plate 83. *'C' and crest of a male griffon segreant holding a spear.*
Plate 84. *'I Porteus Efq^{r}.'.*
Plate 85. *Above 'MAR. . .' (and some illegible letters); below 'L R'.*
Plate 86. *'I M W' and St. George and the dragon; see Appendix II. A good and attractive example of seventeenth century seal engraving, the detail here is quite outstanding. Complete bottles bearing this seal are not known.*

Plate 88

Plate 87

Plate 90

Plate 89

Plate 87. *Cipher of William and Anne Morrell, a crown, 'Ox. . on' and the date 1688. See Appendix II, but note that the 'N' of Oxon is reversed not only on the 1688 stamp, but also on that of 1683.*

Plate 88. *Similar to the previous seal; once again the 'N' is reversed, but the missing date is unquestionably 1688, because the actual cipher letters are somewhat larger on the 1683 version.*

Plate 89. *The only clearly legible part of this seal is the date in the centre 1701. This is all the more unfortunate, as the author has examined a complete bottle with this seal in the same condition.*

Plate 90. *This interesting early seal may represent a merchant's mark, and until it is identified it is probably best categorised as such.*

Plate 91

Plate 92

Plate 93

Plate 94

Plate 91. *'W M R' and a fountain upon a rectangular plinth. The distinctive curvature of the glass body fragment upon which this seal rests immediately suggests a shaft and globe bottle of the seventeenth century. Fountains are not unknown on seal bottles; see also Appendix II, under R.I.T., p.315.*

Plate 92. *'T.M/1717'. Not all seals had careful attention given them; although the seal condition is now bad, it is still possible to note the poor draughtsmanship of this example.*

Plate 93. *This fragmentary seal contains the letters 'P W E', a cross and some other letters encircling this. Few of the words can now be read, but the single digit '3' of a ?date letter, appears beneath the main letter P.*

Plate 94. *?Coat-of-arms; within a shield a lion rampant. The only other decoration to this seal which may be of any significance is the presence of three pellets above and to either side of the shield.*

Plate 96

Plate 95

Plate 97

Plate 98

Plate 95. '*A R*' *beneath a crown; the design of this seal shows close affinities to the A.K.R. seals (see Appendix II), and several Oxford tavern seals have been recovered from the Thames, but this is of course pure speculation. Judging from the fragment attached to the seal an onion wine bottle is indicated.*

Plate 96. *Coat-of-arms: within a shield couche, three berries in base;. crest: upon a knight's helm and mantling a bird's head with wings displayed.*

Plate 97. *Fragmentary seal of Anthony Hall of the Mermaid Tavern, Oxford. Only two digits of the date remain (68). So far this particular mermaid stamp has only been found dated 1682. Several other 'A H' seals are known incorporating the mermaid device, see Appendix II.*

Plate 98. *Rare octagonal seal stamp; there is also an inner octagonal frame to the seal. Within this there would appear to be a coat-of-arms: quarterly, one and four three mullets, two a chough, three a horse rampant.*

Plate 99

Plate 100

Plate 101

Plate 102

Plate 99. *An intact bottle c.1655-60 with a very similar seal to this one is in the Ashmolean Museum, Oxford. On this seal the name is spelt 'R: BILLINGSLEY', and there is the addition of a fine Tudor rose. On the seal on the intact bottle the name is spelt 'RICHARD BILLINGSLEY'. These words are written around the seal edge, but the inclusion of a five turreted castle is common to both. For an illustration of the bottle, see figure 18.*
Plate 100. *'J/Atkin(s)/1735'.*
Plate 101. *'H G' and the head of a hippocampus couped.*
Plate 102. *'G. HOFFMANN'; judging from the remaining fragment of glass with this seal, the bottle was probably square or octagonal.*

Plate 103

Plate 104

Plate 105

Plate 106

Plate 103. *Coat-of-arms: a lion rampant; crest: a dexter hand appaumée. Considerable finesse has been shown in the execution of this seal which is probably seventeenth century. The great majority of the seventeenth century 'gentleman's' bottles are sealed in a like manner.*

Plate 104. *'T.B'; tracing the ownership of initialled seals is virtually impossible unless there are other clues to go on. Where a quantity of such seals are excavated from a particular household or tavern site, however, the problem becomes less acute.*

Plate 105. *This may represent a lamb or a bull, but either way the likelihood is that most early seals with purely a solitary device upon them stem from a tavern or alehouse of that name. Probably seventeenth century.*

Plate 106. *Not all tavern seals were as uninspired as the previous example. This carefully engraved seal, initialled 'I H', is almost certainly one of a particularly interesting group which alludes to the tavern's name by way of an illustrative pun. Some are quite easy to interpret, but others, like this, are not so obvious. Although the author has been unable to explain the strange structure on this seal one is tempted to suppose that the presence of a penguin standing in water, at what could just feasibly be a harbour entrance, points to the seal having emanated from the Coldharbour area close to London Bridge. One would need to identify the 'structure' first, however, for therein lies the key to this seal.*

185

Plate 107

Plate 107. *Six very early separate matrice seals. Although there is no very accurate way of dating these, the great majority are almost certainly seventeenth century. Few complete bottles with this seal type exist, but useful comparison can be made to figure 7, which is one of the earliest wine bottles extant. Separate matrice seals do exist in a few instances well into the eighteenth century, but the delightful, if unsophisticated lettering of the seventeenth century examples, is characteristic and not readily forgotten.*

Plate 108

Plate 109

Plate 108. *Another pair of separate matrice seals, and a fragmentary seal. Note how the remaining glass fragment on the 'I.I.' example curves swiftly away from behind the seal; almost certainly a shaft and globe bottle originally. The strange looking symbol above the letters 'Sy' on the broken seal is also noteworthy.*

Plate 109. *Two crests and a coat-of-arms. Crest: an eagle's head erased upon a cap of maintenance; 'I E S' and a rose slipped and stalked; coat-of-arms; upon an ermine ground a crescent cantoned, crest: a demi lion rampant.*

187

22. Guide to Rarity

In general, disregarding their appeal, the earliest bottles are the hardest to acquire, especially in good condition. Certain types appear quite frequently on the market, and into this category fall cylindrical and squat cylindrical wines. Mallets and onions are far less frequent; bladder onions and octagonals rarer still. Certain sizes of bottle are scarcer than others, particularly miniatures and magnums. The survival rate of magnum onions was obviously poor if the few specimens extant today are anything to go by. This may well have been due to the fact that such large vessels blew unavoidably thin at shoulder level and subsequently were more prone to breakage. Miniatures, although scarce in general terms, survive better.

The collector should not overlook the fact, however, that scarcity and desirability do not always go hand in hand. Investment minded individuals should study the market closely before spending large sums on apparently rare and desirable items. Certain categories of bottle are undoubtedly scarce, but desirable only to a limited market. For instance, the few bladder onion wines I have seen at auction have rarely fetched the equivalent of their onion counterparts. But why? They are a much rarer bottle, more unusual, and to my mind have considerable curiosity and charm, making them rather more desirable than the normal onion wine.

Other unusual forms are often treated in the same manner. Furthermore, many collectors totally disdain the European wine bottles and would not include a single example in their collection. It is true that these bottles are far commoner than their English equivalent, and appear quite readily on the market. In recent years large quantities of Dutch eighteenth century bottles have been discovered in the colonies and at one time the market became so flooded with them that their value dropped dramatically. It is interesting to note that, despite this, the value of English bottles has steadily continued to increase.

As it stands, the English bottle forms the focus of attention for, strangely enough, European seals are scarce, and sealed wine bottles in the main appear to be pre-eminently an English development. Representing as they do a quite considerable fragment of our past, sealed bottles now receive the full and deserving attention of collectors throughout the world. Considering their scarcity the prices of wine bottles had lagged behind other categories of antique glass for many years. Today they have risen quickly to the forefront, and good specimens often attain some of the best prices at auction.

In virtually all categories of wine bottle it normally follows that in order of desirability dated seals rank foremost, followed by undated examples, and finally by plain bottles. Sealed and dated shaft and globe bottles pre-1680 very rarely appear on the market, indeed even good condition unsealed ones are now very difficult to find. Outside museums the number of sealed examples in private hands is few. The major London museums possess a fair percentage of the seventeenth century bottles, many of which came to light during extensive rebuilding of the city following the last war.

Today, the trickle of early bottles that comes on to the market is often the result of digging or excavation but, as large scale rebuilding programmes are now few and far between, the supply is obviously limited. From time to time the auction of a major collection gives the collector a chance to procure an early bottle for his cabinet, but today competition for such items is fierce, and one's chance of a bargain almost nil. Onion bottles of the period 1700-25 are a little easier to acquire, but the transitional linking forms, c.1680-1700, are, again, difficult to come by.

Today it can truthfully be said that any good condition pre-1700 seal is almost worth its weight in gold, and the same applies to unsealed bottles of this period. However, in the latter case, condition really is of paramount importance.

Decanter bottles of almost any type are rare indeed; and sealed examples of the earlier forms can virtually be counted on the fingers of one hand.

The bladder variation of the onion, as previously stated, is a most uncommon bottle, both sealed and unsealed, but possibly not so popular with collectors as its rarity deserves.

Mallet bottles are not too difficult to acquire unsealed and a considerable array of variant forms may be collected. Sealed specimens are uncommon, the early ones scarce, particularly those dated pre-1730.

With the advent of the squat and true cylindrical bottle we arrive at an era from which a much larger proportion of specimens have survived. With these types of bottle only the very earliest dated examples can truly be described as rare. Bottles c.1740 qualify for this rating as they were in existence at a time when most glass houses continued the production of the mallet. Later squats and true cylinders are not uncommon and form the bulk of sealed bottles reaching the market today. Of the two types the squats, which perhaps convey an 'earlier' image, tend to achieve the higher prices. Unsealed examples of both are common. From c.1750 onwards the collector should have no real difficulty in securing a bottle for each decade should he wish to do so.

Commonest of all the true sealed bottles are the three-piece moulded bottles introduced by Henry Ricketts of Bristol. Although much character was lost with the advent of machinery it is only fair to say that finishing off remained a manual process and seals were applied in the traditional fashion. Strangely, dated seals are none too common in this category of bottle, many bearing crests, coats-of-arms, names or initials only.

23. Fakes, Forgeries and Restorations

With the advent of a much wider interest in old English wine bottles and a resultant increase in their value, the inevitable fakes, forgeries and reproductions have begun to appear on the market. Ordinary reproductions of free-blown bottles sporting plainly traceable mould seams, kick-ups without pontil scars and embossed seals are unlikely to fool anyone who has read this book, even if it is the first acquaintance one has had with the subject of antique wine bottles.

Straightforward copies of wine bottles of a slightly more convincing nature do exist, but invariably the modern craftsman has not mastered the techniques employed by the seventeenth and eighteenth century glassmen. Making bottles every day of their lives, the old glass blowers achieved a rare sense of form, proportion and precision, which cannot be achieved today by making a small batch of bottles. Much practice would be required, in addition to the right materials which in themselves may prove difficult to acquire. Suffice it to say that those copies seen by the author are not convincing; rather odd or quaint shapes predominate, incorrectly tooled string-rims, strange pontil scars and kick-ups. Furthermore the glass itself is often all too clear and unimpaired by the multitude of small bubbles and locked in imperfections which are the hallmarks of genuine antique glass. Some exceptions, however, are known; what would appear to be relatively recent copies of early eighteenth century wine bottles tend to lean the other way, and the strange blue and mauvish tinted metal employed is full of swirls and bubbles. With these particular onion bottles the faker has gone 'overboard' in his attempts to simulate old bottle glass, and none too convincingly. See figures a, b and c overleaf.

None the less their overall appearance is not bad, even at arm's length, and it is quite possible that a novice could be fooled. Given a little thought, however, supicions should soon spring to mind. Their shape is a mixture of English and European, the deeply impressed seal is far from legible, and the pontil scar is not only inexpert but of 'odd' diameter. Add the presence of 'applied' wear, and the copy is immediately evident.

Virtually all old glass bears the signs of hard and protracted use, not only on the base but also on the body, in the form of countless small scratches and minor abrasions. Faked wear is too consistent no matter how applied. It is well worth examining the surface of old bottles under a

Figure a

Figure b

Figure c

Figure a. *Not a bad copy for shape, but not one hundred per cent 'English'. Furthermore few onions of this age (the bottle purports to be c.1710) had the seal tucked in so closely to the neck.*
Figure b. *The front view shows the rather dome-shaped body with shoulders falling away, more a Dutch characteristic.*
Figure c. *Close-up of the seal; this is very poor. Because the stamp is deeply impressed the definition should be good which it is not. Naivety was commonplace with the early engravers, but never such extreme crudity.*

Plate 110. *At least half of the neck section and the entire string-rim have been restored on this important seventeenth century seal bottle. The repair is difficult to detect, and it would be difficult to argue that the bottle has not benefited from this particular work of restoration.*

x 10 or 15 hand lens and becoming familiar with what genuine wear really looks like. Once appreciated, the myriad marks occasioned by constant cellar and table use over the centuries is easily remembered and not readily confused with the efforts of the most ardent faker.

With the arrival of four figure sums for early wine bottles came the most insidious fakes of all. These are the plain bottles to which interesting and desirable detached seals have been affixed. This type of fake, which has only appeared during the last fifteen years, can prove the most costly and difficult to detect. As both parts used are genuine, it only needs the faker to affix the seal in a convincing manner, and the job is complete.

There are some safeguards for the collector, and one may as well begin by checking all the obvious possibilities. Does the metal of the bottle and the seal correspond? Is the seal nicely undercut and in the correct position for the age of the bottle, with the same amount of wear as the rest of the bottle? Does the seal conform to the profile of the body. Probably most

Plate 111 *(left). Another late seventeenth century onion bottle, c.1685-88. The neck section and string-rim are badly cracked and the body, too, has a large crack descending from this area. Part of the neck top has been removed and poorly glued back together. None the less, collectors should ask themselves what their individual motives are for collecting; a bottle's value is quite obviously small in this condition, but one cannot take away any historical significance it may have, and this could well be considerable.*

Plate 112 *(right). The entire neck-top and string-rim of this mallet half bottle, c.1735, is a restoration, although few people would spot it. Full translucency to the glass has been achieved, and the colour and light reflecting qualities matched perfectly.*

The whole question of repairs is a 'thorny' one, although quite obviously the job of a skilled repairer is to achieve as perfect a restoration as is possible. It could be argued that those people who consider all repairs as best executed to 'museum standards' (i.e. purposely noticeable) are defeating the object of repairing at all.

important of all, is the seal 'possible' for the age of the vessel upon which it sits? This last criterion is of paramount importance in spotting fakes of this kind. It does entail a sound working knowledge of the genealogical aspect of seals, and willingness on the part of the collector to research the seal on any would-be purchase, but it is well worth the effort involved.

To date fakers have not been very judicious in their choice of seals and bottles, with the result that some very amusing 'marriages' have come to light. For example, the author has seen c.1680 bottles with seals that had not been devised for that particular person or family until at least twenty years later. Other anomalies exist, and no doubt more will come to light.

As with all antiques, it is normally the most choice and valuable that are the subject of the faker's or forger's attentions, sealed wine bottles being no exception. It is as well to remember that all bottles pre-1700, are genuinely scarce and expensive, dated ones especially so; on the other hand broken, fragmentary bottles and detached seals are much more numerous, so plenty of usable materials exist for the unscrupulous. When buying from a reputable dealer insist on a written guarantee of authenticity and if this is not forthcoming it may well be prudent to decline. In any event it is probably wise to avoid the really early sealed bottles until your knowledge of the subject has grown well ahead of your purse.

On the question of repairs, it is considered that any attempt at restoration other than by an expert is to be condemned simply because, with some of the strong resins and glues available today, any poor or abortive attempts are subsequently impossible to rectify. In skilled hands, however, and working with the proper translucent materials, some excellent results are possible. Nevertheless, no matter now skilful, repairs

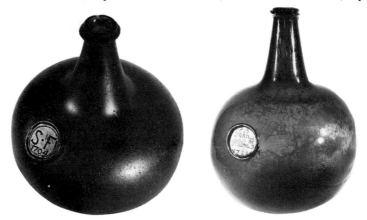

Plate 113 *(left). A badly cracked but otherwise very attractive onion bottle dated 1704, found in the mud of the river Frome in Dorset. The bottle is intact and quite possibly of considerable interest to local historians if it was to be carefully researched.*
Plate 114 *(right). With the unfortunate exception of a very small group of 'star-cracks' to the body, this magnum onion wine dated 1721 is in excellent condition. Very few onions of this size exist; they probably required some considerable skill in making and appear to have blown rather thin in the body section. When full, the bottle must have been very vulnerable.*

to glass items of this nature are totally objectionable to a large percentage of collectors. Fortunately they are normally quite easy to detect.

Unlike china, the light reflecting fractures on glass are virtually impossible to hide. Even where small chips or flakes of glass have been filled, or broken parts rejoined, the fractured break edges are always traceable. The author has seen some quite passable repairs to badly cracked or broken glass articles, by which the use of special adhesives has helped in some small measure at least to hide the light reflecting fractures, but even so it was still immediately evident that some form of restoration had taken place.

The darker the glass, the more care should be taken when examining a bottle. In addition to looking through the bottle against a strong artificial light, the same check should be made in the daylight, and with the bottle held downwards and at arm's length. In the latter position very small or fine star cracks or hairlines will often catch the light, which would not otherwise be apparent.

It is amazing how many collectors have owned a bottle for several years before discovering that it is, in fact, damaged. Small stars and hair lines can be notoriously difficult to detect, and the sombre tones of bottle glass do little to assist. With this in mind, buyers should also beware of a number of bottles which have had their interiors purposely obscured with what appears to be dye, ink or possibly even soot, in order to cover up damage. Some of these bottles have turned up at auction recently, and hapless buyers who, at a later stage decided to rinse their bottles clean of the apparent ages of dirt, were confronted with serious damage, mainly in the form of star cracks.

The danger in buying opaque or virtually opaque bottles even if they have not been tampered with is obvious, since condition cannot be assessed accurately. The same remarks apply to heavily 'marbled' or devitrified bottles. This provides the one exception to the rule as far as repairs to glass are concerned, for with this type of condition, the problems of restoration are no greater than with ceramic articles. If the restorer has the ability to colour-match accurately any repairs, then it is possible to build up entire missing sections, so once again the need to examine carefully any bottles of this type become apparent.

It is hoped that by reading these few remarks, the would-be collector will not be deterred. Collecting antique wine bottles is a thoroughly absorbing pastime with much to recommend it. That there are some pitfalls is inevitable; no form of collecting is without them. Let this in itself be a challenge; you will make some mistakes along the way, but you will learn all the more rapidly for it.

24. Forming a Collection

Firstly let it be said that there is no better way of learning about a subject than by collecting. To collect is ultimately to understand, and by so doing we may increase our knowledge of any given subject in a fraction of the time involved should we have recourse to books alone. And so it is with antique wine bottles, constant contact and handling of the pieces is essential. Even visits to museums, necessary though they are, are no substitute for this. Initially, visits to auctions, dealers' showrooms and close contact with collector friends is desirable. Here at least one can actually handle and inspect the bottles as the need arises.

Patience will be required to assemble a good representative collection, whatever methods are employed, for wine bottles are not the commonest of antiques. There are various avenues which can be explored, however, and obviously the cheapest and most rewarding is to go out with the intent to retrieve them oneself from such sites as ponds, rivers, long forgotten dumps, etc. This is not as impossible as it sounds — witness the amount retrieved to date from such sources.

For results worthy of the effort involved, research into the proposed site by way of local historical archives should be made well in advance of any excavation. Digging early sites can prove both arduous and a little frustrating, for a large number of bottles retrieved prove to be broken or fragmentary. Such fragments together with any detached seals should be preserved for future reference.

When not actively engaged in digging, a close eye should be kept on any large scale rebuilding projects, earthmoving schemes, demolition sites and river widening operations. A casual chat to the workmen involved is beneficial, and just occasionally yields an interesting bottle or two. In addition, river sites near or beneath old bridges are also excellent; dig in the mud and probe the banks; here one is almost sure to find something of interest.

Wells, although awkward to work without specialised knowledge and equipment, are often profitable sources of old bottles. It is amazing just how many artifacts are recovered from such sites in a complete state of preservation. The author recalls a small group of seventeenth century apothecary bottles removed from a well bottom, one of which had remained in mint condition. From the same site came an onion wine c.1690 and, of all things, a Roman cinerary urn, second century A.D.

Searching the neglected corners of old cellars, attics and outbuildings becomes yearly less and less profitable; even finding such a site is difficult.

One of the main reasons is that far more people are aware of the value of what was once 'rubbish'. Consequently most of these locations have been well cleared out in the past.

Having just said that, is it not fun to romanticise about the possibility of a long forgotten hoard of such bottles? In collecting circles one still occasionally hears of such chance discoveries. Publicans themselves were once a good source of old bottles, but today many are ardent collectors and profoundly interested in the past relics of their trade.

Dredgers in harbour areas often uncover an odd bottle or two, in fact certain harbours and estuaries are excellent for 'mudlarking' purposes. Interesting and early bottles from such sites have been seen, including complete onions, mallets, and cylinder wines. One of the author's earliest bottles, although not of glass, was a sixteenth century costrel retrieved from the mud in Langstone Harbour, and he has seen and examined both bellarmines, tavern tankards, and shaft and globe fragments from similar sites.

Plate 115. *An interesting group of bottles auctioned at Christie's, London, June 1978. Left to right: transitional onion-mallet wine bottle 'E/HERBERT/1721'; three-part mould bottle, Jaˢ Gill/1836'; squat cylinder bottle 'I B/1772'; onion bottle c. 1700 with the coat-of-arms of Clarke of Suffolk.*

However, since not everyone has the time or even the inclination to go turning the country upside down in their pursuit of antique wine bottles, here are a few words on purchasing and collecting.

Buying bottles at auction or from a dealer can prove a little expensive; as with all items of this age their overall rarity ensures that prices are

Plate 116. *A collection of wine bottles sold at Lawrence's auction rooms in Crewkerne, February 1980. Left to right: cylindrical wine bottle c.1770-80, with the Bickford crest and motto 'NON DUBIO'; unsealed mallet wine bottle c.1735; squat cylinder, c.1790, with the Bickford crest and 'G B' for George Bickford; onion wine bottle c.1710, with the full coat-of-arms and crest of the Bickford family.*

forever creeping upwards. Regular auction room visits, especially in provincial areas, are bound to pay off eventually, and just occasionally a 'cheap' bottle may be picked up from one of the larger markets or antique shops. It's all a matter of being in the right place at the right time. Short of this, there is little that can be done to minimise the cost of buying bottles for the collection. In view of this, the collector on a tight budget is wise to limit his acquisitions to those of an unsealed nature, especially bearing in mind the quite phenomenal price difference that exists between the two.

Such remarks need not deter the newcomer, bottles turn up in the most unexpected places and, as with any branch of antiques, the possibility of a bargain is very real. For the more seasoned collector close contact with all the major dealers and collectors both here and abroad is vital. Christie's and Sotheby's in London hold regular wine and glass auctions, which invariably include a selection of old wine bottles, relics and related pieces. In addition some of the scarce books on the subject occasionally pass through their hands.

As to what to collect, the scope is virtually endless. The collector of unsealed wines can certainly do no better than assemble the complete cycle of evolutionary forms from the start c.1640-1850. Such a collection will certainly prove of real value and assist in a more complete understanding of the bottles themselves. A further useful addition would be a similar range of European wines for comparison. Some of the differences, often more real than apparent, are very difficult to describe or appreciate from books alone.

Some collectors may prefer to keep to items found only in their own particular county, others may wish to collect certain types of bottle, or even those sealed in a particular fashion. With any collecting, considerable time and effort will be found necessary in order to fill in the inevitable gaps, but such, after all, is the pleasure of the hobby.

The author has travelled many thousands of miles in his pursuit of antique wine bottles and, whether rewarded or not, has always returned home more fully enlightened on the subject, as well as having met many pleasant and interesting people. A good, comprehensive collection almost always reflects the enthusiasm and determination of its owner.

For the collector wishing to correspond regularly and desirous of being able to categorise his finds and acquisitions, the gradings listed overleaf may well prove of assistance. Bottles, like stamps and coins, for instance, can, and should, be categorised.

Other spheres of collecting have this sort of 'condition' code, but the following table, as far as bottles are concerned, is the first of its kind to appear in print. The considerable variation in wine bottle prices unquestionably indicates the need for some form of categorisation. The more recent 'Victorian bottle boom' had a drastic effect on wine bottle prices and values soared.

Until then, the collection of early wine bottles was almost the sole province of the 'glass' collector, and the market was steady. As 'dumps' of one sort or another were explored up and down the country, a new type of collector emerged: the bottle collector pure and simple. It was only a question of time before earlier sites were excavated and old wine bottles found. From then on, the demand for these aristocrats of the bottle world increased dramatically, with the resultant rise in prices already referred to. Ludicrous prices were being asked, and indeed achieved. Ill-informed collectors were 'caught', and large sums of money changed hands for bottles of very questionable condition.

Today, things have improved a little, and there are encouraging signs that more sense now prevails. It is to be hoped that the inclusion of this 'condition' list can only help to serve such ends, and make collectors constantly aware of the radical price differences that should always exist between good and poor condition early wine bottles.

The six basic grades relative to wine bottles can be interpreted as shown overleaf (the 'wear-ring' beneath the base of virtually all bottles is excluded for these purposes).

Grade A Mint	The ultimate condition, which virtually no wine bottle ever fulfils. Unmarked, unblemished; in short — perfect condition. Any bottle in this condition would almost certainly realise a high price, quite likely well in excess of the current market value.
Grade B Near Mint	It is possible to achieve bottles in this state if the collector is both judicious and patient. No major blemishes here, virtually full surface gloss, minor scuff marks if any. Bottles in this grade should always achieve full market value.
Grade C Good	Basically very sound order, but with distinct signs of use. Some scuffing and light abrasions to the body, possibly the minutest of chips to the string-rim or neck top, a limited amount of devitrification, but no surface pitting. What can best be described as satisfactory condition, and the sort of state most likely to be encountered in wine bottles. Possibly current market value, or just a little below.
Grade D Fair	A reasonable amount of imperfections tolerated here; most dug or excavated bottles fall into this category. Scuffing, pitting and abrasions in greater or lesser degrees, often devitrification and iridescence. The string-rim and neck top with some chipping. Half to three quarters of market value.
Grade E Poor	A host of imperfections, together with some of a more serious nature. Possibly some 'star' or hairline cracks, extensive chipping to the string-rim, bad body pitting. Many bottles with all the faults one would expect from either long burial in the soil, or immersion in sea or river water. Devitrification, iridescence, and associated light flaking of the surface glass present. Up to half market value for bottles in this condition.
Grade F Very Poor	All the previous faults with the addition of badly shattered string-rims, whole areas of surface glass missing, often cracks running in the body. Seals where present often chipped or poorly legible. As little as a quarter of market value or even less.

Bottles in an even worse state than this with missing neck tops, compound fractures, and having shed virtually all their actual surface glass, etc., can best be described as of artifact value only.

Whatever type of bottle is collected, those wishing to acquire near mint or entirely undamaged specimens may well have to be considerably more patient than those to whom a certain amount of damage is acceptable.

This whole question of damage has been a much debated one, but in general the following remarks apply. By virtue of the excellent translucent

Plate 117. *A pair of cylindrical wine bottles, c.1780-90. The ideal condition, near mint, and with virtually full surface gloss. Later bottles are, of course, more readily found in this state, and pre-1730 the odds against acquiring such examples become steadily greater. Collectors tend to term good condition bottles with full surface gloss and in an un-dug state, as 'cellar found'.*

and reflective qualities of bottle glass, probably the worst kind of damage encountered is cracking of the vessel. Such damage ruins any chance of display and afflicts the eye upon every encounter. The very beauty of glass lies in its apparent solidity and fragility, and damage of this kind is abhorrent to the majority of collectors. In the same league are bottles with badly broken, shattered, or missing portions, such examples unless very rare, or historically important, are hardly worth acquiring. Only a handful of people exist able to repair damage of this type skilfully.

Bad scuffing, abrasion and flaking of the surface glass consistent with long immersion in water, is bound to detract from the value of a bottle, but opalescence and iridescence can have quite the reverse effect. Were it not for the colourful patina acquired by such bottles, this state of affairs would be much harder to understand. However, for collectors willing to pay over the odds for these bottles, it is as well to remember that attractive or not this condition is indicative of decay and not always of a stable nature.

Of a similar kind is the condition known as devitrification in which the glass has begun to crystallise beneath the surface. Due to long burial in the ground with resultant acid attacks, the glass components have started to separate back to their original elements, leaving the bottle with a

Plate 118 *(left). Damage is of course a matter for the individual, but few collectors would allow the poor string-rim condition on this otherwise fine shaft and globe bottle to colour their judgement of it. Today, more than ever, condition must be balanced out against age and rarity.*
Plate 119 *(right). On an unsealed wine bottle c.1770-80, surface decay such as this is considered both unsightly and unnecessary. Good condition wine bottles of this period abound, and there are plenty for the collector to choose from.*

characteristic brown or grey mottled effect, much reminiscent of marble or stone. In some examples, the condition is so advanced as to render the bottle totally opaque. Strangely, in a fair number of these, the full surface gloss remains unimpaired. As small 'stars' or cracks in the body are rendered difficult if not impossible to detect with such a condition, a certain amount of risk is always attached to their purchase. Any bottles in an even further state of decay with much loss of surface gloss should be regarded as suspect. It is difficult to say at what stage a glass bottle becomes less of a bottle and more of a relic. Such considerations may well be of small relevance to the bottle collector but of paramount importance to the collector of antique glass, it all depends on why one really collects bottles.

Obviously the ideal condition is mint, but as so few remain in this state the addition of light overall scuffing and perhaps an odd chip or two to the vulnerable string-rim is considered acceptable by most. Indeed few bottles

Plate 120. *A pair of late seventeenth century onion wine bottles, left: c.1690 and right: 1700. Varying degrees of what collectors call devitrification are evident here, and the c.1690 example begins to show some very slight surface flaking. This partial (and in some cases complete) decay of the glass does not always result in pitting as the photograph shows, but the change to a marble or stone like colour can, in greater or lesser degree, render the bottle opaque.*

Plate 121. *Onion wine bottle c.1695. Clear evidence of the more advanced stages of devitrification are to be seen here, with localised pitting, and lifting of the actual surface glass. However, conditions of burial vary, and some excavated wine bottles that are completely devitrified and wholly opaque, surprisingly retain their entire surface intact.*

203

Plate 122. *Left: minor and quite shallow surface flaking, as on this early shaft and globe bottle c.1665, often shows patches of quite beautiful iridescence. Here the actual bottle is in quite sound condition, but the iridescence by its very nature can so easily be lost. Centre: a 'water rolled' bottle c.1685, with loss of all surface gloss and characteristic etching to the surface. Collectors will soon come to recognise this condition, the result of long immersion in sea or river water with myriad surface marks occasioned by the continual action of sand and gravel. Bottles retrieved from such places are often in better condition than those found buried when acids in the soil appear to attack the glass far more quickly. This particular bottle has only lost a very minor top layer of surface glass and its overall condition is quite acceptable. Right: prolonged incarceration in soil leads to surface decomposition, then pitting and flaking, followed by an eventual breakdown of whole areas of glass, and finally by total disintegration. The present bottle, an early shaft and globe c.1665, is in rather a sorry state, the dark areas indicating where the decay is at its worst, with complete sections having parted company with the bottle. With sealed examples such an advanced state of decay often renders the seal details difficult if not impossible to decipher, and collectors should remember that bottles in this state are very likely to be of an unstable nature. Long after acquisition further layers of surface glass tend to break away, all too often carrying with them the all important lettering on the seal face.*

have their value impaired by these minor defects.

The author's opinion is that the collector may regret acquiring too many damaged or poor condition bottles; repairs, where skilfully executed, can actually improve or even save a rare bottle from obscurity. Ultimately, the entire question of condition and repairs becomes a decision for the individual. After all, there are no hard and fast guide lines to adhere to; what one incorporates in a collection is purely a matter of personal choice.

Let us examine some of the methods of storage and display. Bottles are most safely stored in a glass-sided cabinet, where not only do they display well but also are relatively free from minor household catastrophes. If pets are kept then cabinets are almost a necessity. Various types of cabinet are available, but those specifically designed for fine porcelain, china and glass are obviously most suitable. All cabinets should allow in plenty of light and have adequate ventilation.

To display antique wine bottles to effect, some form of low wattage lighting is required. Small strip lights fitted in the cabinet behind the bottles will show off the colour of each individual item to advantage. As such lights emit a surprising amount of heat, they must be separated from the bottles by a protective sheet of perspex and ventilation at the top of the cabinet must be provided. Although more expensive, fluorescent lights are suitable since they emit far less heat and do not distort the true colour of the bottles. Alternatively, the complete cabinet may be illuminated from the front by the use of one or two spotlights mounted on the ceiling. In practice however this is more suitable for ceramic items; a fully illuminated display case, as described, does considerably more to enhance the beauty of old glass.

Having said this, bottles casually arranged on furniture, particularly old oak, always look extremely attractive. Court cupboards, dressers and tables provide suitable positions, although care should be taken, as such places are obviously less secure. To anyone restoring or living in an old cottage or period house, there is little to match the decorative charm of an old wine bottle or two.

In the modern home, the centre partition of a large wall unit can be adapted to suit antique wine bottles and, by the addition of sliding or hinged glass doors, the collection can be kept safe and free from dust. The centre alcove of a wall will display bottles very effectively, and it would not be too difficult for the average handyman to devise an integral, purpose-made shelving unit to be mounted on the wall in any desired location. Such a unit would probably be best made of wood, and provided with adequate hanging brackets. Furthermore, in order to allow the collection to alter or expand, adjustable shelving would prove a most useful feature.

One further location which springs readily to mind is the centre room divider so often used in modern homes. Here a most effective area for display is automatically available. So much the better if this is of the glass sectional type which not only allows in plenty of light but also enables the bottles to be viewed at more than one angle.

Wherever one eventually decides to house or display the collection, there remain certain places which should be avoided at all costs. A narrow or high shelf are two obvious danger points; in the first instance, it is always foolish to place fragile items on a base barely wide enough to support them, and in the second, struggling to remove or replace an article on tiptoe can so easily result in that piece being dropped and smashed.

Any area near an open fire or heat source of any kind, including direct sunlight, should also be avoided; extremes of temperature are dangerous to old glass, and any bottles with minor imperfections such as a small 'star' or hairline crack are particularly susceptible. Under adverse conditions such defects have been known to 'run' or open out quite alarmingly; bottles have even cracked clean in half. Much of this is due to the slightly unstable nature of old glass, which was often poorly annealed and consequently subject to certain internal stresses and strains. Fortunately if normal precautions are taken such occurrences are rare, but it is always wise to ensure that glass receives the care and respect it deserves. The answer is quite simply not to break or damage it in the first instance.

Having decided upon a safe position for the collection, and one which shows it to advantage, we move on to consider the all important aspect of data and provenance. When acquiring bottles for the collection any history associated with them should always be preserved intact. Too few bottles, even seals, have this provenance, a state of affairs much to be deplored. It adds considerably both to the interest and value of virtually any early item should this information be available.

To preserve such facts, a small data label can be fixed beneath the vessel to one side of the pontil scar, care being taken to make sure this is permanently done. For this reason, many collectors, including museum staff, prefer to mark their acquisitions in white enamel paint which, if properly executed, is more permanent and, in its situation, cannot detract from the bottle's appearance. Any attempt at merely numbering the bottle and keeping a separate catalogue is best avoided for, as so often happens, in time the catalogue becomes detached from the collection and the written word is lost.

A small stand-up label may be added to the shelf in front of each item which, with relevant information, will enlighten the uninitiated. In fairness, given a little information on a subject previously unknown to them, most people find their curiosity aroused, and only wish to know more about the hobby.

Finally, one further record of the collection is necessary if not imperative. In the unhappy event of a burglary, a complete photographic record, together with the salient features of each individual item, will greatly assist the police in their inquiries. On the same theme, insurance for a valuable collection is also prudent, although premiums tend to be high. Certain firms, mainly in London, specialise in the insurance of such collections and for full cover these are the people to contact. It is true that certain bottles are irreplaceable and, in the event of an accident, a cash settlement will do little to minimise the tragedy; however, once reconciled to the loss, a prompt insurance payment does help to buffer the blow.

Appendix I
Crests and Coats-of-arms

A listing with drawings from *Sealed Bottles* (Chapter Seven — Crests and Coats-of-Arms) by S. Ruggles-Brise, 1949, with supplementary items from the author incorporated in *italics;* captions to supplementary drawings are also in *italics*. Additions to Ruggles-Brise are in [ ].

The supplementary items record the various bottles the author has come across which are not recorded in Ruggles-Brise, and the listing does not purport to be completely up-to-date. No doubt some of the supplementary items will be known and a certain number may even have appeared in print, but the great majority are 'new' so to speak.

In order to keep this listing as complete as possible in future editions, the author would be grateful if readers who know of sealed bottles or detached seals with crests or coats-of-arms, in addition to those mentioned here, would contact him c/o the publisher.

Abercromby crest: A bee volant ppr. c.1770. This may have belonged to Sir Ralph Abercromby (1734-1801), the well-known general. Abercromby got a cornetcy in the 3rd Dragoon Guards in 1756, he married Miss Menzies in 1767, was made a major in 1770 and Lieut-Colonel in 1773. Perhaps he celebrated one of these occasions by ordering himself sealed bottles. He took part in many campaigns, was knighted in 1795, and, to his own great surprise, was considered one of our greatest generals. He was among the wounded at Aboukir Bay as, in his usual reckless manner, he always rode in front. He was carried to the flag-ship *Foudroyant.* "What is this you have placed under my head?" asked the wounded general. "Only a soldier's blanket", answered the aide-de-camp. "Only a soldier's blanket! Make haste and return it to him at once." He died a few days later.

Adams crest: A demi-griffin holding a scallop-shell. Ht. 8ins. c.1770. The glass is white and not green, and it is a carafe and not a bottle, but it bears a seal. It was illustrated in the *Antique Collector,* May, 1932.

TOUJOURS FERME. Arms of an Alsace family: or a band sa. indented az. ensigned with a crown and pastoral staff. Supporters: two naked men with clubs. Motto as above. Ht. 9½ins. This bottle belonged to an Abbess of Messines Convent near Ypres. It was given to the donor C.R. Jennings Esq., by the Royal Institution of Messines, and he gave it to the British Museum, in 1895.

Anchor and rope. Ht. 5⅝ ins. Believed to be American.

Arm with hand grasping axe. Seal only.

A hand grasping an axe.

Arm grasping bow and arrow, and the motto FORTUNA SEQUATUR. Possibly the arms of Cuddon.

Arm raised and embowed and tied with a bow at the elbow and holding a stork's head erased. Found locally. Seal only.

Beckford crest: heron's head erased or, holding a fish arg. Possibly Peter Beckford of Steepleton, Dorset, who married the Hon. Louisa Pitt. daughter of George, 1st Lord Rivers, 1773. He was M.P. for Morpeth. Their only son, Horace, assumed the name of Pitt-Rivers instead of Beckford. But it is also the crest of Stanley, Cobb, Smythe and others.

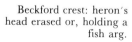

Beckford crest: heron's head erased or, holding a fish arg.

Crest of an arm embowed grasping a scimitar with the motto NON DUBIO. Bickford crest c.1770-80. Cylindrical.

Crest of an arm embowed grasping a scimitar, below the initials 'G.B.', for George Bickford; c.1790. Squat cylinder.

Coat-of-arms: three doves and a chevron wavy, crest: an arm embowed grasping a scimitar, Bickford family arms and crest, c.1710. Onion.

Bird on a cap of estate. From Bristol. Seal only.

Flying bird ensigned by a baron's coronet. Ht. 7½ ins. A broad base and a short neck.

Shield bearing cross potonée. Crest: a bird, probably a goose. Found locally.

Crest: a bird's wing displayed; seal only.

Crest: a bird's wing displayed.

Crest: a boar statant, beneath a baron's coronet. Edgcumbe of Mount Edgcumbe, Plymouth, c.1780. Cylinder.

Crest: a boar statant, beneath a Viscount's coronet. Edgcumbe of Mount Edgcumbe, Plymouth, c.1785. Cylinder.

Bruce arms and earl's coronet. Arms: or, a saltire and chief gu. on a canton arg. a lion rampant az., armed and langued of the second. These were the arms of Robert Bruce, 2nd Earl of Elgin and 1st Earl of Ailesbury (c.1685). He was created Viscount Bruce of Ampthill, Beds., and Earl of Ailesbury in 1663, and was the son of Thomas, 1st Earl of Elgin and Anne, dau. of Sir Robert Chichester of Raleigh, Devon. He was Lord-Lieutenant of Bedfordshire, a Privy Councillor and Lord Chamberlain. He married Diana, dau. of Henry Grey, 1st Earl of Stamford, and by her had eight sons and nine daughters. Wood says of him that he was "a learned person. . . well-versed in English history and antiquities. . . a curious collector of manuscripts" (see D.N.B.). Fragment only.

Bruce arms under an earl's coronet.

Crest: a bull statant, with motto TUTUS-AB-ILIS; c.1730. Bladder onion.

Coat-of-arms: three bulls' heads caboshed; crest: a bull's head upon a knight's helm to dexter.

Coat-of-arms: three bulls' heads caboshed, crest: a bull's head upon a knight's helm to dexter; c.1660. Shaft and globe bottle.

Carew arms: or, three lions passant in pale sa. Ht. 8ins. and 6ins. From the cellars of Sir Thomas Carew.

Carew crest: a mainmast, the round top set off with palisadoes or; a demi-lion issuant thereout sa. Ht. 11ins. from cellars of Sir Reginald Pole-Carew.

Carew crest.

H.C. and baronet's hand of Ulster. c.1805. It belonged to Sir Henry Carew, 7th Bart. (1779-1830), of Haccombe, Newton Abbot, Devon. In the little church at Haccombe there were once four horseshoes, but now only one and a fragment remain. There was once a Carew of Haccombe who challenged Champernoune of Dartington House to a swimming race on horseback. The latter's horse was drowned and Carew returned bringing his opponent with him. Hence the horseshoes.

T.C. and sinister hand appaumée — badge of Ulster borne by baronets. Sir Thomas Carew 6th Bart. (m.1777, d.1805.) of Haccombe, Newton Abbott, Devon. see Sir Henry Carew.

Crest: a castle tower aflame, seal only.

Chadwick arms with date 1785.

Chadwick arms: gules an inescutcheon within an orle of martlets argent.

Ditto with date 1785.

Ditto with date 1788 and the words MAVESYN RIDWARE written round the shield. Ht. 9¾ ins.

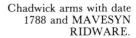

Chadwick arms with date 1788 and MAVESYN RIDWARE.

Malveysin crest: on a wreath a talbot's head of the second vulned and bleeding at the mouth proper, gorged with a collar ermine rimmed and nowed, charged with three chess Rooks with the motto JUXTA SALOPIAM 1791. The above four seals must all be considered together. On the 1791 bottle are two paper labels, one slightly overlapping the other. The under label reads: 'Sir Robert Mowveysin. 23rd. descent of Ridware,' and in another hand 'Juxta Salopiam.' The top label reads: 'The deaths of Sir Robert Malveysin and Sir William Handsacre. August 1791.' These labels have given me [Ruggles-Brise] a lot of trouble, as they suggested that the Sir Robert Mowveysin and Sir William Handsacre died in 1791, which was far from being the case, but I think I have solved the problem. To put it as briefly as I can, there was a Walter Malvoisin who came over with William the Conqueror, who granted him the Manor of Malveysin Berwick in Shropshire, and there was a Hugo Malvoisin, who held Mavesyn Ridware in Staffordshire in the time of Henry I. The male line failed but a daughter married Sir John Cawarden (1399). Again the male line failed and a daughter married Chadwick (1579). The coat-of-arms with eight martlets is Chadwick's.

To go back a little, in 1403 Sir Robert Malveysin and his neighbour Sir William Handsacre (who, I think, was descended from the Conqueror's Malveysin) had a dispute — something to do with fishery rights and a mill. They also took opposite sides in the civil wars of that time (the Hundred Years' War), and when the two rivals met in battle they fell on each other and Handsacre was slain, and Malveysin marched forward to Shrewsbury where he lost his life fighting for the king. So they both died on July 22, 1403.

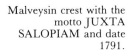

Malveysin crest with the motto JUXTA SALOPIAM and date 1791.

In a history of Staffs. which I consulted, they traced the Malvoisin descent from the first Malvoisin. The first ten generations bore his name; the next seven were Cawardens, and the next six Chadwicks, and now comes the explanation of those paper labels: The 23rd descent was John Chadwick, who, "By grant and exemplification from Garter and Norroy, on August 1, 1791, assumed the crest of Malveysin with variations, viz on a wreath a Talbot's head of the second vulned and bleeding at the mouth proper, gorged with a collar ermine and rimmed and nowed, charged with three chess Rooks with the motto JUXTA SALOPIAM, alluding to the deaths of Sir Robert Malveysin and Sir William Handsacre."

John Chadwick succeeded to his father's property, Healey Hall, in 1756, and, at some date unknown, he had his bottles sealed with the Chadwick coat-of-arms. He did this again, adding the dates, in 1785 and 1788, and, at the latter date, he added the name of Mavesyn Ridware, which property his only son had inherited under the will of his aunt Dorothy Chadwick in 1784. In 1791, having become very Malvoisin-minded and having assumed their crest, he sealed his bottles with that crest, and the date 1791.

Mavesyn Ridware is a village and seat in Staffs. on the Trent, 2½ miles E.S.E. of Rugeley. Handsacre, or Hansacre, is a village and seat 4½ miles W.N.W. of Lichfield. Malveysin Berwick is in Shropshire, and its modern name is Berwick, Maviston, Salop. (Rugeley and Lichfield are not very far apart.)

The *Century Dictionary* says that the names Malvoisie, Malmsey and Mavesyn all have the same origin in *Malvasia,* which is based on the Greek word Μονεμβασια, a seaport on the S.E. coast of Laconia, Greece, a contraction of μονη εμβασια, 'single entrance'. The Malvasia vine produced a wine that was drunk in England through the ages. At the Lord Mayor's Banquet in 1762 four bottles of Malmsey or Sack were consumed, though as 438 bottles of Port were drunk at the same feast, it would not appear that Malmsey was as popular as in the sixteenth century. The word itself is spelt in a variety of ways.

Chatham. see Pitt.

Chetwynd arms: az. a chevron between three mullets or. Ht. 6¾ins. c.1700. Long-necked bottle with handle. Exhibited at Vinters' Hall, 1933 and illustrated in catalogue. This may have belonged to Walter Chetwynd, M.P. for boroughs of Stafford and Litchfield 1703-35, and some time Ambassador at Turin. He was created Viscount Chetwynd in 1717.

Coat-of-arms: on a chevron three balls between three cinquefoils; crest: a stag trippant. Seal only.

Coat-of-arms: a chevron between three crosses; crest: a cockerel; c.1700. Onion.

Clive arms: ar. on a fesse sa. three mullets or. Crest: a griffin pass. ar. ducally gorged gu. Supporters: dexter, an elephant arg. sinister, a leopard guard. ppr. ducally gorged gu. Motto: *Audacter et sincere.* Under a baron's coronet. Ht. 10¾ins. c.1770. Robert Clive (1726-1774), the distinguished general to whom England largely owed her dominion in India, was created Baron Clive (peerage of Ireland) in 1762. He was made Governor of Bengal and described by Pitt as a 'heaven-born General'. He married Margaret Maskelyne and their son Edward was eventually created Baron Clive (peerage of Great Britain) in 1794, and Governor of Madras in 1798. Edward married Lady H.A. Herbert, daughter of the last Earl of Powis of the Herbert family, and he himself was made Earl of Powis of a fresh creation in 1804. In 1807 their son, another Edward Clive, assumed the surname and arms of Herbert. Two bottles, at least, bearing Clive's arms are extant. One was shown at Vintners' Hall in 1933, and described as "full of the spirit brought to England by the first Lord Clive". It came from Powis Castle and was given to the present owners by Lord Powis. As the first Lord Clive left India for the last time in 1766, and the bottle appears to be of a somewhat later date than that, I query whether it did not belong to Lord Clive, Governor of Madras rather than to the Governor of Bengal. But, of course, it may have been bottled at a later date than 1766, and perhaps documentary evidence exists to this effect. One bottle was sold at Sotheby's on December 9, 1947.

Arms of Coker of Mappowder, Dorset. Arms: arg. on a bend gu. 3 leopards' heads, within a bordure engrailed sa. (see RT COAKER, 1718 in Main List [Appendix II].)

Colston crest: Ht. 9¾ ins. An early nineteenth century bottle. Crest: a dolphin naiant ppr. This presumably belonged to Edward Colston, of Roundway Park, Wilts. whose son, Charles Edward H.A. Colston, (1854-1925) M.P. for the Thornbury Division of Gloucestershire, was created Baron Roundway of Devizes, Wilts. in 1916.

Colston crest.

COLYTON HOUSE, DEVON, and Wyvern. see Drake.

A bottle with an unidentified coat-of-arms was bought together with COVENTRY HOUSE. 1702. bottle, for which see Main List [Appendix II].

R.C.C. Crest: a lion passant, dexter paw raised.

R. H. C. Crest: a dragon passant on a wreath.

Two crescents. Seal only.

Three crescents.

Arms: three crescents. Crest: a helmet. Possibly the arms of Oliphant.

Arms: arg. five crosses croslet in saltire gu. Possibly the arms of Cross. Long-necked bottle. c.1650-60.

Coat-of-arms: three daggers within a shield, beneath an earl's coronet; c.1770-80. Cylinder.

Coat-of-arms: three daggers within a shield beneath an earl's coronet.

Coat-of-arms of Daubeney; c.1740. Mallet.

Deane crest: an Indian hunting dog, muzzled, on a castle. This was the crest of John Deane of Bengal and Gray's Inn, London, 1725. Found in the garden of a house called Friarscroft, Aylesbury, on the site of the Manor House of the Pakington family, which was burnt down in the Civil Wars. It stood on part of the site of Grey Friars Monastery. Seal only.

A dolphin naiant ppr. see Colston Crest.

A dolphin under a crown. This was probably from a Dolphin Tavern. see Main List [Appendix II].

Dormer crest: a falconer's dexter glove fessewise arg. thereon perched a falcon, wings inverted, also arg. beaked and belled or under an earl's coronet. Sir Robert Dormer was created Viscount Ascott and Earl of Carnarvon in 1688. This seal was found at Ascott House, Wing, Bucks. see C.C. (Charles Dormer, 2nd Earl of Carnarvon) in Main List [Appendix II]. Seal only.

Dorset. see Sackville.

Douglas crest: a human heart gu. ensigned with an imperial crown and between two wings displayed, all or under a ducal coronet. The second Earl of Queensberry was created Marquess of Queensberry in 1682, and Duke of Queensberry in 1683, and his second son, William, Baron Douglas of Neidpath, at which time the Neidpath property seems to have been acquired from the Tweeddale family. It is possible that this and the succeeding seal belonged to the first Duke, as one seal appears to bear a marquess' coronet and the other one a duke's. The fourth Duke of Queensberry died in 1810 when the dukedom reverted to the Duke of Buccleuch and the marquisate devolved upon a kinsman. Found at Queensberry House, Edinburgh. Seal only.

Douglas crest.

A slightly different version of above. Found at Neidpath Castle, Peeblesshire. Seal only.

Drake. COLYTON HOUSE. DEVON. and arms: arg. a wyvern, wings endorsed, gu. The arms of Drake, a branch of Drake of Ashe, Devon, who owned land at Colyton.

Duke crest: on a wreath a griffin coupled, holding in its claws a wreath. Ht. 7¼ ins. This may have belonged to Edward Duke of Lake House, Wilts. who married Fanny Field, and whose second son, another Edward (1779-1852), an antiquarian, wrote *The Druidical Temples of the County of Wilts.* Seal only.

Duke crest.

Coat-of-arms: on a cross four eagles displayed; crest: a saracen's head; c.1700.

J.E. and Egerton crest: three arrows pointing downwards, banded with a ribbon, c.1650. Sir John Egerton, 2nd Bart (suc.1646, d.1674) married Anne, daughter of George Wintour, Esq., of Dyrrham. Co. Glos.

'I.E.' and Egerton crest.

R. & H. EYRE...WALFREISEN and many-quartered coat-of-arms surmounted by a crown. Eight-pointed star in centre; lions demi-rampant each side; three shields above and three below star; a cross in first and last quarters, and three helms each in third and seventh. Seal only. Evidently foreign. see PYRMONT WATER.

Falcon on a cap of maintenance, surmounted by a baron's coronet. Five bottles, capacity about a pint, all with the same seal, were found quite near the surface in Thornford, Bradford Abbas, Dorset. (*Dorset Field Club Proceedings,* Vol. I, 1877, p.89.)

Crest: a falcon clasping a chapeau beneath an earl's coronet. Possibly the crest of John Worden; c.1690-1700. Onion.

Crest: a falcon clasping a chapeau beneath an earl's coronet.

Arms: az. on a chevron sa. between three falcons' heads erased az. three cinquefoils pierced of the field. Crest: on a wreath a falcon's head. Possibly arms of Jackson.

Crest: five ostrich feathers beneath the letter 'C'. Coham crest; c.1800.

Fish.

Fleece (or possibly a horned animal) under a baron's coronet.

Coat-of-arms: between three fleur-de-lis a chevron charged in its apex a shield, with sinister hand appaumée. Shaft and globe.

Coat-of-arms: between three fleur-de-lis a chevron charged in its apex a shield with sinister hand appaumée.

FORTUNA SEQUATOR. and unspecified crest. Sold at Sotheby's June 1930.

J.F. 1743. and a stag's head. Presumably the crest of John Fothergill. Acquired at the sale at Kingthorpe House, near Pickering, Yorks., which belonged to the Fothergills.

'J.F. 1743' and a stag's head.

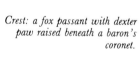

Crest: a fox passant with dexter paw raised beneath a baron's coronet.

Crest: a fox passant with dexter paw raised beneath a baron's coronet. Crest of the Pierpont family; c.1700. Onion.

Wine-glass sealed with a coat-of-arms, a fesse between three garbs, in an arabesque border. c.1735. Straight-sided bowl and opaque twist stem. Recorded by Hartshorne.

Two arms holding a garb. It is believed that bottles with this crest on them are modern fakes.

Gregorie of Pilston, Devon. Arms: az. within three increscents or, as many mullets ar. Crest: large bird holding branch in beak. Ht. 7ins.

Arms: shield with seven daggers; above a baron's coronet; Crest: bird on a wreath. Supporters: two greyhounds.

R.J.C.G. A winged griffin on a wreath.

A griffin segreant between three crescents. Seal only.

Crest: a male griffin segreant holding a spear and letter 'C'. Seal only.

HALL and indecipherable initials. H.B. 1735. This very unusual bottle bears seven seals of which two are illegible, and the other five are as follows:
1. HALL (with initials) and a bird standing on a twig.
2. H.B. 1735 and a bull's head erased.
3. A hunting horn.
4. A wyvern.
5. A coat-of-arms with a cross in the centre, and a helm.

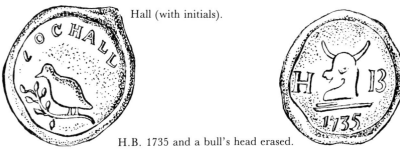

Hall (with initials).

H.B. 1735 and a bull's head erased.

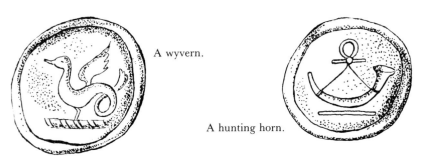

A wyvern.

A hunting horn.

In Fairbairn's *Book of Crests* Vol.1. William Hall, Esquire bears a hunting horn ppr. garnished and stringed gu. Hall of Shropshire has a wyvern in his coat, but it contains other charges as well. This wyvern resembles that of the Drakes of Ashe. Perhaps someone with an interest in and knowledge of heraldry will be able to identify the owner of this bottle.

Hamilton arms and ducal coronet. The Duke of Hamilton. Arms: quarterly, 1st and 4th gu. three cinquefoils erm. Hamilton; 2nd and 3rd arg., a lymphad with the sails ppr. flagged gu. arran. Supporters: two antelopes arg. unguled, ducally gorged and chained or. This seal must be previous to 1761 when the marquisate of Douglas devolved upon the 7th Duke of Hamilton and the Douglas arms were quartered with the Hamilton arms. Found in Edinburgh. Seal only.

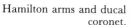

Hamilton arms and ducal coronet.

Open hand and scarf between two branches. see Main List [Appendix II].

Harvey crest: an open dexter hand on a wreath and a crescent above. The crest of the Harveys or Herveys who owned Clifton Maybank, where the bottle was found, and Wyke, Dorset. There are monuments to several of the Harveys in Bradford Abbas Church, one of which, to Sir Thomas Harvey, bears this crest. (*Dorset Field Club Proceedings,* Vol. I, 1877, p.89.)

Haselwood of Maidwell, Northants; Wickwarren, Worcs.; and Oxfordshire. Arms: ar. on a chevron gu. between three owls sa. as many lozenges erm. on a chief az. three hazel branches or. Crest: a squirrel sejant az. collared or charged with three bezants in pale, holding a hazel branch ppr. fructed or.

A chevron between three hawks's lures in various tinctures. This coat-of-arms was borne by the families of Bromwich, Wingham, Skeynert and others.

Three hawk's lures within a border bezantée engrailed. Crest: animal's head (difficult to distinguish). Seal only.

Crest: a head wearing a coronet.

A head facing left. Found in Bristol 1906. Seal only.

A chevron between three small heads couped. Crest: a head couped. Seal only.

HENLY and five five-pointed stars. The Henleys formerly lived at the grange, Glanvilles Wootton, Dorset, where this bottle was found. Sir Robert Henly died in 1758, and Lady Barbara Henly is buried at Glanvilles Wootton. Seal only. (*Dorset Field Club Proceedings,* Vol. II, 1878, p.59.)

Herbert crest and 1678 under an earl's coronet. Crest: a wyvern vert. In present-day illustrations of the Herbert crest the wyvern holds a sinister hand in his mouth; the hand is absent in this and the following seal, as it is also in two Herbert crested memorial slabs on the chancel floor of Salisbury Cathedral. This seal must have belonged to Philip, 7th Earl of Pembroke, who died in 1683 without male issue. In George Cunningham's *London,* I find the following: "It was in Long's Tavern in the Haymarket, a famous resort of the seventeenth century . . . that Lord Pembroke killed a man in 1678 with a blow of his fist." Strange that it should be the year commemorated on his bottles. Seal only.

Herbert crest and 1681 under an earl's coronet. see above. Found at Pitton, Wilts. Seal only.

W. HOLE with crest (unspecified).

A horse (or a deer, or a greyhound). Seal only.

ROBERT HUGHES. 1733. and crest: head of unicorn erased with arrow transfixing neck. Ht. 7ins. Diam. 4¾ins.

Hunloke. see Wingerworth.

H.H. 1823. and crest: pelican vulning himself. H.H. believed to be Heath Hall, Bradford.

H.H. and a horse's head issuant from crest-coronet. This is the crest (in different tinctures) of Higham, Horder and Horsley.

H.H. and a horse's head.

H.H. and a crowned eagle holding a sceptre and orb.

H.H. 1841. and crest: a swan's head and neck with wings displayed. A moulded bottle.

W.P.H. and Royal Coat-of-Arms. Ht. 7¼ ins. Sold at Sotheby's June 18, 1943. From the Berry Collection.

Two increscents. Seal only.

JOHN JEFFERSON. 1652. Arms: a chevron with three mullets between three fetterlocks. The earliest recorded dated seal. Seal only.

Arms of Jermyn family. Ht. 8ins. c.1660. This probably belonged to Henry Jermyn, afterwards Earl of St. Albans (c.1604-1683/4), third son of Sir Thomas Jermyn, of Rushbrooke, Suffolk, by his first wife, Catherine, daughter of Sir William Killigrew. In 1643 he was created Baron Jermyn of St. Edmundsbury for his great zeal in the Royalist cause, and in 1645 he was appointed Chamberlain to Queen Henrietta Maria, whom he accompanied to France and whom he is said eventually to have married clandestinely. He is reputed to have treated her badly: "She had not a faggot to warm herself", while he had "a good fire and a sumptuous table". When she spoke to him he used to say: *"Que me veut cette femme?"* At the Restoration he was created Earl of St. Albans, and for three years he acted as Lord Chamberlain to Charles II (see *Memoirs of Count Grammont* by Count Anthony Hamilton). Hamilton says of St. Albans: "a man of no great genius, had raised himself a considerable fortune from nothing, and by losing at play, and keeping a great table, made it appear greater than it was." But the seal might have belonged to his nephew, another Henry Jermyn (c.1636-1708), son of Thomas Jermyn and his wife Rebecca Rodway. He was Master of the Horse to the Duke of York 1660-1675 (1660 being about the date of the bottle) and was eventually created Baron Dover, and in 1689 Earl of Dover. In 1703 he succeeded to the Barony of Jermyn, but he had no children and when he died in 1708 all his honours became extinct. His wife was Judith, daughter of Sir Edmund Poley of Badley, Suffolk. Sold at Sotheby's, June 1930.

King Arms. Under a baron's coronet. Sa. three spearheads erect ar. embrued gu. on a chief or as many pole-axes az. Supporters: two mastiffs reguardant ppr. each gorged with a collar gu. William 8th Baron King

(1805-1893) was created Earl of Lovelace in 1838, so the bottle must be of an earlier date than that. Sold at Puttick & Simpson's, April 15, 1947.

King's arms under a baron's coronet.

H.K. and a coat-of-arms. Ht. 5¼ ins. c.1660. Sold at Sotheby's, June, 1930.

Coat-of-arms: three leopards passant, guardant; c.1725-30. Bladder onion.

Coat-of-arms: three leopards passant, guardant.

Demi-lion gardant holding a mascle. Seal only.

Demi-lion rampant issuant from a coronet. Found at Cannon's Marsh, Bristol, 1905. Seal only.

Crest: a lion rampant wearing an earl's coronet; c.1660. Shaft and globe.

Crest: a lion rampant wearing an earl's coronet.

Coat of arms: a lion rampant; crest: a hand appaumée. Seal only.

Coat-of-arms: a lion rampant. Seal only.

Coat-of-arms: a lion rampant guardant within three lozenges; c.1740.

Lion rampant with dexter paw raised, standing on a crest-wreath. Ht. 5¼ ins. Small bottle with broad base. Found in neighbourhood of the old castle at Donegal.

Lion rampant and traces of an inscription. Above a small tablet with letter F(?).

Lion rampant between three mullets. Crest: a boar and mantling. Ht. 7ins. This is not a bottle but an ale-jug of transparent brownish-green glass. Second half of seventeenth century. Depressed bulbous body, wide cylindrical neck round which is coiled an applied thread; loop handle. These particulars are taken from the V. & A. catalogue, and a note adds: "A similar jug in the Duke of Rutland's possession at Belvoir Castle February 1926 is dated 1685". Owing to war and post-war conditions it has not been possible to trace the latter.

Arms: 1st and 4th quarterly Maltese cross, 2nd an anchor, 3rd balances. A second coat shows 1st and 4th quarterly two lions passant, 2nd a lion rampant, 3rd probably a unicorn. The label on the base of this bottle associates it with the 'Bonnie House of Airlie'.

Three lions rampant. Seal only.

Arms under an earl's coronet. On left side: chevron between three mullets; on right side: three lions passant.

Lin. Coll. with stag's antlers. see Main List [Appendix II].

Three lozenges, martlet over centre one. Crest: eagle's head. Found at Tylney Hall, Rotherwick, Hants., then in possession of St. John family.

Coat-of-arms: four lozenges conjoined; crest: a helm with dragon's wings displayed; c.1745. Mallet.

Coat-of-arms: four lozenges in fess; crest: a stag's head; c.1730.

Maltese cross on a shield. Seal only.

1828 and a Maltese cross. Paper label: Cognac 1825.

Malveysin crest. see Chadwick.

Chevron engrailed between three martlets. Crest: forearm holding a scimitar.

Chevron between three martlets. Crest: velvet cap (or is it a coronet?). Supporters: two greyhounds.

Chevron between three martlets. Supporters indeterminate, perhaps leopards, lions or dragons.

Masonic square and compass.

Masonic square and compass.

Masonic bottle. Ht. 9ins. A three-sided bottle with the masonic signs of compass and square on the seal. These signs are often used by the Master of a Lodge.

Massingberd crest. Given to the owner by Lady Montgomery-Masssingberd, wife of the Field-Marshall, who inherited the family seat at Gunby Hall, Spilsby, Lincs. The bottle is believed to have been found on the site of the old family house at Bratoft, which was pulled down in 1698. The shape of the bottle fits in with this date.

MAVESYN RIDWARE. 1788. and coat-of-arms. see Chadwick.

Arms: three mitres. Crest: mitre. Applied in horseshoe-shaped shield in red sealing wax. It is always possible that this was a tavern-bottle.

1825. and a mullet. Date and the word Brandy on paper label also.

Three mullets.

Two chevronels between three mullets. Sold at Puttick & Simpson's, April 15, 1947.

F.M. and a royal stag passant. This may have been a tavern-bottle. Found at Dunmow.

Newton arms: quarterly. 1 & 4 Sa. two shin-bones in saltire arg. 2 & 3 arg. on a chevron az. three garbs or. Figure at top holding sheaf or trident.

North arms. "A fine large bottle very clearly sealed." Ht. 9¼ins. Sold at Sotheby's, June, 1930.

N.N. and Estoile. Possibly a merchant's mark. An olive-green bottle of which only a fragment is left. The initials are intertwined and difficult to decipher.

N.N. and estoile.

Crest: an ostrich on a cap of maintenance.

Arms of Peache, Chichester. Ht. 7ins. c.1690. Exhibited at Vintners' Hall, 1933, and illustrated in catalogue.

FRANC(I)S PECHE. 1722 and a crowned lion rampant. Ht. 7¾ins. The old bronze stopper is not contemporary. The glass is blue-tinged.

Pelican. see H.H.

Pembroke. see Herbert.

Phoenix issuant from flames. Seal only.

Coat-of-arms: a phoenix issuing from flames; crest: a shield. Seal only.

Pitt Arms with mantling. Sa. between three besants or. fesse chequy az. and arg. This seal was found at Stratford-sub-Castle, where Thomas Pitt (1653-1726) bought the Manor of Stratford and of Old Sarum in 1690 from James Cecil, 4th Earl of Salisbury. He was known as 'Diamond Pitt' because he bought a famous diamond for £20,000 and eventually sold it to the French crown for £135,000. In 1695 he was elected M.P. for Old Sarum, and again in 1722. He married Jane Innes of Reid Hall, Moray, and had three sons and two daughters. His eldest son, Robert, lived in Cornwall, and was father to William, 1st Earl of Chatham; his second son, Thomas, was created Lord Londonderry; his third son, John, achieved military distinction. His second daughter, Lucy, married General James (afterwards 1st Earl) Stanhope. This seal may have been Thomas Pitt's, or it may have belonged to his grandson, William Pitt, 1st Earl of Chatham (1708-1778), statesman, who was born at Stratford and inhabited the Manor at one time. He began his political career as one of the representatives of Old Sarum, one of the most notorious of the 'Rotten Boroughs'. Two members were returned when there was not a single inhabitant on the site of the old city. Later on he became member for Bath. Dr. Johnson in writing of a debate in which he took part made him make the famous retort to Horace Walpole beginning: "the atrocious crime of being a young man". The eccentric Duchess of Marlborough left him a legacy of £10,000, on account of the noble defence he had made for the support of the laws of England. In 1757 he became Secretary of State "with the supreme direction of the war and of foreign affairs". At the close of the reign of George II he was "in the zenith of his glory", and was known as the "Great Commoner", but when he was created Earl of Chatham in 1766, his acceptance of a peerage was very unpopular, and a banquet that was to have been given in his honour in London was immediately cancelled. His second son was the famous William Pitt who became Prime Minister at the age of twenty-five. (D.N.B.) Seal only.

POUHON-IN-SPA and a coat-of-arms. Ht. 9ins. c.1740-1755. Probably used for bringing back water from Pouhon-in-Spa, a watering place in Belgium. In the *Household Book of Lady Grisell Baillie,* at the time of her foreign tour, there is a note of the payment of £1 1s. "To the women at Geronster Pohon", and of 9s. "To the women at Pohon in Town". This was in 1731. There are several other entries of the same kind. There is also a note "For a water bottle 7d." This is probably one of these sealed bottles. Mr. Willard Connely in his book *The True Chesterfield* gives an amusing account of life at Pouhon in 1741. Patients clad in dressing-gowns assembled at the springs at four in the morning. After two or three hours at the springs they had two hours at the baths, and those who had any strength left, went on to Mass. Subsequently they refreshed themselves at a coffee-house, and during the day they went for walks, to the Ladies' Assembly and to the play. Supper was at six, and soon after seven the doctors drove all their patients to bed. "Damned disagreeable place", said Lord Chesterfield, but he stuck to it and in a fortnight's time found himself much better. Again in 1754 he endured the Pouhon spring, and found "everything detestable except the beef, the mutton, the Champagne, the Rhenish and the Earl of Drogheda". In 1772 Mr. Court Dewes wrote from Spa that he had "sent for a doctor to tell him how to drink the waters", who immediately prohibited the three things he was particularly fond of, viz butter, cheese and fruit, that he rose at six, drank the water of the Pouhon Spring till half-past seven, then rode till nine, after which he breakfasted for the first time in his life without butter, chocolate, milk, a crust of bread or a biscuit!" (see Mrs. Delany's *Autobiography.*)

There are two Pouhon bottles at the Guildhall, but I think they must have been buried a long time for they appear almost to have turned to stone. Another one was found in a wall of the old Court House at

Ramsbury, Wilts., when it was burned down at the beginning of the twentieth century.

Poullett arms. Sa. three swords in pile arg. c.1740. This probably belonged to the 1st Earl Poulett (d.1748), one of the Commissioners for the Treaty of Union with Scotland 1706, a Lord of the Treasury 1710, Steward of the Household 1711, Lord-Lieutenant of County Devon 1702, and *Custos Rotulorum* of Somerset 1712. Created Viscount Hinton and Earl Poulett 1706. He married Bridget, daughter and coheir of Peregrine Bertie, of Waldershare, Kent. Found in November, 1943, in Castle Green, Taunton, in laying a large gas-main. Seal only.

PYRMONT WATER. and coat-of-arms. Quarterly of nine. Overall, in the 5th or an eight-pointed star, sa (Waldeck). In the 1st and 9th ar. a cross ancrée gu. (Pyrmont). In the 2nd and 8th ar. three shields gu. (Rappolstein). In the 3rd and 7th ar. three crows heads sa. tongued gu., crowned or (Hoheneck). In the 4th and 6th ar. semy of billets couchées az. a lion gu. crowned or. Pyrmont, the capital of Waldeck, Germany, possesses many mineral springs. This is doubtless one of the bottles in which the precious liquid was brought home to England. Ht. 9ins. Foreign.

Rivers. see Beckford.

Coat-of-arms: on a bend three roses barbed and seeded. Arms and crest of Cary; c.1700. Onion.

Rowe arms: three holy lambs arg. on a field gu. These belong to the family of Rowe, Launceston, Devon. There is an inescutcheon in the centre which would be from marriage with an heiress. (Dorset Field Club Proceedings, Vol. I, 1877, p.89.)

Rutland. see Lion rampant.

Sa. on a chevron between three fleurs-de-lis or as many spearheads az. Possibly arms of Reeve of Thwayte, Suffolk.

Sackville arms under an earl's coronet. c.1715. Arms: or and gules, a bend vair. Two bottles bearing this coat-of-arms are at Knole, Sevenoaks, Kent, and they almost certainly belonged to Lionel Sackville, 7th Earl and 1st Duke of Dorset (1688-1765). In April 1706 he accompanied Charles Montagu, afterwards Earl of Halifax, on a special mission to the Elector of Hanover. He succeeded his father as 7th Earl of Dorset in 1706. On Queen Anne's death he was sent as Envoy-Extraordinary to Hanover to notify the fact to George I. He was appointed Groom of the Stole and 1st Lord of the Bedchamber in 1714, and Constable of Dover Castle, Lord

Warden of the Cinque Ports and Knight of the Garter in the same year. He assisted at the coronation of George I as bearer of the Sceptre with the cross, and was made a member of the Privy Council. In 1720 he was created Duke of Dorset. He acted as Lord High Steward of England at the coronation of George II, and in 1728 he was reappointed Constable of Dover Castle and Lord Warden of the Cinque Ports. In 1730 he became Lord Lieutenant of Ireland, but left for good in 1755; and in 1757 was for the third time given the appointment at Dover and the Cinque Ports which he now held for the remainder of his life. On one occasion when he was holding this office and England was at war with Spain, he claimed a large consignment of Spanish Mountain wine, which had been washed up at Deal and Sandwich, as the Lord Warden's perquisite. Swift wrote to Lady Betty Germain, Dorset's intimate friend, "I do not know a more agreeable person in conversation, one more easy, or of better taste, with a greater variety of knowledge, than the Duke of Dorset." Lord Shelburne was not quite so civil about him. Dorset married Elizabeth, daughter of General Colyear, and had three sons and three daughters. There are pictures of him by Kneller at Knole. (see D.N.B.)

Sea-Lion under earl's coronet. see Tufton.

Coat-of-arms: a sea serpent issuant from a clam shell. Seal only.

Sheaf of corn. see Garb.

Coat-of-arms: upon a shield ermine a crescent cantoned; crest: a rampant lion. Seal only.

Somerville arms: az. three mullets 2 & 1 between seven cross crosslets fitchée 3-1, 2 & 1 or. Crest: dragon vert spouting fire ppr. standing on a wheel or. Supporters: two greyhounds ppr. collared gu. These were the arms of Baron Somerville. Dormant since 1870.

Coat-of-arms: a squirrell rampant. Octagonal.

Squirrel holding a spray of oak in its mouth.

Coat-of-arms: a stag trippant beneath an earl's coronet; c.1675-78. Shaft and globe.

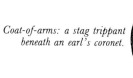

Coat-of-arms: a stag trippant beneath an earl's coronet.

Stork's head erased under a coronet.

TREDEGAR and Tredegar crest: a reindeer's head, from Tredegar, Monmouthshire. Lord Tredegar's ancestor, Sir Charles Gould, was created a baronet and assumed his wife's name of Morgan in 1792. The barony of Tredegar was not created until 1859, so that as the seal is an old one, the word Tredegar would appear to have a territorial significance. Seal only.

Tufton crest: sea-lion issuant from a crest-coronet, with earl's coronet above. c.1730-40. If the date of this bottle is correctly assessed it must have belonged to Sackville, 7th Earl of Thanet, who succeeded his uncle in 1729, and died in 1753. The peerage became extinct in 1849. The Tuftons, originally a Sussex family, were long established in Kent, and fifty Tuftons are buried in the Tufton Chapel in Rainham Church, Kent. (see D.N.B.)

Crest: a unicorn's head erased; c.1670-75. Shaft and globe.

Coat-of-arms; arms of Wallop impaling Bennet. Seal only.

Crest of Warre '91' for 1691. Onion.

Arms of Willoughby. Baldon House, Oxford. Ht. 7ins. Arms: quarterly, 1st and 4th sa. a cross engrailed or; 2nd and 3rd gu. a crossmoline arg., all within a bordure comp. ar. and gu.

WINGERWORTH. 1711. and the crest of the Hunlokes of Wingerworth, Derbyshire.

N.W. and a wyvern.

Wyvern under earl's coronet. see Herbert.

Wykeham Crest: a bull's head sa., armed or., charged on the neck with two chevronels arg. c.1690.

W.W. and crest of lion's head erased. see Wyndham. Main List [Appendix II].

Appendix II
List of Seals

A listing with drawings from *Sealed Bottles* (Chapter Eight — Main List) by S. Ruggles-Brise, 1949, with supplementary items from the author incorporated in *italics;* captions to supplementary drawings are also in *italics.* Additions/amendments to Ruggles-Brise are in [ ].

The supplementary items record the various bottles the author has come across which are not recorded in Ruggles-Brise, and the listing does not purport to be completely up-to-date. No doubt some of the supplementary items will be known and a certain number may even have appeared in print, but the great majority are 'new' so to speak.

The supplementary items have the seal details and bottle type only since full genealogical accounts would occupy a book in themselves.

In order to keep this listing as complete as possible in future editions, the author would be grateful if readers who know of sealed bottles or detached seals, in addition to those mentioned here, would contact him c/o the publisher.

John Abbot; c.1700. Decanter onion.

R.W. ABBY. 1734. Ht. 8¼ ins. diam. 4½ ins.

Thos. Adams Senr. 1714. Bladder onion.

P.A. 1710. ST. SAVUER. GUERNSEY. Ht. 7ins. Onion-shaped bottle. This belonged to a member of the Alles family, and is traditionally supposed to have been a wedding present. The family is said to be extinct.

A.S., C.R. Ht. 11ins. All Souls' College. Common Room, Oxford.

A.S., C.R. Ht. 9¾ ins. All Souls' College. Common Room, Oxford.

ALL SOULS' COLL. C.R. All Soul's College. All Souls' was founded in 1437 by "Henry Chichele and Henry VI, and it is a memorial of Henry V and his men of Agincourt — 'We few, we happy few, we band of brothers'." It has been called "the noblest war memorial in England". (see *Oxford* by Arthur Mee.)

Nichᵠ Amhurst 1719. Straight-sided onion.

A fouled anchor. Seal only.

Ammerdown Park; c.1830. Moulded.

Jnō. Andrews 1770. Cylinder.

JNO. ANDREWS. 1770. Ht. 9¼ins. Octagonal. Left by will in 1852 to George Francis Stuart, Army and Navy Club, London, according to a card attached to it. This may have been John Andrews (1736-1809), historical writer and pamphleteer, who produced numerous historical and other works in the last quarter of the eighteenth century and in the early years of the nineteenth century. He lived at Kennington, Surrey, and his death was announced in the *Gentleman's Magazine* for February 1809, where he is referred to as an ''able historian, profound scholar and politician''.

R.H. ANDREW. TREDMICK. c.1770. Tredmick is in Cornwall. Seal only.

T. Andrews 1799. Seal only.

T. ANSELL. WANTAGE. 1792. Wantage in Berkshire was the birthplace of Alfred the Great.

Samuel Archer; c.1830. Moulded bottle.

JNO. ARFIELD. PORTSMO. COMON. 1765. Portsmouth in Hampshire is said to be the most strongly fortified place in the U.K.

Jos. H. Arlett 1822. Cylinder.

Robt. Arnold 1727. Mallet.

Arthur Tintagel 1755. Cylinder.

F. ARTHUR. 1794. Ht. 15ins. Capacity six bottles.

C. Ashton 1779. Cylinder.

J. Atkin 1735. Seal only.

Auchen Leck 1717. Onion.

John Avery in Winton, around a sun, 1709. Seal only.

'John Avery In Winton 1709', around a sun.

I. AYLIFFE. 1732. Ht. 7½ ins. This was probably John Ayliffe, LL.D. (1676-1732) born at Pember in Hampshire. He was educated at Winchester and New College, Oxford, and suffered from being a "Whig at a time when Oxford was the home of Jacobitism". He published a treatise on Roman law, which is full of learning, but his writings were said to be dull and tedious. He made accusations of misappropriation of funds against Oxford Vice-Chancellors, and in consequence was expelled from the University. The year in which he died (1732) is the date on the bottle, but he did not die until November, so perhaps he had some enjoyment of his sealed bottles — if indeed they are his. (see D.N.B.)

E.A.

F.A. 1728. Seal only.

H.A. the King's Bagnio; c.1685. Onion.

I.A. with head and bust; c.1660. Shaft and globe.

M.W.A. Eighteenth century. Seal only.

N.A. Found near Magdalen Bridge, Oxford. Seal only.

N.A. and a greyhound. Long neck. This is almost certainly a tavern-bottle. There was a Greyhound Tavern in the Borough High St., Southwark. Found in London.

R.A. 1786. This bottle is reputed to come from a descendant of Joseph Addison (1672-1719) of *Spectator* fame, but as he only left a daughter who died unmarried, this cannot have been the case, though it undoubtedly belonged to a member of an Addison family. There was a Joseph Addison who belonged to a yeoman family settled at Lanercost in Cumberland, and who became a prosperous grocer. His son, Thomas Addison (1793-1860) was a distinguished physician and contributed to the fame of Guy's Hospital. It is probable that the bottle belonged to a member of this family.

R.A. with two sprigs of foliage; c.1700. Onion.

R.A.A. and a horse; possibly seventeenth century. Seal only.

W.A.; c.1790-1800. Cylinder.

R. Bake. Seal only.

R. Baker 1729. Mallet.

T. BAKER. 1791. Given to the owner by a member of the Baker family who had lived for some generations at Petersfield where the bottle was found in a cellar with one or two others.

W. BALL. 1825. Maker's name on base: H. Ricketts & Co., Glass Works, Bristol.

I. BANKES. 1780.

S. BANWELL. 1818. Ht. 10½ ins. Bought at Bristol.

WM. BANWELL. WEDMORE. 1807. Ht. 8¼ ins. Wedmore is in Somerset, eight miles from Wells. A treaty was signed here in 878 between Alfred the Great and the Danes. Cheddar cheeses are made here.

I. Barnaby; c.1790. Cylinder.

I. Barnaby 1795. Cylinder.

John Barneby; c.1790. Cylinder.

T. BARNS. WYLDE COURT. Ht. 11¼ ins.

JAM. BARROW. 1734. There were Barrows in Suffolk and at Cambridge in the sixteenth century, but I have not yet identified this one.

J. BARTLETT. SARUM. 1734. Salisbury, Wilts., where the owner of this bottle lived, is famous for its Early English Cathedral.

P. BASTARD. 1725. At the end of the seventeenth century, one of the Bastards (a French family settled in England since the Conquest) married the heiress of Pollexfen of Kitley, since when Pollexfen has been used as a christian name in the Bastard family. This may be one of the Pollexfen Bastards. (see D.N.B.) Two bottles.

W. BASTARD. 1753. Probably William Bastard, who as 'Colonel of the East Devonshire Militia', saved the Arsenal of Plymouth when it was threatened by the appearance of the French Fleet in August, 1779, and was gazetted a baronet. Neither he nor his heirs assumed the title. (see D.N.B.) Or it may have been William Bastard (1689-1766), mason and architect, who with his brother John, rebuilt the town of Blandford, Dorset, after the great fire there in 1731. There is a picture of William in the Town Hall at Blandford. (see *Country Life,* May 21, 1948.)

THOS. BASTERD. EXON. 1709. In spite of the slight variation in the spelling of the name, the owner of this bottle may have been a member of the Pollexfen Bastard family (see P. and W. Bastard). It may have belonged to Thomas Bastard (d. 1720), father of six sons, including John and William Bastard, and four daughters. Thomas, described as ''eminent for his skill in architecture'', married Bridget Creech. All his sons, like himself, were in the building trade. (see *Country Life,* May 21, 1948.)

POLLEXFEN BASTURO. 1730. (see P. Bastard.) The unusualness of the name Pollexfen inclines me to connect this with one of the Pollexfen Bastards; perhaps one who went to live in Italy? But this is pure conjecture. The bottle was sold at Christie's on June 3, 1945, from Col. R.F. Ratcliff's Collection. It was bought by Messrs. Manheim and has gone to the United States.

I. BATS. c.1735. Ht. 8¼ ins. Illustrated in *Apollo,* November, 1938.

JOSEPH BATTERHAM. 1768.

JOSEPH BATTERHAM. 1770.

I. BATTERHAM with a flower. Batterham is believed to have been a builder.

I. BATTISCOME with ornamental scrolls. Ht. 11¼ ins.

William Battishill 1707. Onion.

'*William/Battishill/1707'.*

Ino. Battral, Towedeneck, 1773. Squat cylinder.

H. BAYLAL. 1757.

RICHARD BEACH. 1703. Ht. 5ins.

I. Beague 1785. Squat cylinder.

J. Beague 1773. Squat cylinder.

R. Beal 1828. Decanter.

I.M.B. John and Mary Beaton.

T. BELLAMY. 1773. Was this Thomas Bellamy (1745-1800) who is described as a "miscellaneous writer"? Besides writing verses he started Bellamy's *Picturesque Magazine and Literary Museum* which contained engraved portraits of living persons. (see D.N.B.) (mentioned in Wilmer's *Early English Glass*.)

BELLS TAVERN. see I.M.S., and D.

Benaysh 1713. Onion.

BENEDICTINI in moulded letters and a wax seal with a crest: heads of three Bishops; supporters might be ferns. Mantling includes a Bishop's mitre. Did this bottle belong to a Mitre or a Bishop Tavern?

I. BENNETT. 1727. Ht. 11ins. Trignum size. One of the Bennetts (James Gordon Bennett, 1800-1872) wrote of his family: "The Bennetts were a little band of freebooters in Saxony A.D. 896...They emigrated to France, and lived on the Loire several hundred years...The Earl of Tankerville is a Bennett, and sprang from the lucky side of the race". (see D.N.B.)

Philip Bennett 1707. Onion.

Gam Betts, Ply Dock 1745. Mallet.

J. BHALE. 1787. Ht. 9ins. It is believed that this is a Burgundy bottle. It has sloping shoulders and a shallow kick-up.

J. RICKHAM.

J. BICKNELL. BRADFORD. Bradford, an important wool market, nine miles from Leeds, is in the West Riding of Yorks. But it is quite possible that this bottle comes from Bradford-on-Avon, a market town in Wilts. also celebrated for its wool.

T. Biddick, Bridge; c.1800. Squat cylinder.

N. Bidgood 1773. Cylinder.

RICHARD BILLINGSLY and a five-turretted castle. Date: 'earlier than 1660'. In a list of Oxford City muniments entitled "Almshouses licensed and unlicensed 1640' there is a 'Richard Billingslee'; on the other hand Mr. Leeds has not been able to find a seventeenth-century Castle Inn in Oxford. So the problem of this seal is unsolved at present. (see Leeds, p.53.)

BILLINGSLEY a Tudor rose and castle.

T. Bisson 1708. Onion.

W. Bingham; c.1780. Squat cylinder.

I. BLACKMORE. 1723.

E.B. 1728. Edwin Blagdon or Blagden, of Blagdon House, Keevil, Wilts. The initials and date correspond with those on the lead guttering on the house, which later passed into the possession of the Chamberlaine family. The bottle was given to the present owner by Miss Chamberlaine in about 1936.

Wm. Blomberg 1763. Squat cylinder.

T. Bolitho Jnr; c.1800. Cylinder.

Thos. Bolitho 1817. Cylinder.

JNO. BOOKER. 1734. Ht. 8¼ ins. Illustrated in *Apollo,* November, 1938.

Border Maid 1877. Seal only.

R. Bottral 1726. Mallet.

GEORGE BOWEN ESQ. LLWYNGWAIR. 1838. From Llwyngwair, Newport, Pembrokeshire.

Robert Bowie 1713. Onion.

M.W. Bowle; c.1720.

BOXTED HALL. SUFFOLK. 1774. An Elizabethan moated house in Suffolk, three miles north of Glemsford. The estate was acquired by the Poley family from the Duke of Gloucester in the reign of Henry IV, and the house was built by William Poley, whose descendants still owned the estate in 1908.

DAVID BOYES. Seal only.

BRABSTER. Probably from Caithness. Seal only.

'Brabster'.

J. BRADDON. BRE. RIDGE. Late eighteenth century.

Wm. Braddon Gent Bridge Rule, 1775. Cylinder.

M. Bradford 1723. Bladder onion.

M. BRAGGE, 1734. Ht. 7¾ ins. Sold at Sotheby's, June, 1930.

Brancepath; c.1875. Moulded.

BRANDY, within a beaded border with small decorative star below; three-part mould; c.1830-40.

B.N.C., C.R. Brasenose College Common Room. Brasenose was founded in 1509 by Sir William Sutton, and William Smyth, Bishop of Lincoln, was one of its chief benefactors. The present chapel was begun in 1656, traditionally from the designs of Sir Christopher Wren. ''The brazen nose of its tradition is on the door of the old gatehouse.'' (Arthur Mee.) Among its distinguished graduates are John Foxe (author of *The Book of Martyrs*), Richard Burton (*Anatomy of Melancholy*), Laurence Washington (ancestor of George Washington) and John Buchan (Lord Tweedsmuir) who became Governor-General of Canada and who wrote many books. Seal only.

BRAY OF BARINGTON. Ht. 9ins. Circum. 19ins. c.1650-55. A pair of bottles with this seal on them was bought in Bucks.

R.B. BRAY MORRISH 1786.

'R.B./BRAY/MORRISH/1786'.

S. Brent 1715. Onion.

JNO. BREWSTER OF BRANDON. 1760. Brandon is a small town in Suffolk on the edge of the Fens. The bottle was bought at Lakenheath, Suffolk.

R. BRICKNELL.

B.S. BROADWOOD. 1714

E. BROOK. 1768.

W. BROOK. LYNTON. Lynton is in Devon, on the outskirts of Exmoor.

E. Brown Kidwell 1747. Mallet.

G.I.B. and the Vintners' Arms. George and J(oan) Brown, of the Three Tuns Tavern, Oxford. The name only appears in a lease as an occupier of the house. By her will Elizabeth Pont (q.v.) bequeathed ''to my servants George Brown and Joane Richardson to each of them Tenne pounds. . .and alsoe all the particons that are mine in my now dwelling-house and also Twelve leathern chaires a round table Two pairs of large fflaxen sheetes and all my implements belonging to the Trade in my Cellars equally''. George was buried in St. Mary the Virgin's Church in 1693, and his wife in 1701. (see E.T. Leeds.)

JNO. BROWN LANDRAKE. 1784. Landrake is about five miles from Saltash, Cornwall.

Nich. Brown 1716. Bladder onion.

WILLIAM BROWN. GLASGOW. 1766. Glasgow, in Lanarkshire, is the second largest city in the British Isles, and has eight miles of quays.

T. BROWNE. EXON. 1705. Possibly Thomas Browne (1672-1710) physician, son of Dr. Edward Browne, President of the College of Physicians, and grandson of the author of *Religio Medici*. He wrote ''a curious account of an antiquarian tour through England'' (see D.N.B.). He was admitted a candidate to the College of Physicians in 1704 (the year before the date on the bottle), but died in 1710 by falling from his horse.

H. Browse Yalberton; c.1800. Squat cylinder.

B. 1837 and a ducal coronet. Richard, 1st Duke of Buckingham and Chandos (1776-1839), of Stowe House, Buckingham. He married Lady Anne Eliza Brydges, daughter of the 3rd and last Duke of Chandos. These bottles came from the cellars at Stowe, and are known to have been used when refreshments were provided there by the Duke to celebrate the coronation of Queen Victoria.

'B 1837' and a ducal coronet.

Jno. Bull 1740. Mallet.

T. Bult Nailsbor 1780. Squat cylinder.

G. Burden Surscott; c.1800. Squat cylinder.

I. BURFORD. 1708.

T. Burford 1717. Onion.

JOHN BURROW. Ht. 9½ins. Diam. 5ins. Found in London.

'S./Buscombe/St Brock/1785'.

S. Buscombe St. Brock 1785. Squat cylinder.

ELLIS BUTTON OF UFFCULME. The D.N.B. refers to ''the old family of Bitton or Button, so called from the parish of Bitton, in the county of Gloucestershire''. Two members of this family were successively Bishop of Bath and Wells in the thirteenth century.

Buzza St. Ives. Moulded.

Bydder Thistle Boon 1674. Shaft and globe.

B. 1837 and a ducal coronet. see Buckingham.

C.B. either side of castle with open drawbridge. Seal only.

D.B. in dotted circle. Bottle-decanter c.1720. Ht. 11½ ins. Diam. 6ins.

E.B. 1728. Ht 6¾ ins. see Edwin Blagden.

F.B. Treor 1783. Squat cylinder.

G.B. and a hand holding a scimitar. see also Bickford in Appendix I.

G.I.B. see George and Joan Brown.

H.B. [see below].

H.B., a vintner's brush and three tuns. Belonged to Humphrey Bodicot of the Three Tuns Tavern, Oxford. Bodicot was the predecessor of Richard and Elizabeth Pont. See R.E.P.

I.B. Ht. 8ins.

I.B. 1767.

I.B. 1772. Squat cylinder magnum.

I.B. St. Veep 1795. Squat cylinder.

I.B. and a wheatsheaf. Probably from a tavern. Seal only.

I.B.B.

I.M.B. see John and Mary Beaton.

I.N.B.

J.B. COLUMPTON. Probably J. Blackmore (q.v.). Collumpton is a little town in Devon with a market place dating from 1278. There are various ways of spelling its name.

'I B/Columpton'.

N.B. Dursley 1783. Squat cylinder.

P.B. 1775.

R.B.; separate matrices. Seal only.

R.M.B. Flexbury; c.1800. Squat cylinder.

S.B.; c.1720. Bladder onion.

T.B. c. 1650. Ht. 8½ins. Found in Bishopsgate. From Sir John Risley Collection.

T.B. and a stag's head within a circle of six small pellets. Probably a tavern bottle. Bottle imperfect. Found in London.

T.B. 1727 and a star.

T.B. 1750. Seal only.

T.B. 1797. Squat cylinder magnum.

T.B.; separate matrices. Seal only.

T.B., H.L. c.1800.

W.B. 1769.

W.B. 1796. Seal only.

W.B. and bishop's mitre encircled with rosettes; c.1695-1700. Onion.

W.L.B.; c.1790. Squat cylinder.

RICHARD CALLAWAY and a bunch of grapes. Almost certainly from a Vine Tavern. Found in Winchester. Seal only.

S. Calmady Callington; c.1760. Cylinder.

CAMBRIDGE. E.C. 1684 and a dolphin. The Dolphin Tavern at the Bridge Street end of All Saints' Passage, Cambridge. The initials are thought to be those of E. Clarke who, according to the Hearth Tax. 1674, Schedule of the Parish of All Saints, where the tavern was situated, was the occupier of the largest dwelling. (see *Country Life,* March 30, 1935.)

I.S. CANN. 1794. Ht. 8¼ ins.

I.S. CANN. (W)INDHAM. 1813. An abbreviation of Wymondham, an ancient town in Norfolk.

CANN. WYMONDHAM. 1796. see supra.

T. CARDELL. Nineteenth century bottle. Sold at Sotheby's, December 9, 1947.

Carlisle Spedding 1741. Mallet.

Thos. Carlyon St. Blazey 1708. Onion.

THOS. CARLYON. 1714. Bottle with the short neck and broad base of that period. Thomas Carlyon of Tregrehan was head of the Carlyon family in Cornwall and had considerable interests in the tin and copper mines of that county. He was an ancestor of the present owner.

C.C. under an earl's coronet. Charles Dormer, 2nd Earl of Carnarvon (1632-1709). He married first Elizabeth Capel (d.1678), and secondly, Mary, daughter of the 2nd Earl of Lindsay. Both his wives were buried at Wing, Bucks. He succeeded as 2nd Earl in 1643 when his father was killed at the Battle of Newbury. He died at Ascott House, Wing, where the seal was found. This house, the seat of the Dormers, has now entirely disappeared, the present Ascott House being some distance away.

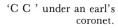
'C C ' under an earl's coronet.

According to Browne-Willis, the Bucks. historian, the 2nd Earl of Carnarvon kept great hospitality at Ascott, "where the neighbouring gentry and clergy were oftentimes well entertained". When he died the title became extinct. (see also Crest of Dormer.) A seal with two C's under an earl's coronet, was dug up at Cornbury Park, Oxon., the home of Viscount Cornbury and Earl of Clarendon (q.v.) but in his case the Cs were interlaced. Seal only.

I. Carrivick 1822. Cylinder.

JAMES CARRUDUS. 1709. This seems to be the earliest known dated Scottish seal. Seal only.

I. Castelman 1720. Late onion.

CASTLE. TAUNTON. The Castle at Taunton, originally built in 702, was at one time in the possession of the Bishops of Winchester. It now houses the Museum. But this bottle very probably belonged to the Castle Inn.

Samuel Caston, Wodbrig, 1725. Mallet.

J. Cave, Chetnol, 1777. Cylinder.

I. CHAPPEL. 1764.

R.M.P. 1657, and king's head in profile, resembling Charles I. Ht. 9ins. The seal probably represents a King's Head Tavern, and the initials those of the licensee and his wife. Found at Wellingborough. This is the earliest recorded dated wine-bottle. (Earliest seal, 1650.)

C.R. 1661. and king's head crowned and in full wig. Ht. 7ins. Charles Rex II. Probably made to celebrate his Restoration. This and the bottle at Hereford are the second earliest recorded dated bottles and the third earliest seals. Exhibited Vintners' Hall, 1933. Was in collection of the late Francis Berry, then A.S. Marsden-Smedley, and was sold at Sotheby's June 18, 1943, for £56.

'C R/1661' and a king's head.

C.R. 1661. R.A.B. and a king's head. see above. Pale green glass; area round date gilded. This was probably a King's Head Tavern bottle and the three last initials would be those of the licensees.

JNO. TRUSTON CHASEFIELD. 1725.

H. CHILTON. 1764.

CH. CH. C.R. c.1780. Christchurch Common Room, Oxford. Cardinal Wolsey planned and endowed Christchurch (1528-1529), beginning with its famous kitchen, and his picture hangs in the Great Hall, said to be the finest of the Oxford Halls. Sir Christopher Wren built the Gateway known as Tom Tower. It is impossible to enumerate all the famous men who were at Christchurch, but among them were Dr. Fell, Vice-Chancellor ("I do not like thee, Dr. Fell"), William Locke, the philosopher, and William Penn, the Quaker. The two latter were expelled in the former's time. C.L. Dodgson (Lewis Carroll), author of *Alice in Wonderland*, was Dean of Christchurch in the nineteenth century. It is always referred to by those who have been there as 'The House'.

CH. CH. C.R. 1771. ⎫
                    ⎬ see above. Seals only.
CH. CH. C.R. 1804. ⎭

I.C. 1790. Sir John Church. Wine still in the bottle.

RICHARD CHURCH. 1678 and a dolphin. This bottle may come from the Dolphin Tavern at Cambridge, and if it does we may have to reconsider the attribution of the CAMBRIDGE E.C. 1684 to E. Clarke. Was there a Church with the initial E, possibly a son of this Richard, who owned the Dolphin Tavern at Cambridge, or does the bottle belong to a tavern of the same name elsewhere?

W. Clapcott; c.1770-80. Cylinder.

℃ (C.C. interlaced) and earl's coronet. c.1705-10. Henry Hyde. Lord

'C C' (interlaced) under
an earl's coronet.

Cornbury and 2nd Earl of Clarendon (1638-1709). He had a remarkably fine collection of medals and was author of the *History and Antiquities of the Cathedral Church at Winchester*. He and his father were friends of Evelyn's, who, as early as 1664, helped Lord Cornbury to plant the park at Cornbury. Henry Hyde is frequently mentioned in Evelyn's *Diary*. He and his wife dined with the diarist on June 10, 1673, and afterwards they visited the Italian glass-house at Greenwich, "where glasse was blown of finer metall than that of Murano at Venice". So he was interested in glass some thirty years before he had his bottles sealed. After an interview with him in October, 1695, Anthony Wood accused him of talking "after a rambling way". His financial difficulties made it necessary for Cornbury to be sold, but he lived there during his lifetime. This creation of earls of Clarendon became extinct on the death of the 4th earl. Found at Cornbury Park, Oxon.

John Clark 1761. Squat cylinder.

I. CLARKE. A squat bottle. Found in Aldwych, London. There are many J. Clarke's recorded in the D.N.B. Jeremiah Clarke (1669?-1707), musical composer, may have been the owner of this bottle. He studied under Dr. Blow, and succeeded him as almoner and master of the choristers at St. Paul's Cathedral. He was also music-master to Queen Anne. Eventually he committed suicide by shooting himself at the Golden Cup in St. Paul's Churchyard. (see D.N.B.)

J.W.C. John Were Clarke (1784-1847) was J.P. and D.L. His commissions are at Bridwell, Uffculme, Devon, where his grandson still lives.

R.H.C. 1815. Richard Hall Clarke (1750-1821) was J.P. and D.L. His commissions are at Bridwell, Uffculme, Devon, where his great-grandson still lives.

C. and a baron's coronet. Ht. 11½ ins. Maker's name on base of bottle: H. Ricketts & Co., Glass Works, Bristol, which shows that the bottle cannot be dated earlier than 1811 (see W. Leman). Baron Clinton. This may have been the eighteenth baron (1787-1832), who was Lord of the Bedchamber to George III, or the nineteenth baron (1791-1866), who bore the great banner at the funeral of George III, or the twentieth baron (1834-1904), who was Lord-Lieutenant for Devonshire 1887-1904.

RT. COAKER. 1718. Robert Coker or Coaker was born in 1657 and died in 1721. Found at Mappowder, Dorset, formerly the seat of the Coker family. (see Arms of Coker.)

W. COCKE. 1723.

OLD CHAMPAIGN COGNAC. 1815. Perhaps a commemoration of the

Battle of Waterloo. Seal only.

OLD CHAMPION COGNAC. 1830.

C. Coker 1721. Bladder onion.

JOHN COLBY. A port bottle of 1822 vintage. Grandfather of present owner of Ffynnonau estate in North Pembrokeshire.

John Colby Fynone 1822. Cylinder.

I. COLE. 1728. A man named John Cole issued halfpenny tokens in Salisbury some sixty years earlier.

Ino. Collard 1725. Bladder onion.

J. Collens 1704. Onion.

I.D. COLLES. PYRLAND. 1807. A place near Taunton, Somerset.

J. COLLINGS. DEC. 1794.

J.P. Collings. 1736. Octagonal.

B.C. 1778. Found in the garden of 21 The Close, Salisbury, the home of Canon Barfoot Colton (d.1803), whose seal it probably was. At the sale of his property were included some sixty dozen bottles of Port wine. Barfoot Colton was elected to King's College, Cambridge, in 1755, and was afterwards made a Canon of Salisbury. The D.N.B. suggests that Charles Caleb Colton (1780?-1832), the eccentric author of *Lacon,* was probably his son. Seal only.

S. Colton 1767. Cylinder.

ROGER COMBERBACH. CHESTER. 1725 with crest (no description). It is impossible to say whether this is one of the tavern bottles or one of the 'gentlemen's'. Chester, with an eleventh-century cathedral, is the capital of Cheshire.

CONSTANTIA WYN. Eighteenth-century Dutch bottle. Constantia wine was so called after Constance, wife of Governor Van der Stell, who gave his own name to Stellenbosch, a pioneer S. African vineyard settlement. Vines were first planted at the Cape in 1653.

B. COOK. PELDON. 1772. Peldon is an old and scattered village near Mersey Island in Essex.

T. COOMBE. 1789. Ht. 11¼ ins. Capacity three bottles.

Joyce Coombs 1730. Seal only.

J. Cornock; c.1780. Squat cylinder.

CORSEBASKET. 1734. Made for the proprietor of The Corsebasket, Lanarkshire, presumably a tavern.

COVENTRY HOUSE. 1702. Coventry House was "the London residence of Henry Coventry, third son of Lord Keeper Coventry and himself Secretary of State to Charles II..." He died there in 1686 "leaving his property in the parish of St. Martin's-in-the-Fields to his nephew Mr. Henry Coventry..." The house is sometimes called Piccadilly House. When Sir William Coventry died at Tunbridge Wells, June 23, 1685, Henry Savile wrote to his brother, the Marquis of Halifax, "He said he had left his will in the hands of my cousin, Nat. Coventry, to whom we have sent to be at Piccadilly House this afternoon at three of the clock, and we have also sent word to both of our uncles Frank and Harry to be there". (*Savile's Corresp.,* Camden Society.) The house stood on the north side of Panton Street and abutted on Oxenden Street, the garden wall adjoining Baxter's Chapel in that street. In the *London Gazette,* July 30 to August 3, 1674, No.908, appears the following advertisement: "Lost, on Friday night last, between London and Barnet, a white Land Spaniel, somewhat long-haired, both ears red, his Tale lately shorne, and a steele collar about his neck; Whoever will give notice to the Porter, at Mr. Secretary Coventry's House, Pickadilly, shall be well-rewarded". (see *London Past and Present* by Wheatley and Cunningham.) A side-light on Mr. Coventry's autocratic character is given in the following quotation written from Oxenden Street, Haymarket: (1676) "Richard Baxter built the first Oxenden Chapel on the west side of this street next to the grounds and residence of Henry Coventry, one of the King's secretaries. Baxter himself was the minister, and the second day he presided Coventry had the drums beaten under the windows to prevent service being held. A continuance of this annoyance caused Baxter to quit and go to preach in another chapel in Swallow Street." (see *London* by George Cunningham.)

R.W.C. c.1800. Ht. 11½ ins. This bottle belonged to the founder of Messrs. W.J. Crabb and Son, wine-merchants.

Cranes. see T.B.D.

Jno. Credito 1730. Bladder onion, magnum.

R. Crig, Merriot 1808. Magnum squat cylinder.

Jnᵒ Croad Esqʳ, Keyham 1797. Cylinder.

'Jnᵒ Croad Esqʳ, Keyham· 1797'.

EDW. CROKER ESQ. 1751.

J. Croombe 1785. Cylinder.

ROB. CROSSE. EXON. 1760. Exeter, an ancient cathedral city, is the capital of Devonshire.

A crown and OXON 1707. Seal only.

A crown and 'OXON/1707'.

CULLODEN. Straight-sided whiskey bottle made at Ferintosh on the estate of Forbes of Culloden. Culloden Moor, six miles east of Inverness, was the scene of the defeat of Prince Charles Edward in 1746, "the last charge of the tribal swordsmen in Scottish history", according to G.M. Trevelyan *(History of England)* who says that Lord President Forbes alone had shown wisdom, and that if his advice had been taken earlier, the issue would have been otherwise. His estates at Ferintosh and Culloden were ravaged by the Jacobites, but in compensation the Scotch Parliament voted his son to the right to "distil into spirits the grain of the barony of Ferintosh".

'Culloden'.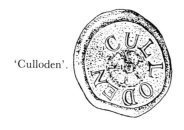

'C' under baron's coronet 1792. Seal only.

C.C. and earl's coronet. see Carnarvon and Clarendon.

C. and a baron's coronet. see Clinton.

A.C. 1833. Decanter bottle.

A.R.C.

B.C. 1778. see Colton.

C.R. & B.C.

G.V.C. Langworthy 1797. Cylinder.

I.C. see Sir John Church.

I.C. Ht. 8ins. and 11½ins.

I.C. 97. Onion.

I.C. and three tuns above; c.1680. Shaft and globe.

I.C. 1700. Ht. 6½ins. Exhibited at Vintners' Hall, 1933, and shown in catalogue. From Francis Berry Collection.

'*I C/1700*'.

I.C. 1700. Not quite the same as the previous seal. A fine 'black' specimen of the seventeenth century.

I.C. 1731. Ht. 9¼ins. Diam. 4¼ins.

I.C. 1748.

J.C.

J.W.C. see John Were Clarke.

L.C. 1707.

N.C. 1710. Ht. 8ins. Exhibited Vintners' Hall, 1933, and illustrated in catalogue.

R.C. and a tulip. This must surely have been a sign of some sort, but not necessarily of a tavern. It came from Bristol. From S.G. Percival Collection. Seal only.

'R C' and a tulip.

R.C. 1695. Found at Bristol. Seal only.

 'R C'.

'R C'; c.1690-1700. Onion.

R.C. 1811. Squat cylinder.

R.C. Polgreen. Moulded.

R.H.C. 1815. Cylinder.

R.H.C. 1818. Cylinder.

R.H.C. see Richard Hall Clarke.

S.C. ESQ. 1769. Ht. 11ins. Cylindrical body.

T.C. 1776. Squat cylinder.

T.C. and crest. see Sir Thomas Carew [Appendix I].

T.C. Ht. 5¾ins. A short neck and a broad base.

W.C. 1775. Ht. 11ins. Diam. 5½ins. Letters and date pricked on and not on a seal. The bottle has been binned upside down. It probably contained port.

W.C.C. the whole intertwined, the W central, the two Cs back to back, above and below two eight-pointed stars. Seal only.

'W C C' intertwined.

W.T.C. 1690.

TRUE DAFFY'S ELIXIR. The original wax seal on the cork, with a complicated coat-of-arms, is intact. This was the most famous remedy in England from the middle of the seventeenth century, when it was invented by one Anthony Daffy, until nearly the middle of the nineteenth century. I should say that this bottle, which is hexagonal, belongs to the early nineteenth century. The words are moulded in the bottle itself and not on a seal. 'Daffy' was tremendously advertised and bogus imitations of it were made. Here is an extract from the *London Gazette* for December 22, 1681:

> "Whereas it has been generally reported by some evil-minded People That the late fire in the Old Baily was in the House of Anthony Daffy, author of the famous Elixir Salutis, and that he himself was therein burnt, to the discouragement of divers persons, who have received benefit from his Elixir. Anthony Daffy is in perfect health, etc. etc."

and another from the *Daily Gazetteer* for December 2, 1743:

> "Daffy's Original and Famous Elixir Salutis, truly prepared by me Susanna Daffy, who for many years prepared the same for my late Mother, Mrs. Elizabeth Daffy, of Fleet St., deceased widow of the late Dr. Elias Daffy, who was the son of Anthony Daffy, the first inventor."

It is amusing to think that this unpalatable compound was still going strong in Charles Dickens' time, as portrayed in *Oliver Twist,* though Mrs. Mann thoughtfully diluted it (or so she told Mr. Bumble) with a little gin, to make it more acceptable to the infant orphans.

I. Dally Esq Thorvertn; 1770. Cylinder.

J. DALLY. 1753.

T. DAMPIER. 1798. There was a Thomas Dampier (1748-1812) who was Dean of Durham, Dean, and afterwards, Bishop of Rochester, and finally Bishop of Ely. But this bottle may have belonged to a descendant of "George Dampier of Porton, near Breadport, in the county of Dorset, Gentln", to whom Captain William Dampier left a tenth of his fortune in 1715. (see D.N.B.)

T. Dampier 1798. Cylinder.

DANIEL. SOUTHON. 1708. These words are written round the edge of the seal and W in the centre. Southampton in Hampshire is the most important mail-packet station in England.

Wm. Daniel 1754. Cylinder.

J. DASON. 1756.

W. DAUBENY. 1776. Daubeny is the name of a well-known Bristol family. One of them, Charles Daubeny, D.C.L. (1745-1827), Archdeacon of Salisbury, was the son of George Daubeny — an opulent Bristol merchant. (see D.N.B.)

J. DAVEY.

M.B. DAVIES. BLAENBLODE. 1821. A port bottle from Blaenblodau, near Lampeter, Cardiganshire.

D. DAVIS. 1801. This bottle has a pronounced kick and is in very good condition.

HENRY DAVIS. 1755.

JNO. DAVIS. MERTHYR. 1770. From Merthyr, Glamorganshire.

WM. DAVIS. MERTHYR. 1770. Merthyr Tydvil ('Tydfil the Martyr') is in the colliery district of Glamorganshire, S. Wales.

ROBT. DAW. c.1765.

D. Denham 1725. Onion.

R. Densham Upton. 1811. Squat cylinder.

'R/Densham/Upton./1811'.

G. DIBBLE. 1805. Ht. 9⅛ ins.

A.D. 1727. Abraham Dobson of Penrith, Cumberland. This is a half-pint squat serving-bottle. Bought from the Dobson home (a small farmer's house) in Penrith in 1940.

Doct. Mill 1755. Cylinder.

F.R. DOCTON. 1775. Ht. 9½ ins. Bought at Bristol.

R. DODWEL. The name occurs frequently in accounts of seventeenth century Oxford. Seal only.

A dolphin. Probably from a tavern.

A dolphin with a crown above. This was most probably from a Dolphin Tavern. There was such a one near Pepys's house, to which he often repaired. On June 20, 1665, he writes: "To the Dolphin Taverne, where all we officers of the Navy met with the Commissioners of the Ordnance by agreement, and dined: where good musique at my direction." Seal only. (see also W.R.)

E. DOMETT JUNR. 1774.

Wm. Dommett 1778. Squat cylinder.

Dommett Junior Offwell 1777. Squat cylinder.

DONERAILLE HOUSE and eight-pointed star. Three-part mould.

John and Elizabeth Dorellpooll 1708. Onion.

DOUGLAS. 1799. This is, presumably, Archibald James Edward, first Baron Douglas of Douglas (1748-1827), the subject of a famous lawsuit. He was created a British peer in 1790. The Duke of Queensberry bequeathed the estate of Amesbury in Wilts. to him. He married 1st Lady Lucy Graham, daughter of the second Duke of Montrose, and 2ndly Lady Frances Scott, sister of the 3rd Duke of Buccleuch, and by his two wives he had eight sons and four daughters. (see D.N.B.) This bottle belonged to Robert Findlay of Easterhill, to whose family it came by intermarriage.

DANIELL DOWSING DE NORWICH. 1700. Was Daniell a son of William Dowsing (1596?-1679?), iconoclast, who, coming of a family of respectable Suffolk yeomen, caused such terrible havoc in Suffolk and Cambridgeshire churches by the destruction of glass, images, pictures, candlesticks, etc., in accordance with Parliament's ordinance of 1643? An eye-witness of his doings describes him as going ''about the country like a Bedlam breaking glasse windows'', and in his own Journal he records breaking down ''about an hundred superstitious Pictures''. (see D.N.B.) This bottle was bought by the late Cecil Higgins for a Museum at Bedford.

'Daniell/Dowsing/de Norwich/1700'.

C. Drake 1790. Squat cylinder.

R. DREWE. 1823.

R. Dugdale Wareham; c.1730. Mallet.

Dunardry. Seal only.

Henry Dunning 1730. Mallet.

John Dunning 1821. Cylinder.

Richd. Dunning 1787. Cylinder.

J.D. Sir John Duntze. This was probably the 2nd baronet (d.1830) who married in 1804 Elizabeth, daughter of Sir Thomas Carew, Bart of Tiverton Castle. Sir John was Receiver-General of land and assessed taxes in Devon. The first baronet, also John, (cr. 1776) was a merchant of Exeter, and M.P. for Tiverton. He died in 1795.

JOHN DYMOND. 1753. There was a well-known Quaker family of this name at Exeter. John and Olive Dymond had five sons, of whom one was Jonathan Dymond (1796-1828), moralist. The owner of the bottle may have been this elder John, or possibly his son.

'D'. *Cylinder bottle fragment.*

D. and four bells out of a possible five (the seal is broken). Probably a tavern bottle. Found on the site of Ascott House, Wing, Bucks. see also Charles Dormer, Earl of Clarendon, Crest of Dormer [Appendix I] and I.M.S. Seal only.

A.D. 1727. see Abraham Dobson.

B.C.D. 1707. Mallet.

C.D. see Palsgrave Head.

C.E.D. and a mitre. Probably from a Mitre Tavern with the initials of the proprietor and his wife. Pepys called at the Mitre in Fleet Street on Jan. 20, 1660, and there was a Mitre in Fenchurch Street, also visited by Pepys, but this was kept by Dan Rawlinson, so the initials would not be suitable for that date. Mitre Taverns usually have an ecclesiastical connection. In the case of the Mitre Tavern between Ely Place and Hatton Garden, it is with the Bishops of Ely who owned a palace in that neighbourhood. The tavern is included ''in the ancient sanctuary of the precinct of the still-existing episcopal chapel. . .where John of Gaunt took refuge. . .'' (Leopold Wagner).

The Mitre at the corner of Chancery Lane and Fleet Street was associated with a Bishop of Chichester who held land in that district. Its mead, malmsey and sack were held in high repute, as well as its roast swan and boar's head. It was later celebrated as a resort of Dr. Johnson, and here it was that Boswell had a first sample of the doctor's conversational powers. A Mitre Tavern in Cheapside had the reputation of making ''noses red''. (Henry C. Shelley). Found in Austen Friars, London.

D.D. Found in Dumfriesshire.

D.B.D. 1820.

D.B.D. 1826.

D.B.D. 1828.

D.B.D. 1830.

D.B.D. 1836.

D.B.D. 1837.

D.B.D. and a star.
   These [D.B.D.] bottles probably belonged to a wine-merchant, and may have been from the west country.

D.Mc.H.D. 1821. Magnum cylinder.

G.D. 1758.

H.A.D. This bottle is divided vertically into four panels by ribbed applied ornaments. It bears a hand-painted floral decoration, and also a representation of Tam o'Shanter and Souter Johnnie, and a painted and gilt wine-label flanked by the initials W.C. and inscribed REAL MOUNTAIN DEW.

I.D. c.1700. Ale jug with three seals all bearing the same initials.

I.D. 1702. Found at Temple Church, Bristol. From S.G. Percival Collection. Seal only.

J.D. see Sir John Duntze.

J.T.D.

M.D. 1836. and masonic symbols. Bottle of very dense glass (Nailsea type) with blue-white speckles on shoulders and neck.

N.I.D. 1715.

R.D. 1713. Onion.

R.D. 1828. Sotheby's, December 9, 1947.

T.B.D. and three cranes. Long-necked bottle. The Three Cranes in the Vintry was a well-known tavern in Upper Thames Street. According to John Stow, the topographer, the Vintry was where "the merchants of Bordeaux craned their wines out of lighters and other vessels, and there landed and made sale of them", and although the sign actually was of three large birds supposed to represent cranes, it was merely a punning allusion to the three iron cranes used for lifting the wine. In the early sixteenth century the tavern was known as The Crane, but by 1574 the one crane had become three; no doubt the import wines had increased and more cranes were required to land them. Pepys speaks scathingly of a dinner he had there with some poor relations of his, and Ben Jonson alludes to it in this sentence: "Your Three Cranes, Mitre, and Mermaid men! Not a corn of true salt, not a grain of right mustard amongst them all". And again in *The Devil is an Ass:*

Nay, boy, I will bring thee to the bawds and roysters
At Billingsgate, feasting with claret-wine and oysters;
From thence shoot the Bridge, child, to the Cranes in the Vintry,
And see there the gimblets how they make their entry.

Found in Southwark.

W.D. 1725.

W.D. 1778.

W.P.D. within a Garter. Ht. 8½ ins. c.1660-80. Long neck. Found in Bunhill Row, London.

Wm. Eddy Cornelly 1799. Squat cylinder.

THO. EDGAR. 1709.

WM. EDGCOMBE. 1793. Ht. 9¾ ins. Diam. 4½ ins. Edgcombes and Edgcumbes are well-known Cornish families who trace their descent from Sir Richard Edgcumbe or Edgcombe (d.1489), statesman. The Earl of Mount-Edgcumbe is one of his descendants, and the original owner of this bottle, presumably, another.

I. EDWARDS. 1729.

T. Edwards, Ninnis. Squat cylinder.

W. EDWARDS. A bottle with a long neck and almost parallel sides. c.1720. (J.M.B's Paper on Bottles and Bottle-Decanters [see Bibliography, Magazine Articles, J.M. Bacon].)

Anne Eilhering^{tn} 1708. Onion.

I. ELLIOTT Stonehouse 1794. Squat cylinder.

C. ELLIS. 1798. Ht. 11½ ins. This may have belonged to Charles Rose Ellis, 1st Lord Seaford, (1771-1845), who entered the House of Commons in 1793, and was created a peer in 1826. In 1798 (the date on the bottle) he married Elizabeth, only daughter and heiress of John, Lord Hervey, and at about the same time he bought the estate of Claremont in Surrey. (see D.N.B.)

H. Ellis 1780. Squat cylinder.

R.D. ELLIS. 1755.

EMAN. COLL. Emmanuel College, Cambridge.

EMMAN. COLL. Emmanuel College, Cambridge. Found in 21 Silver Street, Cambridge. Seal only.
These appear to be the only seals known from a Cambridge College.

R. Erisey 93. Seal only.

R. Erisey. Seal only.

R. Erisey 1718. Onion.

ETTY. Last quarter of eighteenth century. The Ettys appear as lessees or sub-lessees of vaults in St. Aldate's, Oxford: Mr. Etty in 1771 and 1781; Mrs. Etty in 1799; and Simon Etty, Brandy Merchant, in 1802. Seal only.

'Etty'.

'L/Evans/Pant/y candy/1781'.

L. Evans Pant y candy 1781. True cylinder.

Ino. Eveleigh 1736. Seal only.

J.B. EWELL. POUGHILL. 1835. Poughill (pronounced Puffill) is in Cornwall, near Bude.

T. EWIN. CAMBRIDGE. 1722. Found near Soham, Cambs. ⎫

THO. EWIN. 1736. Bought in London. ⎬

THO. EWIN. CAMBRIDGE. 1752. Found in Silver Street, ⎭
Cambridge. Seal only.
   This must have been Thomas Ewin, at first a grocer and later a brewer in partnership with Sparks of St. Sepulchre's, Cambridge. He married the daughter of a Cambridge coal-merchant named Howell and they had a

son, William Howell Ewin, who was born c. 1731 and who was educated at St. John's College, Cambridge. For the son's inglorious career see D.N.B. William Cole writes of him: "Dr. Ewin, by being much of his father's turn, busy and meddling in other people's concerns, got the ill-will of most persons in the town and university...Dr. Ewin, as did his father, squinted very much."

M.C.R. COLL. EXON. 1744. Common Room, Exeter College, Oxford. Exeter College was founded in 1314 by William de Stapledon, Bishop of Exeter, and linked with a west-country school from which all its scholars were to be drawn. The M may stand for Masters (of Arts).

B.I.E. Seal only.

C.E. 1734. Octagonal.

I.E. 1752.

J.E. see Sir John Egerton [Appendix I].

J.M.E. 1833. Nailsea bottle.

P.W.E. and a cross with illegible lettering. Seal only.

R.E. 1762.

T.S.E. IJ. 1726. and a star with seven rays. (Sir John Fagge wrote upon a card attached to it as follows: "This bottle contained the beer which was brewed in 1798 and was drank when I came of age. Mr. George Homersham received it from his mother and gave it to me on Friday, May 2, 1858. John Fagge".) This Sir John Fagge, 7th Baronet, was born in 1798 and died in 1873 unmarried. He was his father's eldest son and heir, and it is interesting to note that beer was laid down the year of his birth (as was also frequently done with wine) to be drunk in twenty-one years' time. The baronetcy dates back to 1660. This was probably a tavern-bottle, the initials being those of the licensees, and the IJ possibly indicating the second month of the year, but this is only surmise.

W.E. (the letters conjoined) 1650. Seal only.

I. Feathers 1789. Cylinder.

J. Fenn 1725. Onion.

W.F. Walker Ferrand, St. Ives, Bingley, Yorks. A leading land-owning family in the parishes of Bingley and Bradford. The bottle came from the cellars of St. Ives.

In FETER LANE. see W.H.

I.W. Fillgate, Lisrenny, around a sheaf of corn; c.1780.

ABY. FILMOR. 1716. Ht. 5¼ ins.

ROBT. FINDLAY. 1755. This bottle was owned (in 1908) by Robert Findlay of Easterhill, great-great-grandson of Robert Findlay, D.D. (1721-1815). He was appointed Professor of Divinity in Glasgow University in 1783, which appointment he held until he died at the age of ninety-three.

A fish with some illegible lettering above. *c.*1670. This was probably a tavern-bottle. It has been ascribed to Glasgow because of the fish (salmon) in the Glasgow coat-of-arms, but it more probably comes from a tavern such as The Pike or The Trout, both of which names are to be found in the vicinity of Oxford.

SAMLL. FISHER. 1712. Ht. 5¾ ins. Sold at Sotheby's, June, 1930.

W. FISHER. 1795.

William Flamary 1719. Onion.

THE OLD FLEECE TAVERN and a Fleece. There was a Fleece Tavern in Cornhill, London, and another in Covent Garden. The latter was frequented by Pepys. On one occasion he went there with Captain Cuttle and two other gentlemen to drink, and there they remained till four o'clock "telling stories of Algiers, and the manner of life of slaves there". Found in Coleman Street.

J. FLEMING. PLYMTREE. 1786. Plymtree is in Devonshire.

R.I.F. above a bear gradient to right. Ralph and Joan Flexney of the Bear Inn, Oxford, on the site of which it was discovered.

I. Fogg 1734. Bladder onion, magnum.

COL. JOHN FOLLIAT [sic]. 1743. From Devonshire.

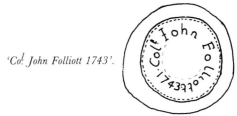

'Col John Folliott 1743'.

Foote-Harwood 1731. Octagonal.

ION FORREST. LAUNCESTON. Launceston is an ancient town in Cornwall, which possessed a mint before the Norman Conquest.

G. FORSTER. Ht. 14ins. c.1740-60. This may have been George Forster (d.1792), traveller and writer, who undertook and in 1782 safely accomplished the "remarkable feat of travelling from Calcutta overland into Russia" (see D.N.B.). But there were many Forsters in the west country and it is not easy to identify this particular one. Found in Trinity Street, Dorchester.

A.H. FORTROS. Fortrose is on the Black Isle opposite Inverness. Seal only.

'A.H./Fortros/1751'.

J.F. 1800. There was a John Fothergill at the Battle of Corunna, of whom there are relics in the Castle Museum, York. This bottle probably belonged to his father, Major Fothergill. It was acquired at the sale at Kingthorpe House, near Pickering, Yorks., which belonged to the Fothergill family.

Robt. Fox. Falmo.; c.1810. Squat cylinder.

Fox 1793. Cylinder.

Fox & Sons; c.1800. Cylinder.

T. Fox 1776. Cylinder.

I. (F)RAMTON. 1703. The Framptons (sic) are a well-known Dorset family. Found at Tyneham House, Purbeck.

I.M.F. and king's bust in profile to right. Ht. 5¼ins. John and Margaret Freeman, licensees King's Head Tavern, Oxford, 1704-1724 (death of John). He was Richard's Walker's (q.v.) nephew and heir. "No license in his name appears in the city records before that of 1711". (see E.T. Leeds.)

I.M.F. 1713 and king's head as above.

C.V., R.W. FROME. Frome is a market town in Somerset and contains the grave of Bishop Ken, the writer of many well-known hymns. A bottle with this seal on it was presented to the Dorset County Museum by

W.H. Bond according to the *Dorset Field Club Proceedings,* 1920, p.7.

Abraham Frost 1701. Onion.

F. Fry; Dear Park 1736. Mallet.

'F Fry/Dear Park/1736'.

JNO. FURSE. 1823. From Uffculme, Devon.

ISC. FUSSELL. Ht. 8⅝ ins.

F (reversed). Found in the Thames. Seal only. (*Dorset Field Club Proceedings,* Vol. II, 1878, p.59.)

E.F. 1702. Onion.

F.D.F. 1705. Onion.

I.F.

I.F. 1811. Squat cylinder.

I.M.F. and king's head.

I.M.F. 1713 and king's head. } see John and Margaret Freeman.

J.F. 1743. and stag's head.

J.F. 1800. } see John Fothergill [Appendix I].

J.F. 1819. Decanter.

L.A.F. and a crude female half-figure, with balloon sleeves and wasp-waist. This was probably a tavern bottle with the initials of the licensees or owners.

L.F. 1740. Octagonal.

R.I.F. see Ralph and Joan Flexney.

R.F. 1809.

S.F. 1704. Onion.

T.F. 1793. Magnum cylinder.

'T F/1793'.

T.F. Ht. 12¼ ins. A large bottle which was found buried in the sand of a beach in the Channel Islands.

J. Gaisford. Seal only.

MOUNT GALPIN. see HOLDSWORTH.

HENRY GALSHELL. 1700. Sold at Trapnell Sale, Sotheby's, 1910, (see Wilmer's *Early English Glass.*)

I. GALTON. TAUNTON. 1715. Taunton, the county town of Somerset, possesses an ancient castle, which now houses a museum with, among many other things, a fine collection of bottles.

GARDINER. CHESTERFORD. ESSEX. Large cordial bottle c.1700. Perhaps Richard Gardiner (1723-1781), author, born at Saffron Walden, Essex, and satirised by himself as Dick Merryfellow of Serious and Facetious Memory.

I.D.G. 1711. DU MILIEU DES ROUVETS. This belonged to John de Garis du Milieu des Rouvets, of which family there are many descendants. In shape and size the bottle is much like the Alles one, also from Guernsey.

GARN. c.1735. Farmers and brewers called Garne have lived for generations in the Cotswolds.

John Garneys 1724. Onion.

GARTHORNE, 1851. Ht. 12½ ins. Sold at Sotheby's, June, 1930.

Gartmore 1802. Double magnum.

'GARTMORE 1802'.

R. Gaskell. 1761.

Edouard Gaston. 1700. Ht. 5ins. From F.A. Crisp Collection. Sold at Sotheby's, June 18, 1943.

General Hospital Bristol; c.1850. Three-part mould.

R. George. Bristol. Found at a depth of ten feet on the foundations of a tobacco warehouse in Cumberland Road, Bristol. Seal only.

Thomas Gerrard Gibbstown; c.1875. Moulded.

Rawley Gilbert. 1722. Sir Humphrey Gilbert (1539?-1583) of Compton, near Dartmouth, was half-brother to Sir Walter Raleigh by his mother's second marriage, and, presumably, brought the name of Raleigh into the family. A few details about the Gilberts may be of interest.
1. Raleigh Gilbert of Compton (d.1634) was the founder of Plymouth College, Sagadahoc River, Maine, in 1606. He is said by Burke to have been granted arms by Camden (Clarenceux in 1620): Ermine on a chevron sa., three roses ar. Crest: a squirrel sejant gu. But there was a different coat already.
2. Raleigh Gilbert of Compton (d.1647), son and successor of No.1.
3. Raleigh Gilbert of Stoke Gabriel, great-nephew of No.1 (b.1688, d. unmarried 1773). The last-named might have been the owner of this bottle.
    The Gilbert estate, according to Burke, was sold about 1775, but some of the land has been bought back by a member of the Gilbert family. Compton Castle is an interesting early fifteenth-century building, and is said to have been well restored without detracting from its ancient charm.

Christor Gill. 1686. From the late Mrs. Radford's Collection. Sold at Sotheby's 3rd November, 1943.

James Gill. 1836.

'Ja:̱ Gill./1836'.

Thomas Glynn, Owner; c.1720. Bladder onion.

T. Godden. 1777. Ht. 10½ins.

T.G. 1801. T. Godsell.

JOHN GOLBY. FYNONE. 1822.

S. GOMOND. 1788.

H. GOOCH; c.1790. Cylinder.

A goose. Ht. 9½ ins. 1650-60. Long-necked bottle sealed with a goose. This is almost certainly a tavern-bottle. There was a Goose and Gridiron Tavern in St. Paul's Churchyard. A favourite musical society gave concerts there, and the sign was put up of a swan surmounted by a lyre. This was christened as above by the town-wits, but whether it had any connection with the bottle sealed with a goose, I cannot say. It was found in Kingsway, which is not very far from St. Paul's. There was a Paddy's Goose Tavern in Ratcliff Highway (now St. George's Street) in the East End.

Cross potonée and goose. From its shape this bottle would appear to date from about 1655, but it has not a very long neck so perhaps it is later. see Birds [Appendix I].

WILM. GORDON. 1743. Seal only.

Henry Gorton, Penrice 1717. Onion.

I. GOULD. 1741.

MAJOR GRANT. 1769. An Irish bottle, which belonged to Major Jasper Grant, of Kilmurry, Fermoy, Co. Cork. a beautiful place on the Blackwater river, and now a Roman Catholic College. He was in the 49th Regiment, and A.D.C. to General Eliott, 1st Lord Heathfield (1717-1790), Commander-in-Chief at the Siege and Relief of Gibraltar. The present owner is Major Grant's great-granddaughter who brought the bottle to England on her marriage.

THOMAS GREAT. COLCHESTER. These words are written round the edge of the seal and there are two twisted posts in the centre. This was the sign

'THOMAS GREAT COLCHESTER' and two twisted posts.

of the owner's tavern in High Street, Colchester, Essex — The Two Twisted Posts, and he, no doubt, was the "Mr. Great of Colchester" who had the honour of presenting Princess Charlotte of Mecklenberg with a "box of candied enrigo root, a product of Colchester" when she arrived in England in 1761 for her marriage to George III. She landed at Harwich and stopped to have tea at Colchester. Enrigo is described as a medicinal sweetmeat with aphrodisiac properties. The bottle is short, and was found upright in the ground, corked, and containing an evil-smelling liquid that was presumably once wine.

GREGORIE of PILSTON.

P. Gregory, Biddeford 1771. Squat cylinder.

A greyhound. see N.A.

John Griffiths of the Mary, Cardigan. Moulded cylinder.

I. Grigby 1792. Cylinder.

S.M. Grimes 1721. Onion.

R. Grose. St Kew. Seal only.

T. Grose, St Kew 1814. Squat cylinder.

T. Grose, St Kew 1820. Seal only.

J. Groves 1828. Cylinder.

GUINNESS & CO., BEST DUBLIN PORTER. SMITH & WEAVER, Sole Agents, BRISTOL; c.1850. Seal only.

GUNTER. LONDON. c.1780. Wide-mouthed. Probably used for bottling cherries or some other fruit. Rare. Brown bottle-glass.

CHAS. GUY. 1774.

CHAS. GUY. 1785.

M. Guy, St Endellion 1816. Cylinder.

D.F.G. 1775. Cylinder.

The Revd. E.G. St Erth. Seal only.

F.G. 1706.

G.G. 1790. Cylinder.

G.G.G. and a pair of crossed keys with heart-shaped ends. This was probably a tavern-bottle (a public-house called The Cross Keys exists to this day in Reading and other places), and the initials those of the licensees. Unfortunately the neck is broken off, but from the shape of the body, it appears to be one of the long-necked and early seventeenth century bottles. It was found in Holborn.

H.G. and the head of a sea horse. Seal only.

H.G. 1854. Ht. 11¾ ins. Sold at Sotheby's, June, 1930.

I.G. 1692. Engraved with two oak trees. Not a seal, but initials and foliage pricked. Reputed to have been dug up at Boscobel. (*Country Life,* May 11, 1933.)

I.G. 1729. Bladder onion.

'I G/1729'.

M.G. 1734.

P.G. OLD BRISTOL PORTER.

R.G. 1777. This bottle was found on a farm in the Glanvilles Wootton district; it is possible that it belonged to Robert Gooden of Over Compton, Bradford Abbas, Dorset. Seal only. (*Dorset Field Club Proceedings,* Vol. II, 1878, p.59)

R.O.G. Ht. 10½ ins. Nineteenth-century bottle.

T.G.

T.G. 1798.

T.G. 1801. see T. Godsell.

W.G. 1801. Ht. 10ins.

W.C.G. Zeals; c.1760. Cylinder.

H and an earl's coronet. c.1714. The only three extant earldoms beginning with the letter H, that existed at this date are those of Haddington, Home and Huntingdon, of which the latter is the most likely. But a far more probable owner of this bottle, which survives in the famous house of Knole, is Charles Montagu, 1st and last Earl of Halifax of the first creation (1661-1715). He was the son of Sir Henry Montagu, 1st Earl of Manchester, and was educated at Westminster School and

Trinity College, Cambridge. He was a lifelong friend of Sir Isaac Newton, and his verses on the death of Charles II attracted the notice of Charles Sackville, 6th Earl of Dorset, who introduced him to William III. In 1706 he went on a special mission to the Elector of Hanover, and was accompanied by Lionel Sackville, 7th Earl of Dorset, and later 1st Duke of Dorset (q.v. [Appendix I]) who, as a youth of eighteen, had just succeeded his father in the earldoms of Dorset and Middlesex. Montagu went into Parliament and displayed great ability as a debater. He was appointed Lord of the Treasury in 1692 and Chancellor of the Exchequer in 1694, and he helped to establish the Bank of England. He was created a baron in 1700, but he had many enemies and fortune began to desert him. He did not hold any office in Queen Anne's reign, although in 1706 he was one of the commissioners for negotiating the union with Scotland. On the death of Anne he acted as one of the Justices until the arrival of George I. In 1714 he was made first Lord of the Treasury and invested with the Order of the Garter and raised to the earldom of Halifax. As he died in 1715, and as the seal has an earl's coronet on it, this fixes the date of the bottle to within a year, 1714-15, assuming it to have been Lord Halifax's. He was a great patron of literature, though Swift declared that the only help he ever gave to literary men was "good words and good dinners". Sarah, Duchess of Marlborough commenting on his economical nature, said "he was so great a manager" that when he dined alone "he eat upon pewter for fear of lessening the value of his plate by cleaning it often". (see D.N.B.)

'H' under an earl's coronet.

J.H. Haddon 1770. Cylinder.

JNO HAINE. CHANKTON. 1721. Ht. 6½ ins. Large bottle with crack in it; broad base; short neck.

A.H. above a mermaid; on right a ship. This is one of the Oxford tavern-bottles. Anthony Hall senior c.1660-1675. The Mermaid Tavern, Oxford. Mayor, 1673. He issued a trade-token: O. ANTHONY HALL AT THE and a mermaid. R. IN OXON. VINTNER. A.A.H. Anthony Hall senior 'at the Meermaid' stood as godfather to Anthony Wood's nephew, Christopher, 1666. In October, 1691, Wood notes the death of "Anthony Hall of the Meremaid" at the age of "35 or therabouts". This was his son. (see A. Clark's *Wood's Life and Times.*) Tablet in Kirklington Church. Sealed bottle and seal only.

A.H. 16(6)7 and mermaid. Ditto. Found at Alverscot, Oxon. Seal only.

A.H. on right; mermaid to left. These bottles probably all belonged to Anthony Hall senior. Two bottles.

A.H. 1682 and mermaid whose tail faces left. Anthony Hall junior (1675-1691). Buried in St. Martin's Church.

ANTHONY HALL IN OXFORD 1685. (The last number is doubtful and it may be 1686.) (see E.T. Leeds.) Mermaid centre; tail to right. Ditto.

'Anthony Hall in Oxford 1685'.

JAMES HALL. Seventeenth-century bottle.

H. Hambly 1768. Seal only.

P. Hambly, Lean, Liskd. 1781. Squat cylinder.

HAMILTON APLIN & CO. 26 Bucklersbury; late nineteenth century. Three-part mould.

R. HAMLEY. 1750. Ht. 9ins. and ditto 8ins. According to tradition these bottles were made in Nottingham, which is possible as glass was made there in the seventeenth and eighteenth centuries.

EDMUND HAMMOND. 1753. Possibly a relation of George Hammond (1763-1853), "first British Minister accredited to the United States", 1791, whose son was Edmund Hammond, Lord Hammond (1802-1890).

Open hand and scarf between two branches. Ht. 10¾ins. *c.*1660-70. Probably a tavern bottle, but I cannot find any tavern with that name. There is, however, a Hand and Shears Tavern, which stands at the corner of Middle Street and Cloth Fair, and which had a connection with Bartholomew Fair. The Fair became so riotous that it was suppressed in 1855. Partly broken. Found in London.

H. HARPER and a King's Head. Ht. 7ins. Long-necked. *c.*1680-1700. Probably from one of the King's Head Taverns. To identify a King's

Head Tavern is not easy — they were so numerous — but in this case the name of the owner H. Harper should be a help. There are several allusions in Pepys to Tom Harper and one to Mrs. Harper; they evidently kept an eating house of some kind, and it may have been situated in Westminster. Jan. 6, 1660, "This morning Mr. Shepley and I did eat our breakfast at Mrs. Harper's (my brother John being with me), upon a cold turkey-pie and a goose." Feb. 31. 1660. "After dinner to Westminster Hall...called in at Harper's with Mr. Pulford..." As the bottle is considered to be 1680-1700 it could not have come from Tom Harper's tavern, but H. Harper might well have been a son or other relation who carried on the business.

There was a noted King's Head in Fenchurch Street, where Princess Elizabeth (afterwards "Good Queen Bess") ate a dinner of boiled pork and pease pudding after visiting a nearby church to give thanks for her deliverance from the Tower of London in 1554. Another tavern of this name stood at the west corner of Chancery Lane, and another in Cannon Alley near St. Paul's Churchyard. There is a King's Head in the Borough High Street, Southwark, and there are many more. Found in Westminster.

W. HARRIS. PENRHYN. 1734. Penrhyn has the largest slate-quarries in Wales. This bottle was exhibited at the Vintners' Hall, 1933, and is illustrated in the catalogue.

G. HARRISON. CHESTER. 1803. An ancient cathedral city and the capital of the county of Cheshire.

W. HARVEY. COCKTHORP. 1800.

HASELWOOD.

Hatcher Careby and letters T H joined; c.1685. Onion.

 'Hatcher Careby'.

JACOB HATT. 1727 with a bird on a bough. Possibly a tavern-bottle.

N. Hawke, St Cleer 1793. Cylinder.

I.N. Hawker; c.1770-80. Cylinder.

R. HAWKER. 1714.

REV. R.S. HAWKER. MORWENSTOW. Robert Stephen Hawker (1803-1875). B.A., 1828. Magdalen Hall, Oxon. M.A., 1836. Vicar of Morwenstow, Cornwall. 1834-1875. He was a poet and antiquary, and also well known for his goodness to those mariners who escaped shipwreck on the rocky coast of Cornwall. A school established by him was largely maintained by his contributions. He instituted a weekly offertory in church, which he advocated in a letter to *The Times,* and he also initiated Harvest Festival services. (see D.N.B.)

R. HAWLEY. 1750. Was this perhaps a misreading of R. HAMLEY. 1750? (q.v.)

CASTLE HAWORD (sic). 1753. Ht. 8½ ins. Castle Howard, Yorks. belonged to the Earls of Carlisle. Henry Howard, 4th Earl of Carlisle, K.G., (1694-1758) would have been the owner at this date. He succeeded his father in 1738, having previously been M.P. for Morpeth (1722, 1727 and 1734-38). He married Isabella, daughter of William, 4th Lord Byron.

M. HAYES. ESQ. 1811.

WILLIAM HAYNE. 1742.

A. HEATHFIELD. 1778. From the late Col. Ratcliff's Collection. Sold at Christie's 3 June, 1943, to Messrs. W.M. & P. Manheim, and has since gone to the United States.

T. HEDLEY. DARLN. 1780. Ht. 12½ ins. Capacity 2 bottles. Exhibited at Vintners' Hall, 1933. Darlington is a town in S. Durham.

LORD HENNIKER. 1810. Ht. 10¼ ins. John, 2nd Baron Henniker (Irish peerage) (1752-1821). Called to the bar 1777 as a member of Lincoln's Inn. Succeeded his father (the son of a Russian merchant) in 1803. M.P. 1805-1818. (see D.N.B.) Sold at Sotheby's, June, 1930.

E. HERBERT. 1721. Traditionally ascribed to Edmond Herbert, Keeper of the Royal Forest at Whittlebury, Northants. Two of these bottles found their way to Mr. H.G. Pierce in British Columbia. (see *Illustrated London News,* Dec. 3, 1932).

SAMUEL HIGGS. FOWEY. 1784. Fowey at the mouth of the Fowey River is a port and yachting resort in Cornwall. Sold at Sotheby's, June, 1930.

CAPT. HILL. 1753. Ht. 9ins. Letters gilded in a gilt frame. On the opposite side of the word GIN.

R. HILL. WYKE FARM. 1781. Ht. 10ins. This might be Sir Richard Hill, Bart (1732-1808). He was returned to Parliament in 1780 to represent

Shropshire. His maiden speech was made on May 19, 1781 (the date on the bottle), and he succeeded to the baronetcy and estates of his father in 1783.

Thos. Hill, Henfield 1723. Seal only.

'*Tho§ Hill/Hen-field/1723*'.

M. HINTON. 1711. Perhaps a relation to Sir John Hinton, M.D. (1603?-1682) physician to Queen Henrietta-Maria, and, after the Restoration, to Charles II and his queen. (see D.N.B.)

HOCK. 1648. An early hock bottle, probably foreign. c.1750. The date refers to the original vintage. The custom in the Rhine valleys was to fill very large casks with wine of a good vintage; these were replenished as and when required with wine of later good vintages, but in the seventeenth and eighteenth centuries they were always classified as belonging to the original vintage. 1648 was one of the great years, and wine would be bottled and sold as 1648 wine more than a hundred years later, although the purchaser knew quite well that there was but a very small fraction of the original wine in his bottle. (see my letter in *The Times*, September 19, 1945.)

R. Hodge; c.1735. Mallet.

T. Hodge, Callestock; c.1780. Squat cylinder.

Wm. Hodge 1800 Lambourn. Squat cylinder.

HOFFMANN.

I.C. Hoffman; c.1800. Cylinder half-bottle.

JOS. HOLDEN & F. LONDON BRIDG. and a Ship. Found in Sumner Street, London. Only a fragment.

ARTH. HOLDSWORTH. DARTM. 1713. Arthur Holdsworth, merchant-adventurer, married Elizabeth Lane, widow of Captain Roger Vavasour. In a Report of the Council of Trade and Plantations dated 1701 he is described as Admiral of St. John's Harbour, Newfoundland, and Commander of the ship *Nicholas* of Dartmouth.

E. HOLDSWORTH. c.1720.

H. HOLDSWORTH. 1807.

HENRY HOLDSWORTH. 1808.

H.J.H. Henry Joseph Holdsworth.

R.H. 1765. Ht. 9½ ins. Robert Holdsworth of Modbury, Devon. Brother of Elizabeth who married Robert Newman as his second wife in 1715. The Holdsworths, a Devonshire family, intermarried with the Newmans for five generations, and were associated with them as merchant-mariners of Dartmouth. The last Governor of Dartmouth was a Holdsworth. The Holdsworths owned Widdicombe House, near Kingsbridge, Devon, a Queen Anne House which has only recently been sold. They also owned a beautiful punch-bowl (made by Paul Lamerie in 1723) which remained in the possession of the Holdsworths of Widdicombe until 1921. It is now at the Ashmolean Museum, Oxford. On one side are depicted eleven of the Adventurers in the Newfoundland Fishery Trade in procession along a quay, and on the other side having dinner. Above is the inscription 'Prosperity to Hooks and Lines'. Two at least of the bottle-owning Holdsworths may have been of this company. This bowl is illustrated in *Country Life,* October 31, 1947, and many interesting particulars are given of the Holdsworth family. (see also Hunt and Newman.)

R. HOLDSWORTH. 1820.

ROBT. HOLDSWORTH. Probably the Rev. Robert Holdsworth, vicar of Brixham, Devon.

Thos. Holdsworth Dartmo; c.1725. Bladder onion.

THOS. HOLDSWORTH. DARTMO. 1755. Ht. 10½ ins.

MOUNT GALPIN. The Holdsworth residence in Dartmouth, Devon.

T. Hole and a hand grasping an axe; c.1840. Moulded.

Thos. Hole 1823. Magnum cylinder.

I.R. Holl St. Neott 1774. Cylinder.

S. Holloway 1725. Late onion-early mallet form.

'*S. Holloway/1725*'.

John Holme 1721. Magnum onion.

'John/Holme/1721'.

H. HOOTON. 1694. Found in Sturminster Newton, Dorset.

Tho. Hopkins Colchester. Seal only.

'THO:/HOPKINS/COLCHES/TER'.

J. Horner Helston 1758. Bladder onion.

R. How at Chedworth 1683. Onion.

'R: How/at/Chedworth/1683'.

S. How. 1705.

HUBARD. Olive-green glass. Fragment only.

'HUBARD'.

Robert Hughes for the owner 1733 and a unicorn's head pierced by an arrow. Mallet.

Saml. HUGHES. BRECON. 1771. Found in Quarrel's Gardens, Sion Street, Brecon.

T.H. HUNT. 1808. Thomas Holdsworth Hunt (1762-?) married Harriet Newman (b. at Oporto 1775) in 1802. She was daughter of Thomas and granddaughter of Robert Newman (q.v.) T.H. Hunt was also related to the Holdsworths (q.v.) and the present firm of Messrs. Hunt and Roope has been built up over a period of three hundred years by the Newmans, Holdsworths and Hunts, all Devonshire families (and, incidentally, all three represented by sealed bottles). Their head office was at Dartmouth until 1820. The Newmans are the only family now left in the firm.

HUBT. HUSEY. 1727.

H beneath a viscount's coronet; mid-eighteenth century. Cylinder.

A.H. FORTROS. 1751. see Fortros.

B.H.

C.H. 1747 within a triangle. Seal only.

C.H.H. SILLATON. 1789. Ht. 9½ ins. Bought at Bideford, Devon.

E.H.

E.H. and a Bell. c.1660. In a footnote to Wood's *City of Oxford* Clarke records of one John Haynes, "that he was a baker, lived at the Bell, Magdalen Street, Oxford..." E.H. may be the Edward Haynes of a Poll Tax List of 1667 who is then at the Globe Inn, located near No. 20 Cornmarket Street. R.T. (q.v.) might well be his successor at the Bell. (see E.T. Leeds.) Seals only. One of them was found in Mitchell Lane, Bristol.

G.H. 1733.

H.J.H. see Holdsworth.

I.H. 1730.

I.H. 1764. Cylinder.

I.H. with a bridge. Seal only.

I.H. and a flower head. Seal only.

I.H. and a Turk's head beneath an arched collonade; c.1680.

'I H' and a Turk's head.

I.H. 1713. PAX. Evidently made to celebrate the Treaty of Utrecht which was signed in 1713. "That Treaty, which ushered in the stable and characteristic period of eighteenth-century civilisation, marked the end of danger to Europe from the old French monarchy, and marked a change of no less significance to the world at large, the maritime, commercial and financial supremacy of Great Britain...The Treaty of Utrecht remains the one great act of statesmanship of St. John, Lord Bolingbroke..." (G.M. Trevelyan). The bottle was exhibited at Vintners' Hall in 1933, and is illustrated in the catalogue.

I.M.H. and a king's head. Seal only.

I.M.H., the letters in pyramidal style; c.1695. Onion.

I.M.H. 1707. H is written over and between the other initials, as on the tavern-bottles at the Ashmolean. It may well have belonged to a tavern, and the initials would be those of the proprietor (or lessee) and his wife.

J.H.; c.1840-50. Three-part mould.

P.H. and a sun, crest a pegasus courant. Seal only.

P.H. Ht. 8¼ins. Long neck. Found in London.

R.H. in a monogram. Seal only.

R.H. 1688 and a globe. Onion.

R.H. 1730. Seal only.

R.H. 1733. Bladder onion.

R.H. 1765. see Holdsworth.

T.H. Seventeenth century.

T.H.; c.1720. Bladder onion.

W.H. flanking a crude figure holding a beer-mug. Probably a tavern-bottle. Found in Sheepen Road, Colchester.

W.H. IN FETER LANE WHIT and a cross. Ht. 8½ins. This was obviously a White Cross Tavern in Fetter Lane, London, with the licensees' initials on the seal. It is a very good example of the early shape with the long neck and the small base, but a fragment of the seal is worn away.

W.P.H. and the royal arms. Ht. 7¼ins. Sold at Sotheby's, June 18, 1943.

D. IAPIE. 1728. Ht. 7ins. Flat-shaped bottle. From Sir John Risley Collection.

I. and an earl's coronet. Moulded bottle c.1820. Name of maker, H. Ricketts & Co., Glassworks, Bristol, on base. This might have belonged to Henry Stephen, 3rd Earl of Ilchester (1787-1858), who succeeded his father in 1802. He was Capt. Yeomen of the Guard, D.C.L.

INFIRMARY. BRISTOL. Bristol Royal Infirmary in Marlborough Street, Bristol, one of the largest hospitals in the kingdom, was instituted in 1735. Found in Newfoundland Road, Bristol, 1907. Seal only.

R.S. & COY. INVERUGIE. Found in Banffshire.

'R:S/& COY/ INVERUGIE'.

B.W.I. Seal only.

I.I. (separate matrices). Seal only.

I.I. 1693 and two mullets. Ht. 6½ ins. Exhibited at Vintners' Hall, 1933, and illustrated in catalogue. Probably a tavern-bottle. From the Francis Berry Collection.

'I I/1693'.

I.I. 1704. Squat bottle. Found in Fetter Lane, London.

M.I. 1756. Seal only.

W.I. This is an early bottle of crude thick glass, a longish neck and a small base.

W.E.I. 1749.

Jno. Jackson 1751. Octagonal.

ST. P. JACKTON. 1726. Seal only.

JOHN JAMES. 1769. Was this John James, D.D. (1729-1785) who became head-master of St Bees' School, Reading, where he remained until 1771?

WM. JANS. 1732. Ht. 8ins. Sold at Sotheby's, June, 1930.

'*G Ieffery/Vicar of/Linkh⁰/1756*'.

G. Jeffery, Vicar of Linkinh⁰, 1756.

ROBT. JEFFERY. HUNTSHILL. 1777. Ht. 9¼ ins.

W. Jeffery, St Enoder; c.1830. Cylinder moulded.

Ben. Jennings, 1728. Mallet.

I.C., C.R. Ht. 12ins. Jesus College, Common Room, Oxford. Jesus College was founded in 1571 by a Welshman, Hugh Price, "chiefly for the education of his own countrymen", and it was the first college to be founded in Oxford after the Reformation. Price was the son of a butcher who made his fortune and gave his children a good education. (see *Oxford* by Arthur Mee.)

ST. I., C.R., OXON. St. John's Common Room, Oxford. Seal only.

ST. JOHN'S COLLEGE. Seal only. The original building was begun in 1437 by Archbishop Cichele. But this was destroyed in the time of Henry VIII and a new benefactor came forward in the person of Sir Thomas White, a clothier's son from Reading. The Quadrangle was completed by Archbishop Laud who had been educated here. Other of its graduates are Archbishop Juxon, Sir William Paddy, physician to James I, and Bishop Peter Mews (q.v.).

THOMAS JOLLY. 1724. Ht. 7¼ ins. Sold at Sotheby's, June, 1930. .

Jonas B 1744. Early cylinder.

BEAL JONES. 1737. Octagonal bottle.

Evan Jones, Llanellyd 1743. Mallet.

John Jones, Colebrook; c.1705. Onion.

R. JONES ESQR. FONMON CASTLE. Late eighteenth century. Robert Jones (1733-1793) lived at Fonmon Castle, Glamorgan, where a portrait of him by Sir Joshua Reynolds still exists.

T.H. JONES ESQ. NEWADD. 1826.

JOHN JOUNES. 1726. Found at the old Glass Factory at Wisborough Green, Sussex. The well-wooded regions of Sussex had long been inhabited by glass-makers, first from Normandy and later on by the Huguenot emigrants from Lorraine. (see *Glass* by W.B. Honey.)

JOHN JOYCE. 1719. Sold at Sotheby's, June, 1930.

John Joyce 1719. Onion.

JUBILEE. 1887. To commemorate Queen Victoria's Jubilee a certain brand of port was bottled in 1887 in bottles bearing this seal.

JUSC; c.1800. Cylinder quarter-bottle.

F.B.J. 1803.

A. Kelly; c.1780. Cylinder.

KELSALL. 1713. Kelsall is about eight miles from Chester. There is also a village in Suffolk, near Saxmundham, with the name Kelsale.

Kempthorne, St. Ives; c.1830. Moulded cylinder.

K and a coronet. Lord Kensington. Found at Westmead, Carmarthenshire.

S. KENT. 1786.

T.A. KENT and a king's head. This is from the King's Head Tavern at the corner of Fleet Street and Chancery Lane. I am told that the date of Kent's tenancy is known, but so far I have been unable to discover what it was. On May 10, 1667, Pepys noted: ''At noon to Kent's, at the Three Tuns Tavern''. Was this the same Kent moved to another tavern? Seal only.

KENTRAUGH; mid- to late-ninteenth century. Three-part mould.

HART KEY. PAWTON. Maker's name on base: H. Ricketts & Co., Glassworks, Bristol, indicating a date not earlier than 1811.

WILLIAM KILLIWICK. 1711.

KILMARNOCK. 1713. Kilmarnock is a town in Aryshire.

Kinahan & Co. Dublin; c.1800. Cylinder.

Bust of crowned and bearded king standing on heraldic garland. Ht. 10½ ins. Probably from a King's Head Tavern.

1699 and king's bust in armour in profile to right. Ht. 6ins. Diam. 5ins. From the King's Head Tavern at Oxford. (see Richard Walker.)

1710 and king's bust in armour. Beaded frame. Good seal but neck of bottle missing. Another similar but bad stamp though neck intact. From a King's Head Tavern.

KINGDOM DEVONSHIRE CHAMPAGNE CIDER.

O. Kingdon 1796. Squat cylinder.

GEO. KIRK. IPSWICH. 1738.

Robert Kitching 1724. Bladder onion.

M. Knight 1739. Mallet.

I. Knill 1781. Cylinder.

JOHN KNOTTESFORD. 1736. There was a William Knottesford of London who made clocks c.1670-80. The Clockmakers' Company own one of his clocks. John Knottesford may have been a relation.

K. and a coronet. see Lord Kensington.

G.E.K. The K is above the other two letters and probably indicates a man and his wife, possibly tavern-keepers.

I.K. (separate matrices). Seal only.

S.K. 1739. Seal only.

S.K. 1775. Ht. 9ins. Sold at Sotheby's, June, 1930.

T.K. 1720.

T.K. 1729. Mallet.

V.H.K. enclosed in two sprays. Long neck. Found on site of the Red Lion, Rochester.

W.K. (separate matrices). Seal only.

LAFITTE VIN. 1864. Not a seal proper but the words moulded in the glass.

J. Lambert, Waghen, 1719. Bladder onion.

'J. Lambert/Waghen/1719'.

Martin Lanyon, Liskeard 1734. Seal only.

D. Lapie 1728. Bladder onion.

Frederic Latimer, Wine Merchant, Oxford; c.1850. Moulded cylinder.

MR. LABBÉ DE LAVILLETTE. 1714. It is thought that this bottle was bought in Paris, and may be a French one.

W. & M. LAW. 1756.

T. LAWRENCE. 1819. Perhaps the painter Sir Thomas Lawrence (1769-1830) who was much patronised by George III and George IV, and was created President of the Royal Academy in 1820. He was also a friend of William Locke of Norbury (q.v.).

W.L. CARDEN. Ht. 7½ins. William Leche of Old Carden or Cawarden Hall, Chester, c.1770. Name engraved not sealed. Carden Hall, a beautiful Elizabethan timbered house, was destroyed by fire in 1912. (Francis Buckley's *Old English Glass.*)

Leckie 1818. Cylinder.

W. LEMAN. CHARD. 1771. Ht. 8½ins.

W. LEMAN. CHARD. 1771. Ht. 9½ins.

W. LEMAN. CHARD. 1771. Ht. 11ins.

Underneath these bottles is the name of the makers: H. Ricketts & Co., Glass Works, Bristol. Bottle-collectors have always been puzzled by this seal because of the date, 1771. The bottle is moulded, not blown. Through the courtesy of Messrs. John Harvey & Son of Bristol I got into communication with Mr. Arthur Balley, a former manager of Ricketts' Works, and he consulted with one of the directors, and this is what he tells me: ''The fact that the bottom of the bottle is marked Ricketts shows that it must have been made at a later date than 1771, because Jacob Wilcox Ricketts and his son Henry and two others did not purchase what was at one time known as the 'Soap-boilers Glass-house' until 1811, and were not engaged in the manufacture of wine- or beer-bottles earlier. Besides it is believed that moulds were first used long after 1771, and until then there was no means of marking a name on the bottom of a bottle. It is generally believed that the date on such seals referred to the date when W. Leman founded his business. The firm of Ricketts amalgamated with that of Powell and Filer, whose premises adjoined, in 1853. For many years the works were carried on by Powell and Ricketts. In 1920 the business was turned into a limited company, and in 1923 was closed.''

There was a Sir John Leman (1544-1632) who became Lord Mayor of

London. The family were descended from John de la Mans, who fled to England from the Netherlands and died about 1485. Sir John owned the Manor of Brampton in Suffolk, and was succeeded in his Suffolk estates by a son of his elder brother, William Leman. (see D.N.B.) A barrel-shaped mug of Lambeth Delft marked JOHN LEMAN. 1654 is mentioned in Hodgkin's *Early English Pottery* and is now in the British Museum. W. Leman of Chard, Somerset, probably descended from one of this family.

Marger(y) Lethard 1721. Onion.

S. Lewis 1740. Octagonal.

A. LIDSTONE. 1728.

Richd. Lidstone, St Huish 1775. Squat cylinder.

'Rich*d*/Lidstone/St Huish/1775'.

LINC. COLL. C.R. Ht. 9ins. c.1770. Lincoln College, Common Room, Oxford.

LINC. COLL. C.R. Ht. 11½ ins. c.1770. Lincoln College, Common Rooms, Oxford.

LIN. COLL. and Antlers (the college crest). c.1760. Lincoln College, Oxford. It was founded in 1427 by Richard Fleming, Bishop of Lincoln. Its most famous scholar was John Wesley, and others were Sir William Davenant, Mark Pattison and John (afterwards Lord) Morley. (see *Oxford* by Arthur Mee.)

ROBT. LINDON. 1819.

LORD LISMORE. 1789. This was Cornelius O'Callaghan, M.P., Fethard, created Baron Lismore of Shanbally, Co. Tipperary, in the Peerage of Ireland (1742-1797). He married Frances, daughter of Right Hon. John Ponsonby, Speaker of the House of Commons in Ireland. Found at Middle Farm, Dorchester.

T. Littlefair 1796. Cylinder.

Thos. Lock. Seal only.

WILLM. LOCK. 1761. Probably William Lock or Locke (1732-1810) of

Norbury Park, art-amateur, and who claimed kinship with John Locke, the philosopher. Fanny Burney (Mme d'Arblay) was a great friend of his and his wife's, and they also befriended Mme de Stael and other French refugees (see D.N.B.). The bottle was sold at Christie's, June 3, 1943, to Messrs. W.M. & P. Manheim who sold it to someone in the U.S.A.

EDW. LOMBE. ESQUIRE. 1736. There was an Edward Lombe who was living at Weston, Norfolk, in 1688. He was High Sheriff of that county in 1700, and he was first cousin of Sir Thomas Lombe, Kt, Alderman of London who, with his brother John, was responsible for the organisation of silk-manufacture in England. He married a Miss Sporle and left by her three sons and two daughters. His will was dated 1703. One of his sons was Edward of Melton. He was High Sheriff of Norfolk in 1714 and he died without children in 1738. He was almost certainly the owner of this bottle. His collateral descendants still live in Norfolk. Captain Evans-Lombe, C.B., R.N., commanding H.M.S. Duke of York (1947) belongs to this family. The bottle was given to the Museum by Major Evans-Lombe of Marlingford Hall, Norwich.

LONDON and a five-pointed star. From Kingthorpe House, near Pickering, Yorks.

LONDON and a crown.

LONDON and a crown and a five-pointed star.

P.I.

Obtained from a sea-captain's grog-chest of six bottles variously marked.

Loop 1777. Cylinder.

L.P. Louis-Philippe (1773-1850), son of Philippe Egalité, and King of France 1830-1848.

CHARLES LOVE. 1709. Could he have been one of the five children left by Christopher Love (1618-1651), who was accused of plotting against the Commonwealth (the affair is known as Love's Plot) and of corresponding with Charles Stuart and his mother (Henrietta-Maria)? He was arrested, tried and exected in 1651. (see D.N.B.)

I. LOWTHER ESQ. UPLEATHAM. 1734. Ht. 8½ ins. This may be Sir James Lowther F.R.S., 4th Bart of Whitehaven (1684-1755). He succeeded his brother Sir Christopher Lowther in 1731. They were the sons of Sir John Lowther who in his marriage settlement appears as Sir John Lowther, Esq. This may explain the Esq. on James' bottle — if it was his. (see *Complete Peerage* by Doubleday and Howard de Walden.) According to Sir Egerton Brydges' edition of *Collins' Peerage,* it was Sir John who opened the mines at Whitehaven (another authority says it was his son James). He disinherited his eldest son Christopher, who died s.p. in 1731. James then "succeeded to the title as he had before to the paternal estate". He was Vice-Admiral of the County of Cumberland, for which place he was Knight of the shire, 1708; was some time member for Carlisle, and also for Appleby. He died unmarried in 1755, supposed to be worth two millions, and was buried at St. Bees in Cumberland.

Upleathem is a small village 2½ miles N.E. of Guisborough, Yorks., and in the vicinity are large iron-stone quarries. The house Upleatham is mentioned by Murray in his *Handbook to Yorkshire* in 1867 as belonging to the Earl of Zetland, and he draws attention to the good gardens, fine trees and agreeable surrounding country. But in the 1904 edition it says that owing to the subsidence caused by the iron workings the walls of the house gave way and it was now a ruin. This was the house built by Sir Robert Smirke who was born in 1781, so there must have been an older one that I. Lowther inhabited in 1734. According to Foster's *Peerage* of 1880, there was a "Sir Lawrence Dundas of Kerse, N.B. of Upleatham, Yorks. M.P." who died 1781. (His grandson became Earl of Zetland.) Sir Lawrence was created a Baronet in 1762. As he was Scottish, and both his father and his elder brother lived in and owned property in Scotland, I think we may assume that, having migrated south, he bought Upleatham — obviously after 1734 (the date on the bottle), and probably in 1755, the year when I. Lowther died.

JOHN LUKE. 1721. A magnum. Was he a son of Sir Samuel Luke (d.1670), parliamentarian, scout-master-general in Cromwell's forces and M.P. for Bedford Borough in both the Short and the Long Parliaments? Sir Samuel married Elizabeth Freeman in 1624, in which year also he was knighted, and he left three sons as well as several daughters. John is perhaps more likely to be a grandson, In the *Gentlemen's Magazine* for 1823 we read: "Samuel...was deformed and dwarfish, defects apparently compensated by superior qualifications of mind". He was reckoned a brave commander, and is supposed to be portrayed in Samuel Butler's *Hudibras*. The family became extinct in his grandson George, who is commemorated on the pavement of the parish church as 'The last Luke of Wood-end'.

LUPTON. Possibly William Lupton (1676-1726), divine, who appointed lecturer at St. Dunstans-in-the-West, London, 1706, and preacher at Lincoln's Inn and the Temple 1714. (D.N.B.) Or was it Thomas Goff Lupton (1791-1873), engraver, and son of a goldsmith? He gave Samuel Cousins his first lesson in engraving, and in 1825 he engraved six prints after Turner. Having neither seen the bottle nor had a description of it, I can give no opinion as to its date.

B.L. LYME. The Leghs of Lyme Park, Disley, near Stockport, are a well-known Cheshire family. William Legh, M.P., for South Lancasire, was created a peer (Lord Newton) in 1892. The seal on this bottle possibly belonged to one of the Legh family, but it is equally likely that it belonged to an inhabitant of Lyme Regis, Dorset, which town was always referred to as Lyme.

S. Lyne 1728. Onion.

'S/Lyne/1728'.

Henry Lyre 1760. Octagonal.

E.L. 1808. Found at Portchester in the upper reaches of Portsmouth Harbour. Seal only.

E.L. 1812.

E:L.; c.1840-50. Three-part mould.

I.L. 1712. Onion.

I:L. 1808. Seal only.

I.L. and a queen's head. This is certainly from a tavern-bottle and the initials are those of the licensee. It was found at Bristol. Seal only.

P.A.L. St Sauver, Guernsey, 1710. Onion.

R E L and a mermaid; c.1700. Onion.

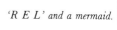

'R E L' and a mermaid.

R.L. 1741. Exhibited at Vintners' Hall in 1933, and illustrated in the catalogue.

T.L. 1686. Shaft and globe.

T.L. 1687.

W.L. CARDEN. see William Leche. The Leches like the Leghs were a Cheshire family.

DRY MADEIRA.

MAG. COLL. C.R. Ht. 8¾ ins. c.1790. Magdalen College, Common Room, Oxford. Magdalen College was founded in 1448 by William of Waynflete, Bishop of Winchester and Lord Chancellor of England. Magdalen Chapel is famous for its music, and it is on Magdalen Tower that the choristers sing on May Day.

I. MALLETT. 1786.

H. MALYEN. 1743.

Geo. Martyn St Teath 1771. Seal only.

Wm. Martyn Ruan; early nineteenth century. Moulded.

SAMUEL MASSE. WISBECH. 1727. Wisbech is in Cambridgeshire, and Samuel Massey was a doctor.

JOSEPH MASSEY. 1794. Massey is a well-known Cheshire name.

RD. MEADE. TAUNTON. 1807. Taunton is the county town of Somerset and the scene of Judge Jeffreys' Bloody Assize.

J. Mearden, Tavistock, 1780. Squat cylinder.

MEDOC. 1810. Probably a French bottle.

C. Menhinick. Seal only.

Merchant's mark: raised oval with triangle in centre; beaded edge to seal, possibly seventeenth century. This may not be a true merchant's mark, but is difficult to categorise. Several seals, but no complete bottles.

Merchant's mark: a pair of 4s above, and a pair below inverted, the whole intertwined. Seal only.

MERMAID TAVERN. see Thomas Wood and F.W.W.

ROBERT METHWEN. 1715. Ht. 6½ ins. A pair of bottles with this seal on them was dug up near Bridgwater. The present Lord Methuen has been applied to, but is unable to identify this Robert. He suggests that he may belong to the Bradford-on-Avon branch of Methuens; perhaps he was one of the rich cloth merchants for which the town was noted.

P.M. and a bishop's mitre. c.1675. Peter Mews (1619-1706), Bishop of Bath and Wells (1672-1684) and Bishop of Winchester (1684-1706), son of Elisha Mews, was born at Purse Caundle in Dorset. He was educated at Merchant Taylors' School, and he married the daughter of Dr. Richard Baylie, President of St. John's College. In 1642 he took service in the King's Guards, and at Sedgmoor in 1685 his horses drew the royal cannon and he himself directed their fire. "He was a loyal soldier and a good bishop". (D.N.B.) He entertained Judge Jeffreys at Farnham Castle in 1685, and when William III landed (1688) King James II thought of taking refuge there. Some verses entitled 'The Ex-ale-tation of Ale (in verse) written by a Learned Pen', published in 1671, were said to be written by Peter Mews. Two seals at least are known bearing his initials and a mitre; one of them was picked up on the battlefield of Sedgmoor and the other was found at Farnham Castle. (see D.N.B. and *Country Life*, December 26, 1947.)

MIDDLE TEMPLE. see Temple.

JOHN MILES. THE FLEET. c.1670. Ht. 8ins. This presumably refers to the Fleet Prison, near Fleet Street, London, notorious for the cruelties practised there, and which was only demolished in 1844. It was also famous for the "Fleet marriages" performed by clergymen who were imprisoned there, and who could not therefore be fined for solemnising clandestine marriages. But it may have belonged to a tavern of that name.

James Mitchell 1794. Squat cylinder.

MITRE TAVERN. see C.E.D.

Modtonham 1737. Mallet.

G. MOOR. Ht. 10ins. This has the appearance of an early nineteenth-century beer-bottle. The seal is near the base and not on the shoulder of the bottle.

GEO. MOOR. 1729. Ht. 7¾ins. From Sir John Risley Coll.

REVD. JNO. MOORE. 1817. Ht. 10¾ins. This was probably John Moore (1742-1821) biblical scholar and writer, son of John Moore, rector of St. Bartholomew the Great, London. He was educated at Merchant Taylors' School where he became head scholar. He matriculated from St. John's College, Oxford in 1759 and graduated B.A. in 1763. He married Sarah Lilley and had a daughter who married Harry Bristow Wilson of the Merchant Taylors' School; their son, Henry Bristow Wilson, became historian of the school. (see D.N.B.)

REVD. JNO. MOORE. 1818. see above.

T. MOORE. BURRINGTON. 1816. Burrington is in Devon, two miles from S. Molton Road Station, and not very far from where the Taw is joined by the Mole, a famous trout stream.

E. MORGAN. DEVYNNOCK. 1822. Devynnock is in Breconshire.

'E/MORGAN/ DEVYNNOCK/1822'.

Thos. Morley 1730. Bladder onion.

W.A.M. either over or under a crown. William and Anne Morrell, licensees of the Crown Tavern, Oxford. 1660-1679. The Crown stood on the site of 3 Cornmarket Street, a house of which John Davenant, Shakespeare's friend, was at one time sub-lessee. It must not be mistaken for the Crown Inn still existing (No. 59a). The Crown Tavern belonged to New College. There are five varieties of this seal, some having no date, some having 74 for 1674, and some having 75 for 1675. In these dated ones the initials have been transformed into a cipher. There are also slight differences in the crowns. Anthony Wood mentions William Morrell (whom he sometimes spelt Murrell) as being the Mayor-elect in August, 1677, and in November of the same year he says: "Morrell, vintner, was mayor; but being sick of the gout, Sir Sampson Whyte did the office for him for that time". He also several times mentions drinking with him at his tavern. (A. Clark's *Wood's Life and Times.*) William Morrell, like Pont, issued a trade token with O. WILL. MORRELL AT YE and a crown, and R. CROWNE IN OXFORD. W.A.M. Three sealed bottles, and six "seals only".

Cipher of Anne Morrell and crown and OXON. 1683. see above. When William died in 1679, Anne carried on alone until 1696. One bottle and two seals only.

Ditto and OXON. 1685. see above.

Ditto and OXON. 1686. see above. Seal only.

Ditto and OXON. 1688. see above. Seal only.
    The N of OXON on the 1688 bottles is written thus: Ͷ

Ditto and OXON. 1701. Anne Morrell's executrix, Joan Turton, her daughter-in-law by marriage to a son by her first husband, 1697-1706. One bottle and two seals. Bottle.

ALEX. MOSS. BADWELL ASH. 1746. Octagonal bottle. Badwell Ash is a small village in Suffolk.

DAVID MURRAY. 1756. There was a Sir David Murray of Stanhope who died at Leghorn without issue in 1777. But a better 'claimant' to my mind is David Murray, 2nd Earl of Mansfield (1727-1796), diplomatist and statesman. It is true that in 1748 he succeeded his father as Viscount Stormont, but he was a scholarly man (who, incidentally, wrote a fine elegy on the death of Frederick, Prince of Wales), and it is just possible that he wrote as David Murray and continued to use that name, for a time at any rate. It may be a coincidence, but it is a fact that he arrived at Dresden in Saxony as Envoy-Extraordinary in the year 1756 (the date on the bottle).

D. Musgrave 98. Onion.

A.M. Nailsea bottle, with pincered glass trails; c.1800.

D.M. CUSTOMS. Large well-shaped bottle from Leith.

D.A.M. NEEDHM. MK. 1764. see Needham Market.

E.M. ESQ. 1739. Exhibited at Vintners' Hall 1933 and illustrated in catalogue.

F.M. 1712.

F.M. Seal only.

G.M. 1720.

G.U.M. 1820. Nailsea.

I.M. 1764. Ht. approx. 15ins. Diam. 6¾ ins.

I.C.M. The M is above the other two letters and probably indicates the initials of a man and his wife, possibly tavern-keepers.

J.S.J.M. STIRLING. 1827. see Stirling.

M.M. 1700. Onion.

M.T.M. with spray between T and M. Long neck. Ht. 9ins.

P.M. 1731.

P.M. and mitre. see Peter Mews.

'P M ' and a mitre.

R.M. Probably from Caithness. Seal only.

S.G.M. 1738. A sack-bottle.

S.I.M. (or I.M.S.) and shield with bells on it. Probably a tavern-bottle. Found in Horseferry Road.

T.M. 1700.

T.M. 1717. Seal only.

T.M. (separate matrices). Seal only.

T.M. 1751. Mallet.

T.F.M. 1712. Seal only.

T.M.M.

W.A.M. } and several similar seals.
W.A.M. Oxon. 75. } see William and Anne Morrell.

WM conjoined; 8 and 1. Shaft and globe.

'W M 81'.

W.M.; c.1735. Mallet.

W.M. 1745. Mallet.

W.M.M. and three stars. Probably from a tavern-bottle. Found at Bristol. Seal only.

I.MC. Ht. 9ins. Diam. 4¼ins. Capacity 1½ pints c.1770. The only seal I know using the abbreviated Mc without the rest of the surname.

J.S. Nance. Seal only.

T. Nankivell, Probus; c.1800. Cylinder.

N. surrounded by laurel leaves. Ht. 12ins. Greenish-white glass, m.s. label: Grande Fine Champagne de Propriétaire. 1809.

N. surmounted by crown, and with paper label: Grande Fine Champagne Impériale.

N. ,urmounted by crown.

  All the three above bottles are supposed to have belonged to the Emperior Napoleon I (1769-1821) but a very great authority (M. André Simon) does not believe that any of them date back to his time. Napoleonic Brandy may at one time have been put into later bottles. This seems to me to be still an open question. see Nicol.

D.A.M. NEEDHM. MK. 1764. Ht. 10ins. Probably Needham Market, Suffolk.

I. NEIGHBOUR. Seal only.

NEWCOMBE. There were two Thomas Newcombes; the elder (1627-1681), king's printer to Charles II. He was office-bearer of the Company of Stationers, to whom he left a silver bowl. His son Thomas Newcombe the younger (d.1691) was king's printer to Charles II, James II and William III. The seal may have belonged to one of these. (see D.N.B.)

JNO. NEWMAN. DARTMO. 1775. Ht. 10¾ins. John Newman (1743-1779), grandson of Robert Newman. Merchant of Newfoundland and Dartmouth, Devon.

JOHN NEWMAN. Ht. 14ins.

R. NEWMAN. 1723. Ht. 6½ins. Robert Newman (1676-1739), merchant-mariner of Dartmouth, Devon. Mayor of Dartmouth 1725, 1728, 1730 and 1731. Dredged up out of the mud in Dartmouth Harbour when dredging for the coal dropped in the Dart by colliers. When found it was covered with barnacles, and had a cork in it which may have been the original one.

RD. NEWMAN. 1766. Ht. 12¾ ins. The Newmans of Dartmouth were merchant-adventurers from 1422 onwards, and in the forefront of the Elizabethan adventurers. They traded with Newfoundland in cod-fish and port among other things. In one of Walter Besant's novels he says: "It is well-known that a certain quantity of the very best Port is sent to mature in Newfoundland and reimported by certain special connoisseurs in Devonshire". Sir Francis Drake started his career as a merchant-adventurer, and in 1596 married Mary Newman, a member of this family. Their fleet of sailing ships seems to have sailed regularly between 1654 and 1907. They still carry on as port wine shippers. The Hunts and Holdsworths (q.v.) were related to them.

JOHN NEWNHAM.

WM. NEWTON. 1771. This may have been William Newton (1735-1790) who exhibited at the Royal Academy 1776-1780. In 1771 (the date on the bottle) he published the earliest English translation of the first five books of Vitruvius. He was responsible for nearly all the decorative ornamentation of Greenwich Chapel. He died at Sidford near Sidmouth, Devon.

I.M. NICHOLSON. 1717.

I.M.N. 1717. This and the last seal must surely have belonged to the same person.

N. with Imperial Crown. Made for Nicol, proprietor of Café Royal, and sometimes passed off as a Napoleon bottle. (But see Napoleon.)

JOHN NOTT. 1736. There was a merchant of that name living in Barnstaple in 1736. The bottle was unfortunately injured by the digger. Dug up in Barnstaple c.1927.

T. NORTHCOTT. HATHERLEIGH. Ht. 10½ ins. Hatherleigh is in Devonshire.

N. see Napoleon and Nicol.

G.N. 1737.

I.M.N. 1717. see Nicholson.

'I M N/1717'.

292

M.N. 1733.

R.N. 1691. Onion.

'R·N/1691'.

R.N. either side of a shield with crossbones 1709. Onion.

R.N. 1709.

T.N. 1705. Wide mouth. A very rare bottle.

JAMES OKES. BURY. 1735. This is in shape like a modern port-bottle, but it is of course, mould-blown, not moulded.

JAMES OAKES. BURY. 1770. Ht. 10ins.

JAMES OAKES. BURY. 1771.

JAMES OAKES. BURY. 1777.

JA. OAKES. BURY. 1783.

JAS. OAKES. BURY. 1785.

JAS. OAKES. BURY. 1787.

JAS. OAKES. BURY. 1788. Ht. 10½ ins.

JAS. OAKES. BURY. 1793.

JA. OAKES. BURY. 1795.

James Oakes was said to be a wine-merchant at Bury St. Edmunds, Suffolk, and from the number of sealed bottles bearing his name he almost certainly was either a wine-merchant or a brewer. But the College of Arms says: "James Oakes of Bury St Edmunds, and afterwards of Nowton Court, Suffolk. Born at Bury in 1741. Died 1829. A Banker". The banker may have been a son of the first James who spelt his name 'Okes'.

N. Oats, L. Lant; c.1790. Squat cylinder.

G. Olliver 1799. Squat cylinder.

O.C. Oriel College, Oxford. Oriel was originally founded in pre-

Reformation days, but the present building dates from the beginning of the seventeenth century. Among Oriel worthies are Sir Thomas More, Sir Walter Raleigh, Archbishop Whately, Gilbert White of Selborne, J.A. Froude the historian, Thomas Arnold and his son Matthew and Sir Cecil Rhodes. Seal only.

J. OTTERWIL. 1783. [This spelling would seem to be incorrect from the bottles the author has examined. See below.]

J. Ottewil. 1783. Cylinder.

'J./Ottewil/1783'.

ROGER OXENHAM. 1731.

OXFORD. see All Souls, Brasenose, Christchurch, Exeter, Jesus, St. John's, Lincoln, Magdalen, Oriel, and Trinity.

D.V.O. 1724. Early mallet.

G.M.O. 1732. Mallet.

'G.M.O./1732'.

L.E.C. 1772. [?L.E.O.]. Ht. 10¾ ins. Sold at Sotheby's, June, 1930.

M.B.O.

R.O. and an animal (?boar). Probably from a tavern-bottle. Seal only.

Pack Horse Inn, St. Blazey; c.1835. Moulded cylinder.

'PACK-HORSE/INN/St Blazey'.

JACOB PADY. COLYTON. 1807. Colyton is in Devonshire, seventeen miles from Lyme Regis.

P. Palmer; c.1780. Cylinder.

W. PALMER. 1727. Seal only.

C.D. PALSGRAVE HEAD, and a man's head. Frederick Palsgrave of the Rhine, and for one winter King of Bohemia, was James I's son-in-law and a 'mighty toper'. The Palsgrave Head was a notorious tavern near Temple Bar. The initials are doubtless those of the licensee. (*Illustrated London News,* Dec. 3, 1932.)

I. Parnel, Kingston, 1728. Mallet.

Thos. Parsons, Luxillion; c.1730. Mallet.

T. Pate Howell 1738. Mallet.

I. Patten, Martock; c.1760-70. Cylinder.

T. PAULL. WEST MONCKTON. 1776. West Monkton is in Somerset.

THE PAULSGRAVE HED TAVERN. C.D.S. Fragment only. see above.

D.S. with head between initials. Presumably Palsgrave Head. see above.

I.H. 1713. PAX. see I.H.

JAS. PEARLE. SOMERTON. Ht. 10ins. Somerton is in Somerset.

(J)NO. PEARCE. 1793. Seal only. This fragmentary stamp from a glass wine-bottle was recently unearthed by a plough in Cornwall.

S. Pears, Cradleigh, 1790. Seal only.

JOHN PEARSE. 1719.

W. Pearse, Chippenham; c.1790. Squat cylinder.

Frances Peche, 1722. Mallet.

Wm. Peckard 1728. Onion.

JAS. PENDER. Bristol or Nailsea flask decorated with blue enamel spirals round the body. Wide mouth.

Arthur Perry 1755. Squat cylinder.

Perry, Bath 1794. Cylinder.

D. PETER. COLQUITE. Late eighteenth or early nineteenth century. Was this David Peter (1765-1837), independent minister, born at Aberystwith? He was appointed President of the Presbyterian College at

Carmarthen in 1795 (which might well be the date of the bottle). He married first a Mrs. Lewis, and secondly a sister of Sir William Nott. He published an account of Welsh religion from the times of the Druids to the beginning of the nineteenth century. Sold at Sotheby's, December 9, 1947.

Edward Peter, Northill. Moulded cylinder.

F. Peter, St Merryn. Seal only.

F.W. PETERS.

W. Peters, 1775. Magnum squat cylinder.

Josh. Phillips 1775. Bladder onion.

PICTON. ISCOED. Probably Sir Thomas Iscoed (1758-1815), a distinguished soldier, and M.P. for Carmarthen. He died at the Battle of Waterloo.

PICTON CASTLE. 1827. Made by Ricketts & Co., Glass Works, Bristol, whose name is stamped on the base.

W.P. and bishop's mitre in centre between initials. This seal is traditionally considered to be that of William Piers, Pierse or Pierce (1580-1670) successively Bishop of Peterborough and of Bath and Wells. His father, called by Wood "A haberdasher of hats", was nephew or near of kin to John Piers, Archbishop of York. (see D.N.B.) But it is possible that it may refer to a Mitre Tavern (see C.E.D.). For July 31, 1665, there is an entry in Pepys' Diary as follows "...that Proctor the vintner of the Miter in Wood-street and his son, are dead this morning there, and was the greatest vintner for some time in London for great entertainments." If Proctor's first initial should prove to be W, I should be inclined to consider the bottle one of his. One was found in Great Smith Street, Westminster, and another at Lambeth Palace.

PIG BAG. Length 5ins. Flask with flat oval body and long neck and broad flanged lip. The name is puzzling. In the Cowper MSS at Melbourne Halle, Derbyshire, there is a letter inscribed "Lady Mary Coke to Thomas Coke at his house at Mell Bourne at Darby Bagg", and in 1720 Mrs. Delany (then Pendarves) addressed a letter to her sister at Buckland, "near Broadway by Campden Bag, Glos." Were these merely postal bags, or could they throw any light on Pig Bag? Having written a letter to the *Sunday Times* on the subject, I received several answers. One writer suggests that it is a misreading of "Pig. Bac., a contraction of *pigmentum baccae,* i.e. olive-coloured pigment, and that the bottle was to contain a dye used for cloth in the Stroud district". This is at least plausible. An Eire correspondent thinks that ''Derby Bag hamlet has been snowed under by the growth of the city and that one of the summits of the Peak was known as Peak Bag''. Yet another suggestion is that ''baec'' is old English for stream or brook, and is still common in West Country dialect as ''bache, bage and batch'', and that ''bage'' is used in Derbyshire of a tract of moorland. I have also had a letter from Wales saying that Bag probably derives from the Welsh ''back'' meaning little. This word appears very commonly in Welsh place-names and always follows the noun it qualifies. ''Pig'' is also probably the unaltered Welsh ''pig'', which means a point, beak or peak, and is the word from which peak is derived. Pig Bag would thus be the ancient British Little Peak. This seems perhaps the most likely solution, and it only remains for a reader to tell me where the Little Peak was.

J. Pitfield 1784. Squat cylinder.

I. Pitt 1724. Bladder onion.

P. under baron's coronet. Sir George Warwick (1786-1858). 6th Bart, created Baron Poltimore, Devon, 1831. He married first, Emma P. Sneyd (daughter of the Chaplain to the King), and secondly Caroline Buller.

R.E.P. and a chevron between three tuns — arms of the Vintners' Company. Richard and Elizabeth Pont, as sub-licensees of the Three Tuns Tavern, Oxford, 1666-1671. Richard Pont also issued a trade token O. RICHARD PONT and Vintners' arms; R. IN OXON. 1668. R.E.P. He was buried in St. Mary the Virgin's Church at Oxford, where a tablet to him and his wife hangs on the west wall. The following extracts are from A. Clark's *Wood's Life and Times:* ''22 July. 1665, at the Mermaid Tavern with Mr. Curteyne, 1s. 6d., of which I gave 6d. to Dick Punt, when we drank wine in the cellars''. ''28 March, 1666, at Dick Punt's new Tavern at Bodicott's where he began to sell wine the 26 day. . .1s.'' Humphrey Bodicott was Punt's predecessor at the Three Tuns. ''December 1668. To Dick Pont for a quart of wine when my brother Kit and his wife dined with us, 2s. 2d.'' (September 1670) ''Afterwards A.W. had them (four Scotchmen) to the taverne against Alls. (All Souls) coll. and there liberally treated them with wine''. A note states that ''Richard Pont, vintner and citizen of Oxford, descended from the Ponts of Moreton neare to Wallingford in Berks., died. . . and was buried at St. Mary's church about the middle of the body, without armes on his hearse. . .(Elizabeth) widow of the said Pont, daughter of. . .Andrews one of the sergeants of Oxon, died 2 Nov. 1687; and was buried (without armes) by her husband, in fine linnen contrary to the act, and in a rich coffin provided by her onlie daughter and heir Elizabeth, an vain fopp of 18 yeares of age. This Elizabeth, who was the onlie surviving daughter of the said Richard Pont, and a rich heiress, was married, the day before her mother died, to. . .Stanley, M.A., fellow of Allsoules College, son of. . .of Wilts.'' see [*H.B.*] Seal only.

R.E.P. There are six similar to the above but with slight differences in tuns or in shield. Three of them are probably assignable to Richard Pont's widow, 1671-1687. Her will was proved in 1687-8. Five bottles and one seal only.

W. POOLY. 1764. Ht. 9ins.

I. Porteus Esq. Seal only.

EARL PORTSMOUTH.

Post House, Newark. Octagonal half-bottle.

B. Powell, 1774. Seal only.

P. under an earl's coronet. Earl of Powis. Obtained by the present owner from the cellars of Powys Castle.

T. PRATT. ?Sir Thomas Pratt (1797-1879).

W. PRATT. 1714. A magnum.

W. Pratt 1714. Onion.

'W Pratt/1714'.

W.S. PRESTON. 1729. Was this Sir William Preston whose brother George (1659-1748) was Governor of Edinburgh Castle at the time of the two rebellions 1715 and 1745? The latter, having no children, settled his property on his brother William and his nephew George.

There was also a west-country family of Prestons, to which he may have belonged. The country gentlemen of the west seem to me to have been particularly fond of having sealed bottles.

Then there was William Preston, writer to the Signet (d.1751), whose second son, another William (1742-1818) was printer and writer on freemasonry. The first edition of his book *Illustrations of Masonry* is very rare. But there may be many claimants for W.S. Preston's seal of 1729.

D.A.P. and mermaid centre, tail to left; an open book — arms of Oxford University; and an ox — arms of the city of Oxford. Daniel and Anne Prince. Prince occurs in a lease of the Mermaid Tavern, Oxford, 1692-3. The only Daniel Prince mentioned in A. Clark's *Wood's Life and Times* is a sergeant in 1663, and again in 1668, "one of the city sergeants". Perhaps the taverner was his son. A bottle and a "seal only".

CHAS. PUGH. 1763.

C. PUGH. 1765.

JOHN PUGH. 1794. Imperial pint.

T. PUTT. 1836. Sold at Sotheby's, December 9, 1947.

Hugh Pyper 1703; crest: a magpie. Seal only.

P. and baron's coronet. see Lord Poltimore.

P. and earl's coronet. see Earl of Powis.

P.I. see London.

A.P. 1713. with a handle. Ht. 6¾ins. by 6ins. A dated serving-bottle of this type is rare.

C.P. 1686. Ht. 5ins. Half-bottle size. Exhibited at Vintners' Hall, 1933, and illustrated in catalogue. A rare bottle in this small size. Found at Railway Works, Bermondsey.

D.A.P. and mermaid. see Daniel and Anne Prince.

E.P. and vintners' arms. see Elizabeth Pont.

E.P. 1760. Bladder onion.

'E P/1760'.

G.P. 1705.

H.P.

H.I.P. and a large fish facing right and branches above it. Ht. 7¾ins. Diam. 4¾ins. Olive-green glass and striations all round the bottle. A long neck and straight sides. Seventeenth-century bottle. It probably belonged to a Fish or Salmon Tavern.

I P.; c.1685. Onion. 'I P'.

I.P. 1794.

J.P.; c.1685. Transitional bottle.

P.P. back to back and inverted. Seal only.

R.E.P. and vintners' arms. see Richard and Elizabeth Pont.

R.M.P. 1657 and king's head. see Charles.

S.P. Moulded cylinder.

T.P. and a sun (full face). Seal only.

W.P. and a mitre. see William Piers.

W.P. 1732.

W.P. c.1750. A gallon flagon.

W.A.P. 1799. Ht. 11ins. Diam. 5ins. The initials on this bottle are said to have been those of William and Anna Maria Pinney, but the dates of their births make it impossible for them to have been the original owners. Colonel William Pinney (1806-1898) was the son of John Frederick Pinney. He was M.P. for thirty-three years; J.P. and D.L. for Somerset; Hon. Col. Somerset L.I. He lived at Somerton Erleigh, Somerton, and his London house was 30 Berkeley Square. His sister, Anna Maria Pinney (1812-1861) lived with him at Somerton. I suggest that he bought the bottle because the initials were his and his sister's, and that he eventually gave it to the Museum at Taunton, to which he gave several things.

W.H.P. and the King's arms; c.1650. Shaft and globe.

'W.H.P.' and the King's arms.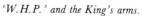

¾ Q. and a horse courant. *c.*1720. Presumably the figures and letters on the seal signify three-quarters of a quart. If so, it is the only seal I have seen showing a measure on it. A horse courant (Westphalia) was part of the arms of Hanover which were added to the shield of the United

Kingdom on the accession of George I in 1714 but no longer used after 1837. This was most probably a tavern-bottle.

Q. Probably the Marquess of Queensberry. Found in Dumfriesshire. Seal only.

Queensberry. see Crest of Douglas [Appendix I].

RACOCZY.

I. RANKS. 1780.

MARY RAYES. c.1715. With the exception of the tavern licensees, a seal with a woman's name on it is unusual, and this is the only one I know of with a woman's name only on it.

S. Read. Seal only.

I.M. Reeve 1738. Octagonal.

W Reeve 1760. Seal only.

'W/Reeve/1760'.

'Rich^d/Rendall/Topsham/1741'.

Richd Rendall, Topsham 1741. Seal only.

R. REYNOLDS. 1712.

RHYD-Y-GROS. This is a corruption of Rhyd-y-Groes, which means the Ford of the Cross. There are many places in Wales to which this name might apply. Seal only.

Rice, Wight 1703. Decanter onion.

Thos. Rich, Over Stowey 1787. Magnum cylinder.

A.K.R. and crown above. Alexander and Kathleen Richmond. The Crown Tavern, Oxford. 1711 to after 1730.

A.K.R. and crown above. Star each side of R. see above. One bottle and one 'seal only'.

A.K.R. and crown above. see above. Was Alexander related to Stephen Richmond, to whom Anthony Wood refers in 1650 as a "godly youth"? Seal only.

A K R Oxon 1706 and a crown. This dated seal considerably extends the known tenancy period of Alexander and Kathleen Richmond.

'*A K R/Oxon/1706'*
and a crown above.

T. RIDGE. 1720. Ht. 7⅛ ins. A six-pointed star each side of initial T.

Wm. Ridgeman, N. Petherwin 1806. Squat cylinder.

I. RIDLEY. 1783.

G.S. RISDON.

I. Risdon; c.1820. Moulded cylinder.

JOS. RISDON. 1818.

JOSH. RISDON. 1821. Ht. 9½ ins. Risdon was the name of a well-known Devonshire family. Tristram Risdon (?1580-1640) wrote a *Chorographical Description or Survey of Devon,* which was not published until 1714.

T. Rivers, Truro 1785. Seal only.

Robert Robbins 1719. Seal only.

W. ROBBINS. BEVERSTOKE CASTLE. 1797.

W. Roe 1717. Onion.

Rog; c.1840. Moulded cylinder.

T. ROGERS. HOTEL. WESTON SUPER MARE. Three-part mould.

ROI DE ROME. 1811. The words are moulded in glass on a champagne bottle but not in the usual form of a seal. The bottle is probably much newer than the wine that was put into it. The son of Napoleon I and Marie-Louise was known as the Roi de Rome (1811-1832).

ROLLE. 1774. Very long neck. This is presumably the seal of John Rolle (1750-1842), who was born the year his uncle Henry, created Baron Rolle of Stevenstone, died. John was the son of Denys Rolle of Bicton House, Exeter, Devon, (d.1797) by Anne, daughter of Arthur Chichester of Hall in the same county. John was M.P. for Devonshire and a staunch adherent of Pitt. He was made the hero of the *Rolliad* but the satire in it was chiefly directed against Pitt and Dundas. In 1796 the revived title of Baron Rolle of Stevenstone was conferred upon him. He married firstly (in 1778) Judith Walrond, and secondly (in 1822) Louisa Trefusis, daughter of the 17th Baron Clinton. (see D.N.B.) At one time this bottle belonged to the Hon. Mark Rollo.

R. under a coronet. John, Baron Rolle of Steventon. see above.

S. ROPER. 1760. There are or were Ropers in Warwickshire, but I have been unable to trace this one.

ROSE. see T.E.S.

Revd. Ino Rouse, 1786. Squat cylinder.

Wm. Rowe, Newlands, 1820. Cylinder.

I. RUMBOLD. CALNE. 1721. There were many Rumbolds in the seventeenth century, both cavaliers and parliamentarians. I have not yet traced this one. Calne is in Wilts.

I. Rumbold, Calne, 1731. Cylinder.

The Revd/Doct Rumney, St. Albans 1734. Mallet.

R. Ht. 8½ins. c.1690. White glass wine bottle decorated with trailed flutes and ribbons, vertical strappings and strawberry bosses, showing evolution from green bottle-decanters to white glass serving-bottles or decanters. Exhibited at Vintners' Hall, 1933, and illustrated in catalogue.

R. with coronet. Ht. 10¼ins.

R. 1809. with crest (unspecified).

R. under a coronet (?duke's) Nineteenth century. Sold at Sotheby's, December 9, 1947.

R. and an earl's coronet. Seal surrounded by a garter and the words HONI SOIT QUI MAL Y PENSE. Ht. 10¾ins. Diam. 13ins. Magnum bottle. Early eighteenth century.

A.R. 1755. Ht. 7¼ins. Sold at Sotheby's, June 1930.

A.R. beneath a crown with a beaded border. Seal only.

D.R. Flint-glass decanter of barrel shape. Ht. 5½ins. Illustrated in the *Antique Collector* in May, 1932.

D.R.R. and a stag; c.1695-8. Onion.

E.R. and coat-of-arms. Ht. 9ins.

E.W.R. 1686. and crown over. This is probably one of the Anne Morrell (q.v.) cipher bottles. Fragment only.

G.R. Seal only.

G.R. with an arrow between the letters. Seal only.

G.R. with a crown. Probably a tavern bottle.

G.R. and a crown; c.1755. Early cylinder.

M.R. 1785. Squat cylinder.

O.R. Bury 1743. Mallet.

R.M.R. and a stag. Ht. 9¼ins. Bulbous body and long neck. Probably a tavern bottle with the initials of the licensees. Exhibited at Vintners' Hall, 1933, and illustrated in the catalogue.

T.R. 1714.

T.R. over X.X. A squat bottle. Found in Duke Street, Aldgate, London.

V.R.

W.R. 1698 with two mullets. Onion.

W.R. Found at the Observatory, Madingley Rise, Cambridge in 1896.

W.R. and a dolphin facing left. There are two versions of this seal with slight differences. They probably come from a Dolphin Tavern. One was found under Parker Street Buildings, Emmanuel College, Cambridge in 1893 and the other at the Observatory, Madingley Rise, Cambridge in 1896 (see also Cambridge. E.C., Richard Church and Dolphin.)

W.M.R. and a statuary urn. Seal only.

REV. E.G. ST. EWETH.

I.B. ST. VEEP. 1795. St. Veep is near Fowey, Cornwall, and is situated on the Fowey River. The name is said to be derived from Wymp or Wennapa, the name of a sixth-century Welsh saint. The bottle was found during excavations in White Hart Road, Old Portsmouth.

A.F. Sampson 1746. Squat cylinder.

H. SANDERS. WATERSLADE. 1738. Waterslade is at Taunton.

I.R. Santard 1723. Seal only.

Wm. Savery 1762. Cylinder.

SAW. 1777.

SCRABSTER. 1830. A port tappit-hen: equals three bottles.

Searle, Ugbro. 1795. Cylinder.

Sedbush 1740. Mallet half-bottle.

PHILIP SERGEANT. 1717. Ht. 9ins. A decanter of pale green bottle metal, oviform, lipped, with handle. It was probably made at Bristol. It is very unusual to find a seal on such a bottle. Illustrated in *Country Life,* September 19, 1947.

Ino. Setter. Seal only.

I. Sharp 1791. Squat cylinder.

BERNARD SHAW. 1802. There are two Bernard Shaws, belonging to the famous writer's family, who might have owned this bottle. One is Bernard (born middle of eighteenth century), son of Robert Shaw of Kilkenny who married Mary, daughter of Bernard Markham (and who presumably brought the name Bernard into the Shaw family) and grandson of Capitan William Shaw of Sandpits, Co. Kilkenny. (This Bernard is great-grandfather of G.B.S.) The other claimant is his nephew Bernard (1755-1808) of Round Tower, Dublin, Collector of Cork. His elder brother Robert was created Baronet in 1821. The seal may well have belonged to the Collector of Cork.

Sheene 1741. Mallet.

S.W. SHEPHERD. 1793.

T. SHILLSON; c.1790-1800. Cylinder.

MOTHER SHIPTON and the seated figure of a woman.

A ship. Long neck. It probably belonged to a Ship Tavern. Found in Storey's Gate, London.

T. SHORY. 1733. Tall hexagonal bottle. Found in garden of 18 North Hill, Colchester.

C.H.H. SILLATON. 1789. (see C.H.H.)

Charles Simpson; c.1770. Squat cylinder.

'W/Skammell/1704'.

W Skammell 1704. Onion.

Skeane 1747. Mallet.

Skene 1742. Mallet.

'Skene/1742'.

I. Skinner 1736. Seal only.

M. SLADE. 1755. Found in Newfoundland Road, Bristol. Seal only.

I. SLOGGETT. 1791.

G.M. Smale, Hatherly; c.1780. Squat cylinder.

B. Smith, Dartmouth; c.1820. Cylinder.

I. SMITH. 1706. Ht. 6¼ ins. ⎱

I. SMITH. 1706. Ht. 5½ ins. ⎰

A silversmith named John Smith made a punch-bowl with hall-mark of 1702 which belongs to the Company of Coach-makers and Coach-Harness Makers. Or it might have been a John Smith of whom Anthony Wood speaks very contemptuously when he was an undergraduate as a notorious atheist and drunkard. (Vol.II, p.3). He died in 1715. Perhaps the most probable claimant is John Smith (1655-1723), politician, who was a student at the Middle Temple, and a member of parliament from 1678 onwards. In 1705 he was elected Speaker of the House of Commons; in 1706 (the date on the bottle) he was one of the Commissioners for arranging the union with Scotland, and when the House reassembled in 1707 with the addition of the Scottish members, he was again elected Speaker. In 1708 he became Chancellor of the Exchequer. Quite a person of consequence and likely to have his own sealed bottles. His daughter, Mary, married in 1705, Robert Herbert, 2nd son of the 8th Earl of

Pembroke, whose elder brother, the 7th Earl, had his bottles sealed with the Herbert crest and the date.

Ino. Smith; c.1735. Mallet.

Jno. Smith Northill. Double magnum cylinder.

Robt. Smith 1710. Onion.

T. SMITH. 1733. Ht. 12¼ ins.

T. SMITH. SARUM. 1735. T. Smith was a chemist at Salisbury, Wilts., and his two large bottles are thought to be tincture rather than wine bottles.

Thomas Smith 1716. Seal only.

Francis Smithson 1705. Seal only.

Smyth 1822. Moulded cylinder.

H. Snell 1786. Cylinder.

P. Soper. Seal only.

R. Spencer 1787. Squat cylinder.

I. Spettigue/Treenegl.⁵/1767. Cylinder.

I. SQUARE. 1804.

Star with five very long rays emanating from it. This indicates a comet year, probably 1811, a good vintage year for both white and red wine, which is rather rare.

Comet.

Eight-pointed star with illegible inscription. Found near Maiden Castle, Dorchester.

Ns. Steer, St Domk. 1791. Squat cylinder.

STEP HENGO. ST. AUSTELL. 1722. St. Austell is in Cornwall.

G & P Stephens, St Tudy 1836. Moulded cylinder.

I. Steutheridge, Lostwithiel, 1734. Seal only.

Ias. Stevens, Launceston; c.1730. Mallet.

THOS. STEVENS ESQ. 1819. Ht. 8½ins. Sold at Sotheby's, June, 1930.

BLYDE STEYN. c.1780. Probably John Blydesteyn (1696-1777) of Stratford Hall, Stratford, E., whose father, a Dutch banker, came over with William of Orange.

J.S., J.M. STIRLING. 1827. Ht. 11ins. This is a sealed bottle of streaked and speckled Nailsea glass, white on black. It has three long and three short rectangular lines of trailed ornament, a short one starting below the seal. Stirling, the capital of Stirlingshire, is surrounded by battlefields including Bannockburn.

William Stonas 1700. Onion.

S.B. STONE. c.1770.

W. STONE. 1772. Ht. 9ins.

STOUGHTON. 1795. Probably Thomas Stoughton (d.1812) who married Sarah Bullard, daughter of the Master of the Norwich Lunatic Asylum (Bethel Hospital). Their son John (1807-1897), was a dissenting minister and writer on religious matters. Thomas' father was an admiral, of whose death I do not know the date. It is just possible that the bottle was his.

STOVER. Stover, near Newton Abbot, formerly belonged to the Duke of Somerset. It is a vast mansion built of huge blocks of granite, and with wine-cellars like the catacombs.

Wm. Strode Esq 1727. Mallet.

W. STRONG. 1772. A short broad brown glass bottle.

Jos. Sunter 1771. Magnum squat cylinder.

SWAN TAVERN. see I.T.

THREE SWANS, the lower one larger than the other two. Ht. 4½ins. This is a very small squat bottle with a broad base, and it may have belonged to a tavern. Found on the site of the new County Hall, Westminster Bridge, in 1910.

I. SWIFT. DEAN. 1727. Jonathan Swift (1667-1745), satirist and writer, was born in Dublin and educated at Trinity College. His career at college was not a distinguished one. In 1685 he was marked "*bene* for Greek and Latin, *male* for philosophy and *negligenter* for theology". (D.N.B.) He became Secretary to Sir William Temple and hoped for political preferment. As, however, he did not get it, he entered the church, and was made Dean of St. Patrick's, Dublin, in 1713. *Gulliver's Travels* and *A Tale of a Tub* are amongst his best-known works. The former appeared in October 1726, and Swift received £200 for the copyright, which, according to him, was the only time he ever made any money by his writings. The second edition came out in 1727 (the date on the bottle). He had a romantic friendship with 'Stella' (Hester Johnson, whom he is reputed to have married privately) and with 'Vanessa' (Esther Vanhomrigh) who made a will leaving him her fortune but who afterwards revoked it. Swift knew Thomas Herbert, 8th Earl of Pembroke, who was Lord Lieutenant of Ireland in 1707, and who in 1683 had succeeded his brother Philip, 7th Earl of Pembroke [q.v. Appendix I], himself the owner of sealed bottles bearing the dates of 1678 and 1681.

THOMAS SWIFT. OXON. c.1690.

S. Ht. 7¾ins. c.1670-80. Small long-necked bottle. Found in Dartmouth Street, London.

S; c.1780. Cylinder.

S 1698 with a merchant's mark. Onion.

A.S. 1834. Nailsea.

A.T.S. Ht. 13ins. c.1775.

D.S. and man's head. see Palsgrave.

E.S. 1688. Onion.

G.S. 1699.

H.F.S. 1811.

T.S. Found at Mildenhall, Suffolk.

I.S. 1728. Seal only.

I.S. and three arrows palewise. Seal only.

I.S. BURY. 1763. This stands for Bury St. Edmunds. The bottle was found at Mildenhall, Suffolk.

I.S. and above a small full-faced head. Eighteenth century. Seal only.

I.E.S. and a five-petalled rose pierced by arrows. The neck is missing. This was probably a tavern-bottle, and the initials those of the licensees. Found in Holborn.

I.E.S. and a Tudor rose. Seal only.

I.M.S. and shield with five bells on it. Ht. 8½ins. Probably a tavern-bottle. Found in Horseferry Road, London.

J.S.; c.1800. Cylinder.

J.E.S. Seal only.

L.S. 1723. Ht. 6½ins. Flat-sided bottle.

M.B.S. Ht. 10½ins. Capacity one pint. Early nineteenth century.

M.I.S. 1711.

P.S. Ht. 6¾ins. Diam. 5ins. Found in London.

R.S. 1716. Ht. 9ins. Diam. 8ins. 26ins. in circumference. A rare bottle in the magnum size. There are two specimens of which one has a pewter mount at the lip. The latter was exibited at Vintners' Hall in 1933.

T.S. 1725.

T.E.S. in a Tudor rose. Long-necked bottle. There was a Rose Tavern in or near Covent Garden where Pepys dined off "half a breast of mutton off the spit", while waiting to get into the King's Playhouse in 1668, (at which place incidentally he noted that he did not see the King laugh once), and another attached to Mary-le-bone Gardens, which was a favourite haunt of the Duke of Buckingham, and the scene of his end-of-the-season dinner at which he always gave the toast: "May as many of us as remain unhanged next spring meet here again". (Henry C. Shelley) There was the Rose Tavern where Pepys "drank some burnt wine" on Christmas Eve, 1667. And there may be other claimants, but until the initials are identified, it will not be possible to say to which Rose Tavern this bottle belonged. It was found in Fetter Lane, London.

W.S. in separate matrices; possibly seventeenth century. Seal only.

W.S. 1776. Bulbous Nailsea shape.

W.S. BOURN HEATH. 1760.

B.M. TABUTEAU Wine Merchant 1821 Dublin. Cylinder.

Iohn Tallamy 1725. Mallet.

Robt. Tanner 1725. Bladder onion.

W. TAYLER. TUREY. 1734.

E. TAYLOR. WELLAND. 1737. Ht. 8ins. A mallet-shaped bottle. Welland is in Worcestershire.

FS. TAYLOR. 1776. This presumably stands for Francis Taylor, but I have not been able to identify him. The bottle was obtained at Bath.

I. Taylor 1807. Cylinder.

J. TAYLOR. WISBECH. 1770. There were many Taylors in East Anglia, but I cannot find any that have a connection with Wisbech, a town in Cambridgeshire, and am unable to identify the owner of this bottle.

W.A.T. and vintners' arms (three tuns). William and Anne Taylor. William is mentioned by Hearne: "1719. Yesterday...died very rich Mrs. Tomlins of the Three Tuns Tavern, Oxon...Her first husband was one Taylour..."(see D.W. Rannie's *Hearne's Collections*). He died 1695. In A. Clark's *Wood's Life and Times* we find on February 26, 1682: "(Nathaniel) Whateley the apothecary was married by Mr. (Baptist) Levinz in Magd. Colledge chappel to Mr. Taylor's daughter". This may refer to William Taylor. He is twice mentioned by name by Wood as an apothecary.

Wm. Taylor, Bossiney 1836. Moulded cylinder.

I. Tazewell 1768. Seal only.

I.T. and horse's head. Crest of Inner Temple, London. Anthony Wagner in *Heraldry of England* notes that "the Pegasus in the arms of the Temple is a misdrawing of the Templars' old device of two knights riding one horse because they were too poor to pay for two". Underneath the bottle is the maker's name: H. Ricketts & Co., Glass Works, Bristol, showing the date to be between 1811 and 1853. (see Leman.) In use until 1938.

INNER TEMPLE. Ht. 11½ ins. c.1780. The words are written on an oblong label three inches from the base, not as is usual on the shoulder.

MIDDLE TEMPLE. These words are written round the seal and the Holy Lamb with a Flag (Middle Temple crest) is in the centre. Port-wine bottles with this seal on the shoulder were in use by the benchers at the Middle Temple in 1878, and, I believe, until a much later date. (*Dorset Field Club Proceedings,* Vol. II, 1878, p.59.)

Templeman of Merriot; c.1780. Cylinder.

FRA THISTLEWASSE. 1716. Found near Abingdon, Berks. Seal only. (*Dorset Field Club Proceedings*, Vol. II, 1878, p.59.)

'E. Thomas, Bath'. Seal only.

Htid. Thomas, Swansea 1770. Nailsea bottle.

R. Thomas, Veryan 1765. Seal only.

Stephen Thomas, Veryan; c.1700. Onion.

W. THOMAS. WEST BUCKLAND. 1775. There are Bucklands in Herts., Kent, Surrey and Devonshire. I think it probably belongs to the latter county.

Thresher 1723. Onion.

T. THROWERTON. 1770.

R. Threxton 1737. Mallet.

Sir James Tillie of Pentillie; c.1700. Decanter onion.

'Sir James Tillie of Pentillie'.

TOKAYER. Probably a foreign bottle. M. André Simon says of Tokay: "The best and best known wine of Hungary. Tokaij Szamorodne is rather dry; Tokaij Aszu is sweet and Tokaij Essencia, or, Tokay Essence, is the richest, best and rarest. The Tokayer Ausbruch is the best value as a rule". Presumably this bottle contained the latter wine. In a letter Swift tells Stella that he dined with a merchant in the city and "drank the first Tokay wine I ever saw; and it is admirable, yet not to the degree I expected". It was hard to satisfy that fastidious man. Fielding mentions Tokay in *The Miser,* and Dr. von Derczen in 1796 imbibed some that was forty years old, which, he says, "on being poured into the glass, filled the whole room with an aromatic, etherial odour".

1707 and vintners' arms. see [C.A.T.] below. Mr. Leeds queries whether this should be assigned to the Three Tuns Tavern, Oxford, without the usual initials, or rather to some member of the Vintners' Company plying his trade in Oxford. Found in the inner quadrangle of Pembroke College. Seal only.

C A T and vintners' arms (three tuns). Culpeper and Anne Tomlinson, 1695-1712. Culpeper Tomlinson (or Tomlins) is first mentioned as occupier of the Three Tuns, Oxford, in 1703. His wife Anne had previously married Taylour (see W.A.T.), when Culpeper was described as her drawer, so she may have been in occupation of the Three Tuns prior to her second marriage. She was a sister of Richard Walker (see R.W.). Culpeper was buried in St. Mary the Virgin in 1712.

'C A T' and vintners' arms.

C.A.T. 1709. OXON. and vintners' arms and bunches of grapes. see above.

A.T. OXON. 1713. and vintners' arms and sprays. Anne Tomlinson, widow, 1712-1719. Buried in the church of St. Mary the Virgin. see above.

A.T. 1715. and vintners' arms and sprays. see above.

W. TOOGOOD. 1780.

THOMAS TREASE. ST. GINNIS. 1815. St. Ginnis is in Cornwall.

N. TREDCROFT. 1784.

Trelaske and star in seal centre; c.1800. Cylinder.

Wm. Tremain, Newlyn. Squat cylinder.

T. TREMEWEN. 1785. Ht. 7ins.

TRENGOFF IN CORNWALL. 1704. Ht. 5¼ins. Diam. 5ins.

I. Trengrouse, Hellston, 1735. Mallet.

H. Tresmarrow P. 1703, and a chevron between three magpies. Seal only.

J. Trevethan. Seal only.

WILLIAM TREVITHICK. 1712. Seal only. Trevithick is a Cornish name. From Chilton Candover, Hants.

Geo. Treweeke 1726. Bladder onion.

T.C., C.R. Ht. 10¾ins. Trinity College, Common Room, Oxford. Trinity College was founded in 1555 by Sir Thomas Pope, who was the son of a yeoman farmer and became a privy councillor to Henry VIII. He was also the friend of Sir Thomas More.

T. COLL. C.R. see above. Seal only.

W. Troyle, 1804. Seal only.

T.T. HANHAM. Ht. 6ins. Early eighteenth century. Thomas Trye of Hanham Hall, between Bristol and Bath.

HENRY TUCKER. 1740.

R. Tucker, Street, 1778. Cylinder.

Wm. Tucker. Nailsea.

JOHN TUPPEN. 1735.

CHA. TURNOR. 1690. A name well-known in Oxford, where it was found, at that date. A Mr. Charles Turner (sic) is committed to Newgate along with other notabilities in July, 1690. (A. Clark's *Wood's Life and Times* III, p.333.)
Also a broken one [see above].

I. TWEED. 1720. A short bottle on a broad base.

T. on a seal on the neck, not the shoulder of the bottle. Nineteenth century.

A.T. 1785. Ht. 9½ins. Octagonal bottle.

E.T. and escutcheon with lion passant. Ht. 8¾ins. Probably a tavern bottle. Found on the site of the Bank of England, London.

E.T. and vintners' arms. Probably a tavern bottle.

I.T. and horse's head. see Inner Temple.

I.T. and a swan. Ht. 8½ins. Long neck. The swan is encircled by what appears to be a hoop. The bottle obviously came from a Swan (or a Swan and Hoop) Tavern. On Sept. 7, 1666, just after the Great Fire, Pepys notes: "To Sir W. Coventry, at St. James's...Thence to the Swan, and there drank, and so home, and find all well". There was a Swan and Hoop at 28 Finsbury Pavement, and a tavern (known as The Olde Swanne as long ago as the fourteenth century) near Old Swan Stairs behind Upper Thames Street. Passengers who were afraid of "shooting the arches" of old London Bridge would disembark here and refresh themselves at the old Swan Tavern before re-embarking at Billingsgate. Johnson and Boswell did this on their way to Greenwich in 1763, and Pepys noted the "very good fish and plenty" in 1660. A tavern with this familiar name existed here until the second decade of the twentieth century. This bottle was found in Westminster, so may have belonged to the first-mentioned tavern.

I.T. 1710. Onion.

I.T. 1783. Cylinder.

I.T. ynys, yplwm, 1808. Squat cylinder.

I.P.T. Ht. 10ins.

L.T. 1810. Squat cylinder.

R.T. and a bell. c.1670-80. Possibly the Bell Inn, Magdalen Street, Oxford. Seal only.

'R T' and a bell.

R.I.T. and a shield containing a fountain with a baluster stem both above and below. Probably a tavern-bottle. Early eighteenth century. Ht. 6½ ins. Sold at Sotheby's, December 9, 1947.

S.T. 1828.

T.C., C.R. see Trinity College.

T.T.HANHAM. see Trye.

T.T. 1688. Ht. 7½ ins.

T.T. Llanvair; c.1770-80. Cylinder.

W.T. c.1720. Ht. 7½ ins.

W.A.T. and vintners' arms. see William and Anne Taylor.

W. UPCOTT. 1778. Name known in Tiverton, Somerset.

M. UPPELL. 1717. Ht. 7ins.

I.V. 1742. Ht. 7ins. Isaac Uppleby. Barrow-on-Humber.

Usk 1724. Magnum bladder onion.

UTRECHT. see I.H. 1713. PAX.

Wm. Vallis 1741. Octagonal.

W. Vassell 176?. Octagonal.

CHAS. VAVAZOR. 1749. Sir Charles Vavasour was a general merchant.

ROWD. VEALE. GWITHIAN. 1778. Gwithian is in Cornwall situated on St. Ives Bay. Its eighth-century chapel (one of the oldest in England) was at one time used as a cowshed.

VELT. 1718. Ht. 5¼ ins. Sold at Sotheby's, June, 1930.

Dl. Venning, Alternon 1793. Squat cylinder.

W. VINER. and a design of grapes and vine leaves. William Viner of the Vine Inn, Salisbury, Wilts., was Mayor of Salisbury 1668, and by his will founded the Great Coat Charity. The design on the seal is a pun on his name and on his inn. He also issued a token. His brass is in St. Thomas' Church, Salisbury. Seal only.

I.V. 1742. see Isaac Uppleby.

I.V. 1776.

I.E.V. Found at Manning College, Oxford. From the arrangement of the initials (that of the surname above and those of husband and wife at each side below) this would appear to be a tavern-bottle.

P.C.V. and a double-headed eagle. Ht. 7ins. This is one of the early long-necked bottles, but the top is broken off and there is a large hole in the side of the bottle. Probably it was a tavern-bottle; with the initials of the licensees.

T V 1771, with vine and grape decoration. Cylinder.

'T V/1771'.

Rev. I.M. Wade, Forrabury, 1798. Squat cylinder.

Jno. Wade, Downrow, 1826. Cylinder.

Stephen Wade, Trethevy 1794. Squat cylinder.

W. Wade, Trethevy 1794. Squat cylinder.

Wm. Wade, Tintage^ll 1804. Squat cylinder.

William Wade, Tintagel, 1794. Squat cylinder.

J. WAKEFIELD. SEDGWICK. Ht. 11½ ins. c.1780-1800.

JOHN WAKEFIELD. 1802. Ht. 11½ ins.
The Wakefields were bankers operating as Wakefield and Crewdson (now Martin's Bank) at Kendal, Westmorland. For many years two branches of the Wakefield family lived at Kendal and Sedgwick respectively. Their descendants now reside at Milnthorpe and Kendal.

H. WALDEN. 1715.

H. Walker 1764. Squat cylinder.

R.W. 1693. and a king's head full front, robed and crowned. Richard Walker, 1687-1704, The King's Head Tavern, Oxford. He was apprenticed to William Morrell (q.v.) 1668. He was buried in St. Michael's Church in 1704, and described on his tombstone as *'oenopola notissimus'*. Seal only.

R.W. 1695. and king's head. see above.

R.W. 1696. and king's head, full face, crowned. see above.

R.W. 1697. and king's head in profile, robed. see above. Seal only.

1699 and king's bust in armour in profile to right. see above.

R.E.W. 1699. and king's head as last. Richard and E(lizabeth) Walker. She was apparently his second wife with the same initial and possibly the same name as his first wife.

R.W. 1699. and king's head. see above.

Four of the above-mentioned bottles were excavated from the foundations of Market Place, Oxford in the 1890s, bought by Mr. Handley and given by him to Mr. R.G. Bell, a director of Handley's Brewery, Oxford, who had them mounted with silver and subsequently bequeathed them to members of his family.

R.W. 1690 and king's head. see above. Sold June 3, 1943, at Christie's, from the late Col. Ratcliff's Collection. Bought with ninety-six other bottles by Messrs. D.M. & P. Manheim (for £90) and sold by them, with one or two exceptions, to the U.S.A.

R.W. 1690. and king's head. see above. Found on the site of Powell's Glass-house, Whitefriars.

W. WALKER. YORK. and Prince of Wales' feathers. Ht. 5½ ins. Octagonal. On base: YORK. 1882.

JOHN WALL. WEST BROMWICH. 1761. West Bromwich is in Staffs. This may have been John Wall (1708-1776) physician, who was born in Worcestershire. He devoted his spare time to painting. His son, Martin Wall (1747-1824) edited and published his essays. Seal only. (see D.N.B.)

Chas. Walley, Exmouth 1770. Seal only.

R. WALLINGTON. 1719.

Wm. Walters, Goldrift; c.1760. Squat cylinder.

C.H. WANSBOROUGH. SHREWTON. Shrewton is on Salisbury Plain, Wilts., about a mile and a half from Stonehenge. The Wansboroughs were of Dutch extraction, and the owner of this bottle was a well-to-do farmer. He is incidentally, an ancestor of the present Director of the South Wilts. Museum, Mr. Frank Stevens, O.B.E.

Genl Warde 1809. Cylinder.

 'Genl/Warde/1809'.

I. WARREN. 1764. Possibly John Warren (1730-1800) successively Bishop of St. David's and Bangor. He was appointed the seventh prebend of Ely in 1768, and also appointed to the rectory of Snailwell in Cambridgeshire. He was buried in Westminster Abbey. (see D.N.B.)

W. WARREN. TAUNTON. 1807. Taunton is the county town of Somerset.

P. WATKINS. BRECON. 1764. Brecon is the county town of Breconshire.

I. WATSON ESQE. BILTON. Ht. 9ins. Diam. 4ins. Early eighteenth century. The owner of this bottle, John Watson, lived at Bilton Park, a fifteenth-century house one mile from Knaresborough, Yorks.

E. WATTS. 1725. Isaac Watts (1674-1748), hymn-writer, had a brother Enoch who went to sea. Does this bottle commemorate him? Their father, Isaac, had nine children, and their grandfather Thomas Watts, commander of a man-of-war under Blake in 1656, died from an explosion on his ship. (see D.N.B.)

J. Webb 1700. Seal only.

I. WEBBER. Was this the landscape painter, John Webber (c.1750-1793), son of Abraham Weber, a Swiss sculptor? He was draughtsman to Captain Cook's third and last expedition to the South Seas, and was afterwards employed by the Admiralty. His portrait of Captain Cook is now in the National Portrait Gallery. (see D.N.B.)

T.I. WEDGWOOD. BURSLEM. 1770. This was probably Thomas Wedgwood, cousin of Josiah Wedgwood (the great potter) who was taken into partnership by latter in 1766. From then until 1788 Thomas was "at the head of the useful works both at Burslem and afterwards at Etruria". (*Life of Josiah Wedgwood* by Eliza Metayer [?Meteyard]). There are five or more Thomas Wedgwoods, all potters, and of one of them the following was written: "In the inventory of the personal estate of Thomas Wedgwood of Burlsem taken July 30, 1773, there are forty-four pewter plates, valued at 7½ d. each, and 24 dishes at 2s. each; no household pottery is set down, though the warehouse stock of the same date included '295 dozen of table-plates; best white ware.' " (ibid) Evidently the great potters preferred pewter to pottery for their own personal use.

Ino. Wellar 1735. Mallet.

Robt. Wellar 1711. Onion.

N. Wells, London 1717. Onion.

T. WELMAN. 1723. Thomas Welman (1693-1757) settled at Poundisford Lodge, Pitminster, near Taunton, Somerset, a property which had been purchased by his uncle, Dr. Simon Welman. Thomas served as High Sheriff for Somerset in 1733. In 1731 he married Mary, daughter of Benjamin Hawkins, Esq. of Exeter, and by her (who died in 1760), left at his death an only daughter, who married William Hawker, Esq., nephew of the Rev. M. Towgood, and dying in 1769, left Prudence and Hannah.

J. Wenfley, N. Tawton; c.1780. Cylinder.

J. Wensley 1742. Mallet.

ROBERT WENSLEY. WALLSUTON. 1717. This is Walsoken, a suburb of Wisbech, Cambridgeshire.

W. WERE, Wellington, 1805. Cylinder.

EDWARD WERGE. 1774.

I.E West, Tilbury Hall. Squat cylinder.

'*I.E/WEST/TILBURY/HALL'.*

WESTHILL.

T. Weston 1742. Mallet.

WHICKER. The various occupiers of the Mermaid Tavern, Oxford, were "occupiers under leases from the City held first by John Whicker and later by John Whicker Moreton both of Tackley, Oxon." (see E.T. Leeds.) cf. initials F.W.W. and I.M.W. The latter might be I.W.M.

Thos. Whipham 1816. Cylinder.

A. WHITE. 1725. Found on the site of the Regal Cinema, Newbury, Berks.

S. White 1731. Mallet.

T. WHITE. 1791.

J. Whitethorn, Charlton; c.1800. Squat cylinder.

SAML. WHITTUCK. 1751. Ht. 9ins.

J. WHITWEL. KENDAL. 1805. A wine-merchant. The original license to sell wines was granted to John Whitwell in 1758; and succeeding members of his family operated the business up to 1883 when it was sold to Whitwell, Mark & Co. Ltd., brewers at Kendal, Westmorland, who carry on to this day. They possess the old license referred to above.

Whl. Fortune Mine; c.1790-1800. Squat cylinder.

'*Wh^l/Fortune/Mine*'.

WILLIAMS & HUMBERT DRY SACK. Ht. 11ins.

H. Williams Colon, 1771. Cylinder.

In. Williams 1774. Cylinder.

Jno. Williams, Ruan 1815. Squat cylinder.

R. Williams. St Issey, 1789. Squat cylinder.

W. WILLIAMS. SURGEON. LLANDOVERY. Llandovery is in Carmarthenshire.

WILLOUGHBY.

Geo. Wilmott, Axminster; c.1790. Squat cylinder.

WINCHESTER HOSPITAL. Octagonal.

Wingerworth 1711 and cockatrice. Onion.

JOS. WOOD. 1740. Ht. 9¼ ins. Octagonal flat-fronted bottle.

WM. WOOD. TOPSHAM. Topsham is near Exeter, and must be pronounced Tops-ham and not Top-sham.

T.W. and two tennis-players. Thomas Wood (d.1663), who in 1647 sought and obtained a license to hang out the sign of the Salutation in St. Martin's Parish, Oxford. Behind his house was a tennis-court which he ran in connection with his tavern. This is probably one of the two earliest of the Oxford tavern bottles. (see Leeds.) The following entry occurs in A. Clark's *Wood's Life and Times* I, 241. ''1658...A.W. did give him (Davis Mell, violinist and clockmaker) a very handsome entertainment at the taverne cal'd The Salutation in St. Marie's parish Oxon, own'd by Thomas Wood, son of...Wood of Oxon, sometimes servant to the father of A.W. The company did look upon Mr. Mell to have a prodigious hand on the violin...'' In the Harleian Ms. Thomas Wood is described as a dancing master.

C. Woolley 1756. Seal only.

J. Worden, St Kew; c.1800. Squat cylinder.

W. WRATHER. 1776. Ht. 5½ ins.

J.T. WRIDE.

Charles Wright, Opera Collonade, Haymarket, London; c.1800. Cylinder.

P Wynall, Polruan; c.1710. Onion.

'Charles Wright/Opera Collonade
Haymarket/London'.

'P/Wynall/Polruan'.

WYNANDROCK. INK. AMSTERDAM. An early eighteenth-century Dutch wine-bottle has this inscription in raised letters on the base of the bottle.

T.W. 1767. This and the two following bottles belonged to the Wyndhams of Dinton, near Salisbury, Wilts., where they were found. In the account of Sir Wadham Wyndham (1610-1668) in the D.N.B. it states that his third son William, "is the ancestor of the Wyndhams of Dinton, Salisbury".

J.S.W. Mid-nineteenth century. see above.

W.W. and crest of lion's head erased. Early nineteenth century. see above.

Sir Wm. Wynn, Sandown Fort, Isle of Wight; c.1840. Cylinder.

W. moulded in bottle itself and not on a seal. Ht. 11ins.

A W, a mullet above and below. Seal only.

'*A W*'.

B.W. 1758. Mallet.

C.V.R.W. Frome.

E.T.W. Ht. 9ins. Sold at Sotheby's, June 18, 1943.

F.W. 1764.

F W; c.1690. Onion.

'*F W*'.

F.W.; c.1720. Mallet.

F.W.W. and mermaid with comb and mirror, from the Mermaid Tavern, Oxford. see Whicker.

G.M.W. and an eagle with wings displayed; c.1660. Shaft and globe.

G.S.W. 1720. Ht. 4½ ins. A tankard of green bottle-glass with trailed work round the body near the rim. It has a patterned handle and is sealed four times as above. It holds a little more than a pint and it was found in Norfolk.

I.W. 1695. Onion.

I.W. 1732. Seal only.

I.W. 1747. Seal only.

I.W. 1768.

I.W. 1775. Cylinder.

I.W. IN COLCHESTER. The two latter words are written round the outer edge of the seal, and the initials in the centre. Colchester is a market town in Essex, with an old castle.

I.C.W.; c.1685. Onion.

I.M.W. and St. George and the dragon. Ht. 5ins. Diam. 4ins. Seventeenth century. This is almost certainly a tavern-bottle. see Whicker. Found in Thames Street, London.

J.S.W. see Wyndham.

K.W. and two eight-pointed stars. Seal only.

M.W. 1761.

R.W. 1687. Onion.

R.W. St. Just. Squat cylinder.

R W 1690 and a king's head. see Richard Walker.

'R W/1690' and a king's head.

R.E.W. 1688. and a king's head. see Richard Walker.

R.W. 1693. and a king's head. see Richard Walker.

R.W. 1695. and a king's head. see Richard Walker.

R.W. 1699. and a king's head. see Richard Walker.

R.E.W. 1699. and a king's head. see Richard Walker.

1699. (no initials) and a king's head. see Richard Walker.

R.W. 1739. Ht. 9ins. Flat-sided, which is unusual at this early date. Perhaps an early attempt at binning. Exhibited at Vintners' Hall, 1933, and illustrated in catalogue.

S.W.

T.W. Seal only.

T.W. and two tennis-players. see Thomas Wood.

T.W. 1767. see Wyndham.

W.W. see Wyndham.

W.W., a queen's head with fleur-de-lis beneath. Seal only.

W.W.; c.1840. Moulded cylinder.

W.W.; c.1700. Onion.

YNYS Y MAEN GWYN. 1738. lit: The Island of the White Stone. This is the name of a house and estate near Towyn on the Merionethshire coast, which belonged to the Corbett family in the eighteenth century. It was sold in the early nineteenth century to another family of the same name.

M. YEO. 1728. Ht. 5ins.

CHATEAU YQUEM. HAUT-SAUTERNES. GRAND CRU. On a paper label is the date 1869.

O.Y.

S.Y. and possibly a merchant's mark above.

Bibliography

Books

Some elementary remarks on wine bottles are to be found in many of the more recent books on bottle-collecting, but these are mainly concerned with Victorian examples and therefore of limited usefulness.

In addition, many of the excellent earlier books on glass often failed to mention wine bottles altogether. Bearing this in mind, the following list is reasonably complete in relation to reliable and useful works to date.

Davis, Derek, *English Bottles and Decanters,* 1972.

Hume, Ivor Noel, *A Guide to Artifacts of Colonial America,* New York, 1970.

Hume, Ivor Noel, *All the Best Rubbish,* 1974.

London Museum, *Glass in London,* catalogue of London Museum Exhibition, 1970.

Morgan, Roy, *Sealed Bottles,* Burton-on-Trent, 1976.

Powell, H.J., *Glassmaking in England,* 1923.

Ruggles-Brise, Sheelagh, *Sealed Bottles,* Country Life, 1949.

Truro Museum, *The English Glass Bottle,* catalogue of Truro Museum Exhibition, 1976.

Vincent, Keith, *Nailsea Glass,* 1975.

Vintners' Hall, catalogue of the Wine Trade Loan Exhibition of Drinking Vessels held at Vintners' Hall, London, 1933.

Wills, Geoffrey, *Bottle Collectors' Guide,* 1978.

Wills, Geoffrey, *English Glass Bottles for the Collector,* 1974.

Wills, Geoffrey, *English and Irish Glass,* 1968.

Journals

Haslam, Jeremy, 'Oxford Taverns and the Cellars of All Souls in the 17th and 18th Centuries', *Oxoniensia,* XXXIV, 1969.

Haslam, Jeremy, 'Sealed Bottles from All Souls College', *Oxoniensia,* XXXV, 1970.

Hinton, D.A., 'A Glass Bottle Seal from Oxford', *Oxoniensia,* XXXII, 1967.

Hudson, J. Paul, '17th Century Wine Bottles at Jamestown', *Journal of Glass Studies,* III, Corning, New York, 1961.

Hume, Ivor Noel, 'The Glass Wine Bottle in Virginia', *Journal of Glass Studies,* III, Corning, New York, 1961.

Jones, Olive, 'Glass Bottle Push-Ups and Pontil Marks', *Historical Archaeology,* V, Lansing, Michigan, 1971.

Leeds, E.T., 'Bottles of the Crown Tavern', *Oxoniensia,* XIV, 1949.

Leeds, E.T., 'On the Dating of Glass Wine Bottles of the Stuart Period', *The Antiquary,* 1914.

Leeds, E.T., '17th and 18th Century Wine Bottles of Oxford Taverns', *Oxoniensia,* VI, 1941.

McNulty, R., 'Dutch Wine Bottles of the 17th and 18th Centuries', *Journal of Glass Studies,* XIII and XIV, Corning, New York, 1971-72.

Price, Rees, 'Notes on the Evolution of the Wine Bottle', *Transactions of the Glasgow Archaeological Society,* 1908.

Robertson, W.S., 'A Quantitative Morphological Study of the Evolution of Some Post-Medieval Wine Bottles', *Science and Archaeology,* 17.

Sands, T.O., 'A Collection of Late 18th Century Bottles', Archaeological Society of Virginia, quarterly bulletin, 28, No. 4.

Magazine articles

Bacon, J.M., 'Bottle Decanters and Bottles', *Apollo,* XXX, 1939.

Berry, F., 'Dated English Glass Wine Bottles', *Country Life,* March 30th, 1935.

Buckley, F., 'Curious Marked Bottles', *Antique Collector,* May, 1932.

Campbell, A., 'Bottles of Great Charm', *Antique Dealer and Collectors Guide,* September, 1954.

Davis, F., 'Down Among the Dead Men', *Illustrated London News,* December 3rd, 1932.

Dunsmuir, R., 'Old and Rare English Wine Bottles', *Antique Collector,* August, 1976.

Gordon, L., 'Wine Containers Through the Ages', *The Decanter.*

Hughes, B., 'When Wine was Bought by the Butt', *Country Life,* April, 1969.

Lewis, M., 'Vintage Bottles', *Art and Antiques,* August 23rd, 1975.

Michaelis, R.F., 'Old Bottle Seal Finds', *Antique Dealer and Collectors Guide,* April, 1962.

Ruggles-Brise, S., 'More Bottle Seal Discoveries', *Country Life,* October 24th, 1952.

Stuart, S., 'Old English Glass, *Antique Dealer and Collectors Guide,* April, 1962.

Thorpe, W., 'Glass: The Evolution of the Decanter', *Connoisseur,* April, 1929.

Wade, A.G., 'A 17th Century Bishop's Seal', *Country Life,* December 26th, 1947.

Books not specifically on wine bottles, but containing relevant chapters or passages

Douglas, R., and Franks, S., *History of Glassmaking,* 1972.

Guttery, D.R., *Broad Glass to Cut Crystal,* 1956.

Hughes, G.B., *English Glass for the Collector.*

Mackay, J., *Price Guide to Collectable Antiques,* Antique Collectors' Club, 1976.

Meigh, E., *Story of the Glass Bottle,* 1972.

Perceval, M., *The Glass Collector,* 1918.

Phillips, P., *Collector's Encyclopaedia of Antiques,* 1973.

Wills, G., *Antique Glass for Pleasure and Investment,* 1971.

Wills, G., *Country Life Pocket Book of Glass,* 1966.

Wyatt, V., *From Sand-core to Automation,* 1972.

Price Guide and Auction House Records

In many respects a price guide on any subject is a difficult thing to write; so much depends on the vagaries of the market, that no sooner has one completed it than it is almost out of date. This does not imply that every change is an increase in price, often quite the reverse.

Fluctuating prices normally reflect both demand and availability. For example, a sudden influx of uncommon bottles on to the market can affect their value quite drastically; collectors do not feel encouraged to spend large sums of money on what they always imagined were genuinely scarce items. Conversely, where the demand far outstrips the supply prices tend to escalate; this has certainly been the case of recent years with the very early wine bottles.

The position is such, that certain unsealed bottles can now realise prices previously reserved for good condition sealed ones only. This trend appears to continue unabated, with the result that all but the most affluent of collectors are forced to seek early specimens in places well away from the rooms of major London dealers and auctioneers.

On the other hand, the prices of mid- to late eighteenth century bottles have remained noticeably more stable, due largely to the more ample supply available. As a very general rule, the values of dated bottles begin to rise sharply c.1730, and the earlier the more difficult they are to find, and hence more expensive to buy.

One of the more phenomenal increases concerns the unsealed bottles of the seventeenth and eighteenth centuries. Good condition examples of this era now command very respectable prices. The same remark applies to interesting or ancient bottles in a damaged condition previously disregarded by all but a few. It is surely a sign of the times, and proof of their scarcity, that the major auction rooms and dealers accept them at all. As supplies dwindle, this trend is bound to continue and the number of early English bottles 'fresh' on the market will always remain a limited one.

European bottles provide a rather different case; being relatively common, they rarely attain comparable figures to English examples, though sealed ones are very scarce. So many factors affect the prices of bottles (rarity, availability, desirability, even trends) that rarely do two similar examples realise the same eventual selling price. Saleroom competition between buyers will occasionally inflate the price of rare items way beyond the bounds of reason. On occasions, none of these criteria seems able to account for the incongruity of the market. For these reasons alone, it is with considerable trepidation that I have added a list of the main wine bottle types together with the prices a dealer is likely to ask for good condition bottles in each category. Naturally I speak of those dealers principally in antique glass and thoroughly conversant with their subject.

It would be foolish to regard this list as anything other than a general guide, for the very reasons just set out above. However, preceding this first list, I have given a selection of auction room and dealers' prices for the years 1976, 1977, 1978 and 1979, and from these I will allow the collector to draw his own conclusions; throughout I have separated the London and provincial auctions and dealers. This move seemed necessary, as the major London rooms reflect more accurately a bottle's current value. Such sales are attended regularly by collectors and the trade alike and, although few bargains are to be had, close monitoring of these auctions will give a pretty accurate guide on the present state of the market. Just occasionally a scarce bottle will sell quite cheaply at a country auction, but this is of little relevance when one considers the few that ever crop up in such places. Good luck to the collector 'in the know', however.

In addition, I thought it interesting to include a small section on some prices realised for damaged or poor condition bottles by both auctions and dealers.

In conclusion, auction room prices speak for themselves, the facts are there for everyone to read and the prices quite obviously reflect the growing interest there now is in antique glass of this category.

Abbreviations used on the following pages

BLD	Bladder Onion
c.	Circa
D	Dated
ML	Mallet
OC	Octagonal
ON	Onion
S	Sealed
S&G	Shaft and Globe
SQ	Squat Cylinder
TC	True Cylinder
U/D	Undated
U/S	Unsealed
3PM	Three-piece Mould Cylinder

Selection of auction room and dealers' prices 1976-1979

1976

LONDON AUCTIONS

Type	Category	Description	Year	£
ON	S U/D	Fox with coronet above	c.1700	390
ON	U/S		c.1690	54
SQ	S D	C. Pugh	1763	130
SQ	S D	John Pugh	1794	100
TC	S D	J. Mearden, Tavistock	1780	130
TC	S U/D	All Souls C.R.	c.1760	54
TC	S U/D	Linc Coll C.R.	1770	42
TC	S U/D	Trin Coll C.R.	1780	44
3PM	S U/D	R O G in script	c.1840	37
ML	U/S	Magnum	1735	100
OC	U/S	Half bottle	c.1740	115
SQ	S D	R. Crig, Merroit	1803	360

PROVINCIAL AUCTIONS

Type	Category	Description	Year	£
S&G	U/S		c.1660	100
ON	S D	W. Roe	1717	175
ON	U/S		c.1690	36
ML	S D	T.M.	1751	70
ML	U/S	Half bottle	c.1725	16
TC	S D	T. Godden	1777	60
TC	S D	Juxta Salopiam	1797	130
TC	S D	Jas Oakes Bury	1788	75
TC	S U/D	Flaming comet	c.1811	40
3PM	S U/D	Charles Simpson	c.1825	35
3PM	S U/D	R.H. Andrews	c.1770	26
SQ	S D	Sir Will. Strickland Bart.	1809	30

LONDON DEALERS

Type	Category	Description	Year	£
ON	U/S		c.1690	40
ON	U/S		c.1700	52
ON	S D	T. Burford	1712	500
BLD	S D	D. Lapie	1728	350
ML	S D	R. Threxton	1737	300
SQ	S D	James Bay, Kilkhampton	1785	250
SQ	S D	T. Dampier	1789	200
TC	S U/D	.S.	c.1790	25
TC	U/S		c.1780	15
ML	U/S		c.1740	38
3PM	S D	Rousden Jubilee	1887	25

PROVINCIAL DEALERS

Type	Category	Description	Year	£
ON	U/S		c.1700	55
ML	U/S		c.1725	38
TC	U/S	With full provenance	c.1760	15
SQ	S D	John Clarke	1761	245
ML	S D	Col John Folliot	1743	265
TC	S D	All Souls Coll C.R.	c.1760	75
TC	S D	J.F.	1800	125
TC	S U/D	A lion and swan	c.1810	65
TC	S U/D	R.H.C. and dragon	c.1805	75
TC	S U/D	W.C.G. Zeals	c.1780	85

LONDON AUCTIONS

Type	Category	Description	Year	£
ON	S D	T.W	1712	700
ON	S D	S. Lyne	1728	680
ON	S U/D	Crest and coat of arms of Lowther		
ON	U/S	Magnum	c.1690	480
ML	U/S	Half bottle	c.1710	150
ML	S D	I. Knottesford	c.1730	50
OC	U/S		1736	110
BLD	U/S	Magnum	c.1740	135
SQ	S D	James Mitchell	c.1730	165
TC	S U/D	T.C. and a hand in a shield	1793	170
3PM	S U/D	Lupton	c.1770	50
			c.1850	23

PROVINCIAL AUCTIONS

Type	Category	Description	Year	£
S&G	U/S	Almost a half bottle	c.1665	100
S&G	U/S		c.1675	100
ON	U/S		c.1700	30
ON	U/S		c.1710	55
SQ	S D	I. Sharp	1781	170
SQ	S D	I. Taylor	1807	150
SQ	S D	Wm Dommett	1778	200
TC	S U/D	W.A.	c.1800	55
TC	S D	Loop	1777	110
ML	U/S	Half bottle	c.1725	30
3PM	S U/D	E.L.	c.1830	44

LONDON DEALERS

Type	Category	Description	Year	£
ON	U/S	Half bottle	c.1700	150
S&G	U/S		c.1670	100
ML	U/S		c.1735	76
ML/ON	U/S	Transitional, magnum	c.1720	85
SQ	S D	S. Buscombe, St Brock	1785	285
ON	S D	William Battishill	1707	300
ON	S U/D	Anne Morrell cipher	c.1690	700
TC	S U/D	H.C. and a raised hand	c.1780	75
TC	S U/D	.R. a crown above	c.1790	60
SQ	S D	Rd. Hill, Wyke Farm	1781	500

PROVINCIAL DEALERS

Type	Category	Description	Year	£
S&G	U/S	Half bottle	c.1675	40
ON	S D	M.M.	1700	500
ON	S D	Anne Morrell cipher	1684	500
BLD	S D	I.G.	1729	300
ON	U/S		c.1715	45
ML/ON	U/S	Transitional	c.1720	87
SQ	S U/D	G.B.D.	c.1780	110
ML	U/S		c.1735	38
ML	U/S	Half bottle, long neck	c.1740	30
S&G	S U/D	Goose	c.1660	830
BLD	U/S		c.1730	45
TC	S D	Magdelen College, half bottle	1760	125

1978

LONDON AUCTIONS

Type	Category	Description	Year	£
S&G	U/S	With full provenance	c.1660	780
ON	S U/D	With a Saracen's head	c.1680	1,600
ON	S D	J. Collens	1704	750
ON	U/S		c.1680	230
BLD	S D	Thos Adams Senr	1714	620
ML	S D	E Herbert	1721	540
ON	U/S		c.1700	160
TC	S D	W. Pooly	1764	180
ML	U/S		c.1730	77
ON	U/S	With full provenance	c.1710	210
SQ	S D	I.B.	1772	155
3PM	S D	Jas Gill	1836	75

PROVINCIAL AUCTIONS

Type	Category	Description	Year	£
ON	S D	R.N.	1691	330
ON	U/S	Magnum	c.1690	55

LONDON DEALERS

Type	Category	Description	Year	£
S&G	S D	Bydder. Thistle Boon	1674	5,000
ON	S U/D	Northampton coat of arms		350
ON	U/S		c.1695	145
ML	S D	Wm Strode	1700	550
ML	S D	Sedbush	1727	450
SQ	S U/D	T.G. Bond	c.1790	225
SQ	S D	J. Fleming, Plymtree	1786	245
ML	S D	O.G.M	1732	275
ML	U/S		c.1740	125

PROVINCIAL DEALERS

Type	Category	Description	Year	£
S&G	U/S	Quarter bottle	c.1765	550
ON	S U/D	Shield, three daggers, etc.		725
BLD	S D	I. Pitt	c.1695	300
ML	S U/D	G.R. and a crown	1724	145
ML	U/S		c.1755	75
SQ	S D	Wm Daniel	c.1740	350
SQ	S U/D	J Browse, Yalberton	1754	150
SQ	U/S	Magnum	c.1790	80
ON	U/S		c.1770	65
TC	S D	Thos Whipham	c.1710	150
SQ	S D	R. Densham, Upton	1816	160
SQ	S D	I.W.	1810	220

1979

LONDON AUCTIONS

Type	Category	Description	Year	£
SQ	S U/D	H with coronet above	c.1780	46
TC	S U/D	A.S.C.R.	c.1770	32
TC	S U/D	T.C. and a shield	c.1795	72
SQ	S U/D	I. Watson, Bilton, a pair		
ML	U/S		c.1800	190
ON	U/S		c.1730	40
ON	S D		c.1720	58
ON	S D	I.T.	1710	480
ON	S D	I. Smith	1706	680
ON	S D	W. Skammell	1704	620
ML	S D	Saml. Whittuck	1751	340
ML	S D	T. Weston	1742	540
S&G	U/S		1660	660
S&G	S U/D	Coat of arms	c.1655	1,400

PROVINCIAL AUCTIONS

Type	Category	Description	Year	£
ML	S D	Revd. Doctr. Rumney, St Albans	1734	520
ON	S U/D	A.T., a chevron and three tuns	c.1716/9	380
ON	U/S		c.1685	80
ML	U/S		c.1730	80
S&G	S U/D	W.H.P. and the king's arms	c.1655	820

LONDON DEALERS

Type	Category	Description	Year	£
SQ	S U/D	H with a viscount's coronet	c.1780	85
ML	S D	I. Fogg	1734	400
ON	S D	R.H. with globe?	1688	1,650
S&G	U/S	Short necked bottle	c.1675	150

PROVINCIAL DEALERS

Type	Category	Description	Year	£
TC	S U/D	JUSC. quarter bottle	c.1800	200
TC	U/S	Miniature	c.1760	150
SQ	S D	Gartmore	1802	85
ML	U/S		c.1730	90
ON	U/S		1710	85
ON	U/S		c.1720	45
OC	U/S	Squat form in amber metal	c.1760	130
ON	S U/D	Two Cs beneath an earl's coronet	c.1695	450
ML	S D	T.K.	1729	120
S&G	U/S	Short necked bottle	c.1675	225

General guide to prices, 1980-81

Type	Year	Category	£
S&G	1630-60	S D	1,500 +
		S U/D	800-1,000
		U/S	300-400
S&G	1660-80	S D	1,000 +
		S U/D	700-800
		U/S	250-300
ON	1680-1700	S D	500-650
		S U/D	400-450
		U/S	70-80
ON	1700-30	S D	400-500
		S U/D	350-400
		U/S	50-60
BLD	1710-75	S D	350-400
		S U/D	250-300
		U/S	40-50
ML	1725-50	S D	200-350
		S U/D	150-200
		U/S	30-40
OC	1730-90	S D	350-400
		S U/D	250-300
		U/S	40-50
SQ	1740-1830	S D	120-180
		S U/D	80-110
		U/S	20-25
TC	1740-1830	S D	100-150
		S U/D	60-70
		U/S	5-10
3PM	1811-1900	S D	60-80
		S U/D	30-50
		U/S	2-3

Prices realised for damaged or poor condition bottles at dealers and auctions, 1977

Mallet bottle, c.1735, heavily barnacled and large portion of one side replaced with resin, £35.

Onion, 'W. Pratt, 1714', body with large continuous crack at shoulder level, almost encircling bottle, glass with full gloss, £150.

Onion, 'P. Wynall, Polruan', c.1700, badly cracked, and string-rim shattered, full shine to glass, £110.

Shaft and globe, rampant lion, c.1660, iridescent and bottom third of seal missing, £1,870.

Shaft and globe, unsealed, c.1660, rather deep surface flaking, with large portions missing; no apparent internal damage however, £660.

Onion, 'Wingerworth 1711', small crack in bottle, otherwise an attractive example with little or no other faults, £300.

Onion, unsealed, c.1685, deep and ugly surface pitting due to long incarceration in the soil; no apparent internal damage visible.

Prices realised for damaged or poor condition bottles at dealers and auctions, 1976-1978

Sealed bottles

Shaft and globe form, 'M.W. (16)81'. Bottle buried for some considerable time, devitrified and neck top missing, £210.

Onion, early form, 'F.W.', c.1690, neck top detached but present crack running from neck down to shoulder; devitrified, £82.

Onion, 'S.F. 1704', oval shaped crack around base and shoulder, overall abraded condition, £150.

Onion, 'F.D.F. 1705', good condition except for a small line and a small star crack in the body; one would assume from the price that these imperfections were not noted, £620.

Mallet, 'F. Fry, Dear Park 1736', impact mark to base of bottle with resultant crack running in base for at least two and a half inches; full gloss to glass, £155.

Mallet, 'Skene 1742', multiple cracks in neck, full gloss, £170.

Mallet, 'Henry Dunning 1730', quite large portion of neck top and string-rim missing, star to shoulder, £240.

Onion, coat of arms, c.1700, neck top completely detached but present, dull overall, £75.

Squat cylinder, 'T.B. 1797', impact mark at rear of bottle, with radiating cracks, full gloss to glass, £45.

True cylinder, 'I.B. Columpton', similar damage to above, if not worse, some attempt at gluing, £15.

True cylinder, 'Linc Coll C.R.', large chunk cut of neck top on one side, affecting all but a very small part of the string-rim, otherwise mint, £9.

Unsealed bottles

Shaft and globe, c.1660, surprisingly no chipping to bottle at all, but a bad series of cracks running around body, and neck has been detached, abraded, £100.

Shaft and globe, c.1680, heavily devitrified, opaque, large chunk out of one side of neck top, £115.

Onion, early form, c.1685, water rolled with layers of surface glass missing and neck top badly eaten away, £65.

Onion, c.1690, small size, bad cracks in area of base, and surface glass beginning to decay, £22.

Flat sided onion, c.1690, scarce bottle, but large crack encircling the entire neck, glass outwardly good, £30.

Onion, c.1710, water rolled, somewhat iridescent, and surface becoming flaky, virtually opaque, £25.

Mallet, c.1720, sea-washed, barnacled, and having lost many layers of surface glass resulting in rough uneven finish, the top badly nibbled, £15.

Onion-mallet form, transitional, c.1715-20, small stars in area below shoulder, and nearly half of string-rim missing, smooth with slight shine to glass, £30.

Octagonal, early two-piece mould, c.1760, heavily scale like and iridescent with crack in corner and missing portion of glass, nearly opaque, £8.

Mallet, half bottle, c.1720, partially iridescent with string-rim and neck top entirely missing, £32.

Squat cylinder, almost a mallet, c.1750, full gloss to glass but two small stars around shoulder, £15.

Index